William Howard Taft
and United States Foreign Policy:
The Apprenticeship Years
1900-1908

RALPH ELDIN MINGER

———

William Howard Taft
and United States Foreign Policy:
The Apprenticeship Years
1900-1908

———

UNIVERSITY OF ILLINOIS PRESS

Urbana   Chicago   London

Publication of this work was supported in part by a grant
from the Andrew W. Mellon Foundation

LIBRARY OF CONGRESS CATALOGING IN PUBLICATION DATA

Minger, Ralph Eldin, 1925–
    William Howard Taft and United States foreign policy.

    Bibliography: p.
    Includes index.
    1. United States—Foreign relations—1901–1909.
2. Taft, William Howard, Pres, U. S., 1857–1930.
I. Title.
E756.M56   327.73   75-6691
ISBN 0-252-00427-2

DEDICATED TO
my father, Rudolph Eldin Minger
my mother, Avis Isabel Minger
AND
my wife, Julia Maria Minger

Preface

WILLIAM HOWARD TAFT'S apprenticeship for the presidency, as well as his term in that office, lies within the period during which the United States began to assume a position of consequence not only in the Western Hemisphere but in the world. Placed as he was in the presidential succession between two giants, Taft's contribution to the American position has received less attention than it deserves. While colorful personalities attract scholarly inquiry into all aspects of their lives, there is an inertia which frequently immobilizes any serious consideration of conservative figures. So it was with Taft. As president, he was largely concerned with the policy of the United States regarding Latin America and the Far East. To the presidency of the Second Philippine Commission, Judge Taft brought in 1900 only vague and general conceptions of United States foreign policy. To the presidency of the United States, former Secretary of the War Taft brought in 1909 a coherent set of ideas, based on experience in the Philippines, Panama, Cuba, Japan, and China under Presidents William McKinley and Theodore Roosevelt. He was unusually well prepared for the problems which would face him.

The purpose of this monograph is to trace the origin and

development of Taft's concept of the proper foreign policy for the United States, through a study of his role in the conduct of foreign affairs from 1900 to 1908. These years constituted his apprenticeship in foreign affairs, and I was not entirely satisfied with the previous accounts of Taft's activities within this period. The definition and description of that role in meaningful terms represented an exciting challenge. Thus, the study of this period is interesting and significant not only for the light it throws on Taft's actions as president, but also for relating and analyzing an important—and neglected—segment of American diplomatic history. Taft was, in the Philippines and elsewhere, one of our most effective foreign representatives, and his work had a permanent effect on the course of United States history.

My main source for this study was the William Howard Taft Papers, a huge collection numbering over a thousand portfolios on deposit in the Manuscript Division of the Library of Congress. In addition, I consulted other relevant collections in the Manuscript Division, such as the Theodore Roosevelt Papers, the Elihu Root Papers, and the William McKinley Papers. I wish to express my thanks and appreciation to Mr. David C. Mearns, the recently retired Chief of the Manuscript Division of the Library of Congress, and to his able staff. In particular, I should like to acknowledge my special indebtedness to the now retired Dr. C. Percy Powell, long in charge of the William Howard Taft and Theodore Roosevelt Papers, for his encouragement and sympathetic guidance.

It was necessary to visit Cornell University to examine the Willard Straight Papers, now available in the Collection of Regional History and University Archives. The Straight Papers bore upon an important phase of this study. I am indebted to Mr. Michael Straight, former editor of *The New Republic* magazine, who granted me permission to use his father's papers; to Mr. Foster M. Coffin, Director of Willard Straight Hall at Cornell University; to Mrs. Edith M. Fox, Curator and University Archivist; and to Miss Kathleen Jacklin,

Assistant Curator. In particular, I wish to thank Mr. Foster M. Coffin for arranging my accommodations at Willard Straight Hall, showing me the grounds of Cornell University, and taking such a keen interest in my work.

I found it helpful to visit the National Archives located in Washington, D.C., for additional materials relating to the substance of this study. I wish to express my appreciation for assistance rendered to Mrs. Julia Carroll and Mr. Phillip Sneider of the Foreign Affairs Section and to Mr. Richard S. Maxwell and Miss Jane F. Smith of the Interior Section of the Natural Resources Records Branch.

This book represents three years of concentrated research, analysis, and writing. The year spent in the Washington, D.C., and adjacent areas gathering research materials was one of the happiest of my life. To my parents, Doctor Rudolph Eldin Minger and Avis Isabel Minger, who instilled in me a love of history and the duty of exercising an independent judgment, my eternal love and gratitude. To my wife, Julia Maria Minger, who assisted me at every stage of the work with magnificent typing and with uncommon sensitivity, managed to detect shortcomings, and made me aware of them without precipitating domestic crises, my everlasting love and respect. To my two lively daughters, Avis Isabella and Elda Maria, and inquisitive son, Rudolph Manuel, who have patiently borne with their father's preoccupation, my deepest love and appreciation. The final draft of this manuscript was prepared during the Fall semester of 1972–73 when I was granted a sabbatical leave by the Faculty Appointments Committee of Loyola University of Chicago.

In the course of a long preoccupation with this subject, I have contracted intellectual debts from fellow scholars that I shall never be able to repay, and cannot even fully acknowledge. A study of the footnotes and more especially the bibliography will indicate that this book could not have been written without the aid of their works. In preparing this book I have been aided and influenced by the notations of four distinguished scholar-teachers. Professor Richard W. Van Alstyne, distinguished scholar of United States diplomatic history, did a careful evaluation and criticism of this work. Professor George E. Mowry, renowned scholar of the eras of Theodore Roosevelt and William Howard Taft, read the manuscript with painstaking care, graciously shared with me his vast fund of information about Taft and his family, and made valuable and practical suggestions about publishing the manuscript. Averill J. Berman, Ph.D., a fellow historian and close friend of many years, made perceptive comments and did much to clarify the arguments that I have attempted to make. Finally, I acknowledge gratefully the assistance of my uncle, Paul Jordan Monroe, a superb editor and my severest critic. Because he was impatient with vagueness, scornful of pomposity, and ruthless with verbiage, I am greatly indebted; the reader has also profited. I wish, last, to express my appreciation and gratitude to Mrs. Mary Anne Connelly for her superb typing and editing of the final manuscript. The Loyola University Research Committee provided funds for typing the final manuscript.

Contents

xi

CHAPTER I

From Law to Diplomacy: The Summons
to the Philippines

ON MONDAY AFTERNOON, January 22, 1900, William Howard Taft, presiding judge of the Sixth United States Circuit Court of Appeals, received a telegram from President William McKinley: [1] "I would like very much to see you in Washington. If you could come Thursday it would be convenient." [2] On Wednesday night Taft took a train to Washington, D.C., and upon his arrival went promptly to the White House, where McKinley received him at once.[3] The president disclosed that he intended to establish a civil government in the Philippines, that he proposed to appoint a commission to carry out this task, and that he wanted Taft to serve on the commission, possibly as its president.[4] But when

1. Henry F. Pringle, *The Life and Times of William Howard Taft* (2 vols., New York, 1939), I, 159 (hereinafter referred to as Pringle, *Taft*); Margaret Leech, *In the Days of McKinley* (New York, 1959), 483 (hereinafter referred to as Leech, *McKinley*). The date is not given in any published work, but has been established via information provided by William McKinley and William Howard Taft in their correspondence. William McKinley to William R. Day, Jan. 30, 1900, William McKinley Papers (Division of Manuscripts, Library of Congress); William Howard Taft to W. F. Wakeman, Sept. 11, 1908, William Howard Taft Papers (Division of Manuscripts, Library of Congress).
2. Charles S. Olcott, *The Life of William McKinley* (2 vols., Boston, 1916), II, 175 (hereinafter referred to as Olcott, *McKinley*).
3. Pringle, *Taft*, I, 159; Leech, *McKinley*, 484.
4. W. H. Taft to Henry W. and Horace D. Taft, Jan. 28, 1900, Taft MSS.

McKinley asked for Taft's views on American policy toward the Philippines, Taft's response was complicated. He had disapproved of our taking the Philippine Islands in the first place, because it meant "the assumption of a burden by us contrary to our traditions and at a time when we had quite enough to do at home." [5] He was opposed to free trade with the Philippines, and would deny United States citizenship to their inhabitants, because the United States Constitution did not extend automatically to such new dependencies.[6] However, he disagreed with such Americans as Senator George F. Hoar of Massachusetts who contended that the Filipinos were capable of self-government, and who found that our actions in the islands violated our principles of government and the Declaration of Independence.[7] Taft believed it a national obligation, a "sacred duty," to create a government adapted to the needs of the Filipinos, one that would help to develop them into a self-governing people.[8]

5. *Ibid.* Taft's point of view was profoundly influenced by members of his family. The impact of his younger brother, Horace, and of his mother, Louise, is evident here. Horace wrote in June, 1897: "If we could have any assurance that Hawaii was fit for any place in your government system, I should be willing to risk any foreign complications. However, you know my objections to anything like vigorous foreign policy. It seems to me that the whole work of America is the civilization of America and the building up of a nobler democracy than has yet been seen." Horace D. Taft to W. H. Taft, June 18, 1897, Taft MSS. This was a favorite theme with American anti-expansionists. In his written statement of January 24, 1898, to the Associated Press which dealt with the then proposed annexation of the Hawaiian Islands, Grover Cleveland wrote: "I regarded, and still regard, the proposed annexation of these islands as not only opposed to our national policy, but as a perversion of our national mission. The mission of our nation is to build up and make a great country out of what we have, instead of annexing islands." *Letters of Grover Cleveland 1850–1908*, ed. Allan Nevins (Boston, 1933), 491–492. Indeed, for Horace Taft, even the admission of new states into the Union was a matter of the "greatest misfortune" and the "greatest folly," creating as it did the problem of the "Wild Western Senators" from "sparsely settled and uncivilized sections of the country." Horace D. Taft to W. H. Taft, June 18, 1897, Taft MSS. Taft's mother was also pessimistic about expansion. She could see no advantage in gaining sovereignty over "those savages" in the Philippines. Indeed, she believed that the United States already had more aliens than could be managed comfortably. Louise Taft to W. H. Taft, Jan. 8, 1899, Taft MSS.

6. W. H. Taft to Henry W. and Horace D. Taft, Jan. 28, 1900, *ibid.*; Leech, *McKinley*, 484.

7. W. H. Taft to Henry W. and Horace D. Taft, Jan. 28, 1900, Taft MSS.

8. *Ibid.* There is strong evidence that President McKinley agreed with Taft's views. W. H. Taft to W. F. Wakeman, Sept. 11, 1908, Taft MSS; Olcott, *McKinley*, II,

By background, principle, and temperament, Judge Taft opposed the annexation of the Philippines, though he accepted it as a *fait accompli.* There were other difficulties in accepting the position: he was not a Spanish scholar, and he had to consider his judicial career.[9] President McKinley and Elihu Root, the secretary of war, attempted to meet his objections. Root appealed to his patriotism, stating that Taft owed it as a duty to his country to take a place on the Philippine Commission.[10] McKinley pointed out that the position offered on the Philippine Commission was only temporary, and implied that acceptance might well advance his judicial career in the near future.[11] Taft delayed his decision, asking for time to consult his family and friends.

A week passed, and Taft had still not decided. The president, anxious as ever to obtain him, decided to press his decision. Fortunately, McKinley's old friend and a former secretary of state, Judge William R. Day, had reason to go to Cincinnati. McKinley wrote to the judge, asking his help:

> Indeed, on some accounts I am rather glad you are going to Cincinnati because Judge Taft will consult you about a matter which I have brought to his attention. I want him to go to the Philippines on a Commission to establish civil governments in provinces where there is peace. I have had him down here; have gone over the whole ground with him. He took a week to reply. This morning a letter comes, that he wants a little more time that he may consult with his brethren on next Monday. I want you to appreciate, Judge, that this is a very important mat-

15–16, 26–27, 108–111, 144–145, 165–172, 175; Julius W. Pratt, *Expansionists of 1898: The Acquisition of Hawaii and the Spanish Islands* (Baltimore, 1936), 215, 326–340; Theodore Roosevelt to Douglas Robinson, March 30, 1898, *The Letters of Theodore Roosevelt,* ed. Elting E. Morison (8 vols., Cambridge, 1951–54), II, 805–806 (hereinafter referred to as Roosevelt, *Letters*); H. H. Kohlsaat, *From McKinley to Harding: Personal Recollections of Our Presidents* (New York, 1923), 66–68; Archie Butt to Mrs. Lewis F. Butt, Aug. 5, 1911, *Taft and Roosevelt: The Intimate Letters of Archie Butt Military Aide* (2 vols., Garden City. N.Y., 1930), II, 732–736.

9. W. H. Taft to Henry W. and Horace D. Taft, Jan. 28, 1900, Taft MSS.

10. For a full account of Elihu Root's appeal, see Mrs. William Howard Taft, *Recollections of Full Years* (New York, 1914), 34 (hereinafter referred to as Helen Taft, *Recollections*).

11. W. H. Taft to Henry W. and Horace D. Taft, Jan. 28, 1900, Taft MSS.

ter and I invoke your aid to get the consent of Judge Taft to go. It is a great field for him, a great opportunity, and he will never have so good a one again to serve his country. I think he is inclined to accept. You must not make it harder for him to accept.

The Commission which I shall send will have large powers and a wide jurisdiction. They can accomplish great good and help me more than I can tell you in the solution of the important problem in the East. Besides, a Commission made up of men of the character of Judge Taft will give repose and confidence to the country and will be an earnest [*sic*] of my high purpose to bring to those peoples the blessings of peace and liberty. It will be an assurance that my instructions to the Peace Commission were sincere and my purpose to abide by them.[12]

It was, in fact, a difficult decision for Taft to make, involving as it did the interruption of a promising judicial career and the risk of great responsibility in a field where he had no experience.[13] But his family urged him to undertake the assignment; his friend Elihu Root was also strongly in favor of it, and Judge Day's arguments were no doubt also persuasive.[14] Finally, McKinley informed Taft that he would

12. William McKinley to William R. Day, Jan. 30, 1900, McKinley MSS. This letter is a revealing illustration of what one historian has described as McKinley's "magnetic charm and ability to bend people to his will." Richard W. Leopold, *Elihu Root and the Conservative Tradition* (Boston, 1954), 194. It also lends strong support to Elihu Root's belief that McKinley's judgment of men was of a superior caliber. Elihu Root to Thomas F. Ryan, Jan. 13, 1904, Elihu Root Papers (Division of Manuscripts, Library of Congress).

13. Although President McKinley had told Taft that he would not need to resign his judicial position as the work in the Philippines would not take longer than nine months to complete, Taft soon saw that it would be years before the Philippine problem would be solved. Helen Taft, *Recollections*, 34–35. So, on March 15, 1900, William Howard Taft resigned from his position as a federal circuit judge. *Dictionary of American Biography*, ed. Dumas Malone (22 vols., New York, 1928–35), XVIII, 268 (hereinafter cited as DAB). By his wife's testimony, it was the hardest thing he ever had to do. Helen Taft, *Recollections*, 35.

14. Horace D. Taft to W. H. Taft, Jan. 31, 1900, Taft MSS; Helen Taft, *Recollections*, 34; Elihu Root to W. H. Taft, Jan. 31, 1900, Root MSS. At a much later date, Taft credited Elihu Root with sending him on his mission to the Philippines. Root put the problem before him in such a way, Taft said, as to permit only one decision. Address by William Howard Taft at the University Alumni Luncheon, Hamilton College, Clinton, New York, June 23, 1913. *Addresses and Articles*, XXXi, 70, contained in Taft MSS.

definitely be the president of the new commission.[15] Taft preferred this arrangement, because if he were to have the responsibility for the success or failure of the mission, he wanted as much power as possible to meet it.[16] Taft's decision seems also to have been influenced by his feeling that the problem in the Philippines was primarily one of reshaping the government—which was a job for a lawyer.[17]

After two weeks, Taft made up his mind. On the morning of February 6, 1900, he called at the White House in the company of Judge Day.[18] After a Cabinet meeting, McKinley announced Taft's appointment as president of the new Philippine Commission. Taft attended this meeting of the Cabinet and was fully informed about the plans of the McKinley administration.[19] As he left the White House, Taft stated that the special mission of the commission would be the establishment of a civil government for the Philippine islands; beyond that he was not at liberty to speak.[20]

The general reaction to the appointment was favorable. Charles Dawes noted in his diary that "We all expect great things from Taft in the Philippines." [21] Theodore Roosevelt wrote to Taft that of all the men he knew, Taft was best fitted for the position and would "do a great work for America." [22] Elihu Root wrote to a friend that Taft's acceptance was a sacrifice made under "the impulse of the highest and most unselfish sense of duty to his country." [23]

Jacob Gould Schurman, who had been chairman of the first

15. W. H. Taft to W. F. Wakeman, Sept. 11, 1908, Taft MSS. Taft said later: "I went under the influence of Mr. McKinley's personality, the influence he had of making people do what they ought to do in the interest of the public service." As quoted in Leech, *McKinley*, 485.

16. W. H. Taft to Elihu Root, Feb. 2, 1900; W. H. Taft to W. F. Wakeman, Sept. 11, 1908, Taft MSS.

17. W. H. Taft to Elihu Root, Feb. 2, 1900, *ibid.*

18. W. H. Taft to W. F. Wakeman, Sept. 11, 1908, *ibid.; New York Times*, Feb. 7, 1900, p. 1.

19. Leech, *McKinley*, 485.

20. *New York Times*, Feb. 7, 1900, p. 1.

21. Charles G. Dawes, *A Journal of the McKinley Years* (Chicago, 1950), 214. This diary entry was for February 7, 1900.

22. Theodore Roosevelt to W. H. Taft, Feb. 7, 1900, Roosevelt, *Letters*, II, 1175.

23. Elihu Root to M. E. Ingalls, Feb. 10, 1900, Taft MSS.

Philippine Commission, wrote enthusiastically to McKinley, hailing Taft as a scholar, gentleman, jurist, and man of affairs who was not so young that he lacked experience, nor so old that he was incapable of vigorous action.[24] He thought Taft fully qualified for the position, and believed his appointment would refute the "prophetic lies which some so-called reformers" were spreading about the Philippine service.[25]

The New York *Times* called attention to a prevailing impression that Taft would be made the first civil governor general of the Philippines, as soon as the commission had succeeded in replacing the existing military government with a stable civil government.[26] It also described Judge Taft's record as one "of continuous and brilliant success." [27] What then was this record? Who was the man?

William Howard Taft was born on September 15, 1857, in a large two-story brick house located in a suburb of Cincinnati on a height known as Mt. Auburn.[28] His father, Alphonso Taft, had moved westward from Vermont two decades before, settled in Cincinnati, and built a substantial law practice.[29] Subsequently, he was to attain success in a career devoted to public service. After holding the posts of secretary of war and attorney general in the Cabinet of President Ulysses Simpson Grant, he rounded out his career with service in the diplomatic corps.[30] A self-made man, his career was substantial but

24. Jacob Gould Schurman to William McKinley, Feb. 8, 1900, McKinley MSS. The first Philippine Commission arrived in Manila during March, 1899, one month after hostilities had commenced between the Filipinos and American troops. This commission tried to diminish Filipino resistance by explaining the American position, but to little avail. David Bernstein, *The Philippine Story* (New York, 1947), 82. The Schurman Commission completed its work in January, 1900, by submitting a four-volume report. Then, the commission disbanded, and Dr. Schurman returned to his post as president of Cornell University. Pringle, *Taft*, I, 159.

25. Jacob Gould Schurman to William McKinley, Feb. 8, 1900, McKinley MSS.

26. *New York Times*, Feb. 7, 1900, p. 1.

27. *Ibid.*

28. Robert Lee Dunn, *William Howard Taft American* (Boston, 1908), 262 (hereinafter referred to as Dunn, *Taft*); Francis McHale, *President and Chief Justice: The Life and Public Services of William Howard Taft* (Philadelphia, 1931), 18 (hereinafter referred to as McHale, *President and Chief Justice*).

29. Pringle, *Taft*, I, 4.

30. Alphonso Taft came to Washington in March, 1876, to serve in the cabinet of President Ulysses S. Grant as secretary of war. Less than three months later, he was

6

undistinguished. Like so many men of all periods, Alphonso Taft was determined to lay a solid foundation for his children and it was noticeable that Taft, the elder, transferred many of his unfulfilled ambitions to his son, William Howard. He was always proud of William and much of the success that the young man achieved in his studies and in his preparation for public life he owed to his father.[31]

Young William's mother, Louise Taft, a native of Millbury, Massachusetts, was a striking woman of strong intellectual fiber who wielded enormous influence over William Howard throughout a large part of his career.[32] She was to live long enough to see her son rise to high office and become a presidential possibility, and to him her voice was always one of wisdom and insight in both personal and world affairs. She surpassed the other members of the Taft family in her understanding of her son's temperament and aspirations. Her counsel and influence were enlisted on behalf of a judicial career which she felt to be best suited to his qualities of mind.

William Howard Taft was the favorite child in the family, but this favoritism, shown to the child of destiny, did not arouse any animosity on the part of his brothers and sister.[33]

William Howard's closest fraternal relationship was with his younger brother, Horace. Horace, a schoolmaster, maintained an intimate personal correspondence with his older brother and sought to influence William Howard generally in a more liberal direction. Horace, a mugwump, was, in effect, the keeper of his brother's conscience. Experiencing a vicarious satisfaction in the progression of William Howard's public career, Horace, removed from the hurly-burly of public

attorney general. In 1882 he was appointed minister to Austria-Hungary by President Chester A. Arthur. On July 4, 1884, he was transferred to Russia, where he remained until August, 1885. DAB, XVIII, 264–265.

31. Pringle, *Taft*, I, 16; McHale, *President and Chief Justice*, 20.

32. McHale, *President and Chief Justice*, 20; Pringle, *Taft*, I, 12.

33. William Howard was the third of five boys, the sons of Alphonso Taft, who had married twice. William Howard, Henry Waters, Horace Dutton, and their sister, Frances Louise, were born of the second union with Louisa Maria Torrey. Charles Phelps and Peter Rossen were born of Alphonso Taft's first marriage to Fanny Phelps, who died of tuberculosis on June 2, 1852. Pringle, *Taft*, I, 10–14.

life, never lost touch with his more famous brother. William, for his part, listened to his brother's counsel, and was in part shaped by it. Remote from the rapacity of the Gilded Age and alienated by it, Horace entertained views that were somewhat heretical for a Republican. These he imparted to his older brother and they were of some influence in shaping his thinking. Horace's estimate of the abilities of William Howard Taft was accurate and incisive: "My brother was a hard worker, had a clear, strong mind, and, though certainly not brilliant, was outstanding in ability." [34]

To underscore his brother's enormous vitality, Horace has pointed out that in the Philippines "he did an amount of work that would have crushed an ordinary man and that required a great deal of physical exertion." [35] William Howard Taft's innate generosity and genuine concern for the welfare of those who were close to him was put down by Horace as one of his most endearing attributes. And the Taftian sense of humor was legendary. Here was a man who could and would tell a joke which made himself the butt, and there was much of the humane and of the compassionate in his interpersonal relationships.

The impact of Taft's brothers, Charles Phelps and Henry Walters, was also important. It was Charles Phelps, a prominent lawyer and newspaper publisher in Cincinnati, who provided the necessary financing so that William Howard could assume various governmental posts. This was true for an age-old reason in American history—the inadequacy of governmental salaries and hence the utter impossibility of maintaining the required standard of living on such limited stipends. Although he exercised less influence intellectually than Horace, Charles Phelps's voice was that of a more orthodox conservative. The role of Henry Walters is more difficult to define. His main usefulness in relation to Taft's public life stemmed from a wide and apparently intimate acquaintance with the key public figures of the day. And Henry was most

34. Horace Dutton Taft, *Memories and Opinions* (New York, 1942), p. 107.
35. *Ibid.*, p. 108.

ambitious for his brother's preferment. Behind the scenes he played a most unostentatious but highly effective role in advancing his brother's career. Henry seemed to enjoy the role of the inobtrusive arranger of great events; he undertook representations with Secretary Root and even with President Roosevelt on behalf of William Howard when necessity arose. The point is that the combined services of all the Taft brothers presented a formidable team and a unique one devoted to the single purpose of advancing a political career. But it is also a tribute to Taft on the personal level that he was able to command such unselfish devotion and generosity.

William Howard's wife, Helen Herron, played a role far more significant than that of the traditional, genteel wife of a public figure.[36] She was charming, bright, and totally consumed by one overpowering obsession. She, above all else, and more than anyone else in the family, sought for her husband the biggest prize of all—the presidency of the United States. His wife always had great plans for him, plans first formulated in the early stages of their common life. Nellie, a loyal helpmate, accompanied her husband on many of his far-flung journeys, such as those to the Philippines and Panama. Taft loved her dearly and seemed to be willing always to serve her. Despite the eminence of her husband's various positions, and the demands they made upon his time, Mrs. Taft insisted—and successfully—upon the performance of some rather routine tasks. Thus, for example, William Howard undertook such prosaic correspondence as answering social courtesies and renewing his wife's magazine subscriptions.

Although the Cincinnati of William Taft's youth had a population of better than 200,000 by 1870, it was little more than a series of villages.[37] Hence, William's formative years were

36. I am indebted to Professor George E. Mowry for a correct understanding of Helen Herron Taft's character and plans for William Howard Taft. The reader should see Professor Mowry's splendid book *The Era of Theodore Roosevelt 1900–1912* (New York, 1958), 233–234, 269.

37. Pringle, *Taft*, I, 20.

spent in a comparatively small-town atmosphere. The fortunate son of a well-bred family in comfortable circumstances, he had a happy, uneventful childhood.[38] He was reading and spelling when, six years old, he entered the Nineteenth District Public School, although he was less proficient in arithmetic and writing. He soon demonstrated that he combined a fine mind with an ability to concentrate. At Woodward High School in downtown Cincinnati, which he entered in 1870, Taft was a splendid student, standing second highest in his senior year.[39] Although an active, outdoor boy, he was an omnivorous reader, not only of the usual children's books, but also of technical and historical works.[40] His interest in current events was fed by newspapers and magazines.[41]

In the fall of 1874 Taft was admitted to the freshman class of Yale.[42] He did well there, graduating on June 27, 1878, the second in scholarship of a class of 132. The faculty appointed him salutatorian for the commencement; his classmates elected him class orator. In addition, he won several special honors in subjects to which he devoted particular interest.[43] He was singled out for membership in Skull and Bones, a senior society which sought men "of outstanding personality and great force in undergraduate life." [44]

It was preordained that William Howard should study law upon his graduation from Yale, for as his younger brother Horace observed later, "all of us Tafts went into the law as naturally as we went from junior year to senior year in college." [45] So, William Taft went back to Cincinnati, where in

38. Herbert S. Duffy, *William Howard Taft* (New York, 1930), 5.

39. Pringle, *Taft*, I, 22–28; Dunn, *Taft*, 215.

40. McHale, *President and Chief Justice*, 20.

41. Meditating on these years, William wrote to a close friend: "My memory of your mother goes back as far as anything I can recall. I spent a large part of my boyhood in your house, either playing with you or the boys, or reading *Harper's Weekly* in those great volumes of which I was so fond. It is sad to look back and see how closely associated we all were in those days and how time and circumstances have set us apart now." W. H. Taft to Mrs. Sallie Shaffer, Jan. 7, 1909, Taft MSS.

42. Dunn, *Taft*, 216.

43. Pringle, *Taft*, I, 44; Dunn, *Taft*, 217.

44. Pringle, *Taft*, I, 40.

45. Taft, *Memories and Opinions*, 48.

1880 he received his law degree from the Cincinnati Law School and was admitted to the Ohio bar.[46] There followed several years during which he engaged in politics, held various minor political offices, practiced law, and toured Europe. The latter experience broadened his interest in and perspective about world affairs.[47]

William Howard Taft went on the bench, the place where he was happiest, in March, 1887, when Governor Joseph B. Foraker appointed him to the Superior Court of Ohio for the unfinished term of Judge Judson Harmon, who had resigned.[48] After serving the unexpired term of fourteen months, Taft was renominated by the Republican party and in April, 1888, was elected for a five-year term, winning by a vote of 21,025 to 14,844 for William Disney, the Democratic candidate.[49] This was the only office except the presidency of the United States which Taft achieved by popular vote.[50] Few of the youthful judge's opinions were of great legal significance. They revealed a thorough judicial mind, coupled with a tendency toward verbosity in writing.[51]

With such a limited judicial background, it is astonishing that Judge Taft was seriously considered in 1889 for associate justice on the Supreme Court of the United States. It even astonished Taft. Although he exerted all the influence that he could to obtain the appointment, he did not share the optimistic view of those who felt he might get it.[52] He wrote to his father: "My chances of going to the moon and of donning a silk gown at the hands of President Harrison are about

46. DAB, XVIII, 266.

47. The following passage from a letter shortly after the renewal of the Dreiksasiserbund treaty, and while Alphonso Taft was minister to Russia, is representative: "Father was not present I suppose at the kissing of the three Emperors. It is hard to understand why they should kiss each other when next year they may be shooting at each other. Judging from the extraordinary preparation made for dynamiters, the life of an Emperor is not a happy one." W. H. Taft to Louise Taft, Sept. 22, 1884, Taft MSS.

48. DAB, XVIII, 266.

49. McHale, *President and Chief Justice*, 45.

50. DAB, XVIII, 266–267.

51. Pringle, *Taft*, I, 100.

52. DAB, XVII, 267; Pringle, *Taft*, I, 106.

equal. I am quite sure if I were he I would not appoint a man of my age and position to that bench." [53]

Harrison lived up to Taft's expectations, but shortly thereafter offered him a valuable consolation prize, the post of solicitor general of the United States. Taft accepted and assumed office on February 4, 1890.[54] The prime appeal to the work of solicitor general during the first year was its variety.[55] The issues were less interesting than the ones which had come before him while serving on the Superior Court of Ohio, but Taft acquired a detailed knowledge of federal procedure.[56] This was to change in January, 1891, however, when Taft was faced with the case of in re Cooper, which developed out of the Bering Sea controversy.[57] The facts in this case were, briefly, as follows: The W. P. Sayward, a Canadian sailing schooner engaged in the seal trade and owned by a British subject named Cooper, was seized by a United States revenue cutter. This action was taken because the United States government claimed control over seal fishing in the entire Bering Sea. The schooner was ordered forfeited and condemned. Cooper presented, through the British Foreign Office, a claim for damages. The secretary of state, James G. Blaine, rejected the claim, and Great Britain then proposed arbitration. However, before any determination was reached, the British government abandoned diplomacy and turned to law, appealing formally to the Supreme Court of the United States for a writ of prohibition to prevent the sale of the vessel by the Federal District Court of Alaska.[58]

53. W. H. Taft to Alphonso Taft, Aug. 24, 1889, Taft MSS.
54. DAB, XVIII, 267; Pringle, Taft, I, 116.
55. Ibid.
56. Ibid.
57. Ibid.; Duffy, Taft, 29–30. This controversy arose when the United States began its protective policy of the seals in Alaskan waters. It was only one of the long series of issues which produced friction between the United States and Great Britain. For a detailed, scholarly analysis of this controversy and its settlement see Charles S. Campbell, "The Anglo-American Crisis in the Bering Sea, 1890–1891," The Mississippi Valley Historical Review, XLVIII (Dec., 1961), 393–414, and the same author's "The Bering Sea Settlements of 1892," Pacific Historical Review, XXXII (Nov., 1963), 347–367.
58. Duffy, Taft, 31–32; Pringle, Taft, I, 118.

Taft and the attorney general, William H. H. Miller, prepared the answer to the application.[59] Although annoyed because the application had been made abruptly and without proper notice, Taft did not reflect the popular temper by baiting the British government. Instead, he observed mildly: "I think Great Britain had departed from diplomatic courtesy in going by the executive and State Department to the courts, and I shall not be at all surprised if they go out of the court with a flea in their ear on this point."[60]

Taft's prediction proved correct, for the Supreme Court refused to issue a writ of prohibition, concurring instead in Taft's argument that "an application to a court to review the action of the political department of the Government upon a question between it and a foreign power, made while diplomatic negotiations were going on, should be denied."[61]

While this dispute was being adjudicated, the United States became involved in a major diplomatic controversy with Italy.[62] Many Sicilians, some burdened with criminal records and a number of them alleged to be members of the Mafia Black Hand Society, had gathered in New Orleans, where they carried on their vendettas, chiefly among themselves. When a chief of police who was tracking down the criminals lost his life by foul play, a number of Italians were put on trial. None of them were convicted, however. Aroused by what they believed was a perversion of justice, a mob of several thousand broke into the jail on March 14, 1891, and killed eleven Italians, who had either been acquitted or were being detained as suspects. The inflamed feelings produced

59. W. H. Taft to Alphonso Taft, Jan. 23, 1891, Taft MSS.
60. *Ibid.*
61. Duffy, *Taft*, 32.
62. Thomas A. Bailey, *A Diplomatic History of the American People* (4th ed., New York, 1950), 499–550. For a valuable assessment of this Mafia controversy see Jules A. Karlin, "The Indemnification of Aliens Injured by Mob Violence," *Southwestern Social Science Quarterly*, XXV (March, 1945), 235–246. Karlin believes that the incident produced a war scare that contributed to a new sense of national unity in the United States. See Jules A. Karlin, "The Italo-American Incident of 1891 and the Road to Reunion," *Journal of Southern History*, VIII (May, 1942), 242–246. See also John E. Coxe, "The New Orleans Mafia Incident," *Louisiana Historical Society*, XX (Oct., 1937), 1067–1110.

by this act, particularly in Italy, led to much talk about the possibility of war.

In a letter to his father on this episode, Taft pointed out one of the consequences of the Constitutional doctrine of states rights: "The recent outbreak in New Orleans against the Italians has raised some rather embarrassing international questions, and emphasizes the somewhat anomalous character of our Government, which makes the National Government responsible for the actions of the State authorities without giving it any power to control that action." [63] This is a point of some importance. More than once in our history (as in the California segregation incident of 1906 involving Oriental pupils or the California land laws which long made it impossible for Chinese and Japanese nationals to own land) a state has complicated the foreign relations of the nation.

During his two years as solicitor general, Taft argued twenty-seven cases before the Supreme Court and won a national reputation as an able and promising counselor.[64] The circle of his friends and acquaintances widened to include such sparkling personalities as Theodore Roosevelt, John Hay, and Henry Cabot Lodge.[65] He was on good terms with President Harrison, who sought his advice on judicial appointments.[66] However, he formed his closest friendships with the members of the Supreme Court and the attorney general.[67] Strangely enough, despite his many accomplishments, reflected in the spectacular advance of his career, Taft was plagued with doubts and convinced that mediocrity was to be his future lot.[68] Perhaps he was uneasy as to where he would go from the solicitorship. He had reason to feel some frustration.

63. W. H. Taft to Alphonso Taft, March 18, 1891, Taft MSS. This incident was closed officially when the United States paid $25,000 to Italy. Bailey, A Diplomatic History, 451–452.
64. Duffy, Taft, 33.
65. Pringle, Taft, I, 113–114; Theodore Roosevelt to W. H. Taft, Aug. 19, 1891, Roosevelt, Letters, I, 258–259.
66. Pringle, Taft, I, 115.
67. Ibid., 144; Helen Taft, Recollections, 28.
68. Pringle, Taft, I, 120–121.

But once again, circumstances were to shape the course of his career. The volume of litigation in the federal courts had been increasing for some years and in March, 1891, Congress took action to correct the situation by creating an appeals court in each of the nine circuits in the United States, and by requiring the appointment of an additional judge for each of the new courts. Taft was the logical choice for the opening in the sixth circuit and was recommended for it by members of the Cincinnati and Ohio bar.[69] Senator John Sherman of Ohio provided additional support, speaking directly to President Harrison on Taft's behalf.[70] Despite such impressive backing, months passed and nothing happened.

Finally, on March 21, 1892, William Howard Taft resigned from his post as solicitor general to become United States circuit judge for the Sixth Judicial Circuit and ex-officio member of the Circuit Court of Appeals of the sixth circuit.[71] The sixth circuit of the Federal Circuit Court was a court of precise and strict traditions.[72] Its jurisdiction spread over the states of Kentucky, Michigan, Ohio, and Tennessee, and its judges had to cope with a wide variety of legal problems. For Taft, a man of pronounced judicial tastes who was also developing into a profound legal scholar, the appointment was ideal.[73] He served on this court with great distinction for eight years, which were among the happiest years of his life.[74] In 1896 Taft also became the dean and professor of property at the Cincinnati Law School.[75] The additional work was congenial to him because of his loyalty to the school, his alma mater in the law, and because of his intense interest in legal education.

Taft's increasing prestige during his years on the bench was reflected in the fact that he was sounded out for the presi-

69. Duffy, *Taft*, 33.
70. Pringle, *Taft*, I, 122.
71. *Ibid.*
72. Duffy, *Taft*, 34.
73. DAB, XVIII, 267.
74. Helen Taft, *Recollections*, 30.
75. Pringle, *Taft*, I, 125.

dency of Yale in January, 1899.[76] His refusal to be considered is interesting because of the light it throws on his character. He believed there were "two insuperable objections" which made him unsuitable as the president of Yale.[77] The first of these was religious: he was a Unitarian, while Yale found its strongest support among the members of the orthodox Evangelical churches. Taft was convinced that "it would shock the large conservative element of those who give Yale her power and influence in the country to see one chosen to the Presidency who could not subscribe to the creed of the Orthodox Congregational Church of New England." [78] The election of such a person would stimulate a bitterness of feeling and suspicion among his co-workers that "would deprive him of all usefulness and would be seriously detrimental to the University." [79]

His second objection was that he lacked the background and professional training necessary for the post. While Taft conceded that a great university needed a man of affairs, with executive ability, as its leader, and while he was attracted by the power of the position for good "in the discussion of public affairs and the guiding of public thought," he believed that the main function of a university made mandatory the selection of an educator as its chief officer.[80] He saw the educator as belonging to a distinct profession, like law, or the ministry, and believed that education for the first should be as distinct as for the other two. As a man specifically trained for law and, since his graduation, exclusively occupied with its practice and study, Taft felt himself "necessarily lacking in the wide culture, breadth of learning, and technical preparation in the science of education" needed by a university president.[81] Yale's loss was probably the country's gain. The

76. Henry W. Taft to W. H. Taft, Jan. 14, 1899, Taft MSS.
77. W. H. Taft to Henry W. Taft, Jan. 23, 1899, *ibid.*
78. *Ibid.*
79. *Ibid.*
80. *Ibid.*
81. *Ibid.*

very scrupulousness which characterized Taft's refusal would, I think, have made him as president of Yale unavailable to McKinley in 1900. He was no more the man to abandon an obligation lightly than he was to assume it lightly.

The closing years of the nineteenth century were full of provocative incidents and controversial issues affecting foreign policy which forced themselves upon public attention.[82] In terms of their impact upon Taft, however, only the most provocative crises, those which actually held out the possibility of war, caught his attention, and then only fleetingly. Thus, the day after Grover Cleveland sent Congress his famous, ill-tempered pronouncement on the dispute between Great Britain and Venezuela over the boundary line between British Guiana and Venezuela, Taft expressed disapproval:

> Cleveland's message, it seems to me, is phrased in such a way·as to make it difficult for the country to avoid a war with England without a backdown that will be humiliating. It might have accomplished the same purpose, had it assumed a more conciliatory tone and still recommended an investigation into the boundary question in order to determine whether England's course had been in fact an attempt to steal by force a large territory under the guise of a contention over a mere boundary difference.[83]

This short paragraph illuminates Taft's approach to foreign affairs. His primary concern was that the United States avoid international complications which might lead to war. The inference can be drawn from the first sentence that the United States could not afford a war with Great Britain. The remainder of the paragraph, with its judicious approach and steady focus on the substantive issue in question, reflects the conditioning of a legal background. Although critical of the president's belligerence, Taft assumed that Cleveland de-

82. Richard W. Van Alstyne, *American Diplomacy in Action* (2nd ed., Stanford, 1947), 617–618.
83. W. H. Taft to Helen H. Taft, Dec. 18, 1895, Taft MSS.

sired to have a genuine investigation into the entire boundary question. This in actuality was the case.[84]

But the comment reveals decided limitations in Taft's knowledge of foreign affairs at that time. The power-political aspects of the boundary dispute largely eluded him. He did not seem to grasp the central point of Cleveland's message—that the government of Great Britain recognize the right of the United States to assert an overriding authority in any affair of the Western hemisphere. Although the relating of the Monroe Doctrine to this dispute can be, and I believe should be, considered farfetched, it is a commentary on Taft's understanding of these events that he did not even mention that doctrine. Finally, it seems strange that Taft, who did not share the widespread Anglophobia that engulfed the nation, should ignore entirely the role played in the Venezuela crisis by Richard Olney, the secretary of state. Although Olney's famed dispatch of July 20, 1895, was published shortly before President Cleveland's message and presented views in direct contrast to those held by Taft, the latter at least in written form did not react.[85]

The other crisis sufficiently perilous to goad Taft into expressing an opinion was the Cuban uprising of February 24, 1895, against Spanish rule, which after a long and tortuous path ended on April 21, 1898, in war between Spain and the United States. In late March, 1896, after paying a social call on John Hay, Taft wrote to his wife: "Hay is wild about Cuba and is in favor of war to free her from Spain." [86] This brief and noncommittal remark was the only allusion by Taft to the Cuban question until the end of March, 1898.

In January, 1897, his friend, William Hallett Phillips, wrote a scathing denunciation of the Congress and of President McKinley for their indifference to the plight of the Cuban people "who are making one of the most glorious struggles in

84. Van Alstyne, *American Diplomacy*, 212.
85. Samuel Flagg Bemis, *A Diplomatic History of the United States* (4th ed., New York, 1955), 418–419.
86. W. H. Taft to Helen H. Taft, March 24, 1896, Taft MSS.

the century, for emancipation from the Spanish yoke." [87] Taft did not respond to the challenging points; in fact, he did not answer at all. Phillips may not have expected a reply, for near the end of his letter he observed: "But I know the subject is not one which interests you as it does interest me nor do you attach to it the importance which I do." [88]

Phillips was to be proved correct on both counts. Even the publication of the de Lôme letter on February 9, 1898, with its caustic comments about President McKinley, or the destruction by explosion of the battleship *Maine* six days later failed to elicit a response from Taft. Finally, on March 30, 1898, as the mania for a war with Spain rose to fever pitch, Taft wrote directly to President McKinley, praising his conduct:

> The courageous stand you have taken to avert the horrors of war if it can be avoided with honor, and the brave resistance you have made against the thoughtless jingoism of some and the blatant demagoguery of others in and out of Congress have won for you the deep and abiding admiration and gratitude of the American people. The shallows murmur while the deeps are decent. The froth of public sentiment is often its greatest impurity.
>
> No one can know the pressure to which you have been subjected to induce you to depart from the wise and conservative policy you are pursuing, but it is the duty of those of us who faintly realize it to express the strong feeling of sympathy we have in the position you have taken and the pride we feel that our nation has at its head a humane, clear headed, able statesman who can not be frightened from the course which honor, patriotism and a love for humanity marks out for him by a pseudo-popular clamor. If war comes, it must be a just war and it can not be just if all that war could accomplish can be wrought by peaceful methods.
>
> I earnestly hope that the serious strain to which the present crisis must subject you will not affect your health.[89]

87. W. Hallett Phillips to W. H. Taft, Jan. 13, 1897, *ibid.*
88 *Ibid.*
89. W. H. Taft to W. McKinley, March 30, 1898, McKinley MSS. There were powerful countervailing forces that were leading the nation almost irresistibly toward

Taft remained unsympathetic to the popular outcry for war.[90] The progress of the war with Spain held little interest for him, and his comments about it were few and of little significance. Two days after the Spanish fleet was swiftly and totally destroyed outside the harbor of Santiago, Cuba, Taft observed that in Cincinnati the sky was full of balloons and the people were in a good humor.[91] He took notice, also, of the exploits of Theodore Roosevelt and the American troops at the battle of San Juan Hill. His only comments, however, were that Roosevelt had thus far escaped injury, and that the losses among the officers had been much greater proportionately than among the men.[92]

If the Spanish-American War failed to capture Taft's interest or enlist his sympathies, the Boer War produced exactly the opposite effect. One day after the famous "black week" (December 9–15, 1899) during which the British suffered three defeats and found their forces beleaguered in Ladysmith, Kimberley, and Mafeking, he showed pronounced concern in a letter to his wife: "The English are suffering serious and humiliating defeats in South Africa. I am very sorry for my sympathies are with them. The world will see how powerful England is before she gets through with this struggle for she is now fighting for her prestige as a colonial power and that is her life." [93] Here, Taft felt that a vital national interest was at stake, and hence saw that war was necessary to protect it.

To sum up: McKinley's appointee as president of the Second Philippine Commission was a man of excellent family, well educated in a profession to which he was devoted. He was ambitious, like most men of his ability; but his ambition was qualified by a deep and strict personal integrity. His per-

war. Theodore Roosevelt was an eloquent and powerful spokesman. T. Roosevelt to Douglas Robinson, March 30, 1898, Roosevelt, *Letters*, II, 805–806.

90. Pringle, *Taft*, I, 154.
91. W. H. Taft to Helen H. Taft, July 5, 1898, Taft MSS.
92. *Ibid.*, July 8, 1898.
93. *Ibid.*, Dec. 16, 1899.

sonal qualities and professional accomplishments had won him high reputation and many friendships. Admittedly, he had shown little interest in or knowledge of American foreign affairs. But how many of his contemporaries were better equipped, particularly with regard to the Orient? The general enthusiasm over Taft's appointment indicates that Oriental specialists were difficult to come by in the United States. No one seems to have mentioned an alternative choice.

On the same day, February 6, 1900, that President McKinley announced Taft's appointment as president of the new Philippine Commission, the two conferred at the White House regarding the details and personnel of the commission.[94] McKinley said to Taft: "I propose to give you the full power of appointment of those who are to assist you." [95] This proved to be no idle promise, for McKinley consulted Taft before selecting any of the other four members of the Philippine Commission.[96] The other members were Vice-Governor Luke E. Wright of Tennessee, a Democrat and former attorney-general of that state, Dean C. Worcester of Michigan, a zoologist on the faculty of the University of Michigan and the only member of the commission who had ever been in the Philippines, Henry Clay Ide of Vermont, formerly chief justice of the United States Court in Samoa and therefore a man with some experience in colonial government, and Bernard Moses of California, a professor of history at the University of California and a writer of note on the history of the Spanish colonies in America.[97] Taft was highly pleased with McKinley's other appointments, because he felt that through

94. *New York Times*, Feb. 7, 1900; Duffy, *Taft*, 79; Leech, *McKinley*, 485.

95. Olcott, *McKinley*, II, 178; Leech, *McKinley*, 485. McKinley's grant of appointive power to Taft, his provision for an efficient and honest civil service, and his vigorous speeches were an effective answer to the accusation that the McKinley administration of the Philippine Islands would be crippled by spoils politics. Leech, *McKinley*, 485–487.

96. W. H. Taft to W. McKinley, Feb. 26, 1800, McKinley MSS.

97. W. Cameron Forbes, *The Philippine Islands* (2 vols., Boston, 1928), I, 124–125; Pringle, *Taft*, I, 165. The appointments of the members of the Philippine Commission were dated March 16, 1900. Dean C. Worcester, *The Philippines Past and Present* (New York, 1930), 269.

the diversified talents of its members the commission was broadly qualified for work both in practical government and research.[98]

On March 29, 1900, the members of the commission met in Washington and completed preparations for their departure.[99] Much of their three-day stay was spent with Elihu Root, secretary of war, discussing the powers, functions, and duties that the commission would have.[100] The members made many suggestions, which they discussed with Root at great length. From his notes of their meetings, the secretary drafted a set of instructions for the commission, which were issued, after some minor changes by President McKinley, on April 7, 1900.[101] These instructions were "the magna carta of the Philippines." [102] They contained the germ of all future government and advancement for the Philippine Islands, as well as valuable suggestions for future legislation.[103]

Henry F. Pringle, his biographer, states that Taft knew "as much—and as little—about the Philippine Islands as the average American." [104] At a later date, Taft admitted that this was indeed the case.[105] But Taft did have some general ideas about what should be done in the Philippines. First, the commission had to convince the Filipinos of its desire to give them individual liberty and a large measure of political self-government.[106] Their individual liberty should be secured by

98. Helen Taft, Recollections, 45.

99. New York Times, March 30, 1900; W. H. Taft to Charles P. Taft, April 2, 1900, Taft MSS.

100. W. H. Taft to James LeRoy, Dec. 1, 1905, ibid.; New York Times, March 30, 1900.

101. Garel A. Grunder and William E. Livezey, The Philippines and the United States (Norman, Oklahoma, 1951), 63. Because it was deemed unwise to do so, these instructions were not released publicly. W. H. Taft to Charles P. Taft, April 15, 1900, Taft MSS.

102. James Ford Rhodes, The McKinley and Roosevelt Administrations, 1897–1909 (New York, 1922), 197.

103. Arthur Wallace Dunn, From Harrison to Harding: A Personal Narrative, Covering a Third of a Century, 1888–1921 (2 vols., New York, 1922), 256.

104. Pringle, Taft, I, 157.

105. Address by William Howard Taft at Nashua, New Hampshire, on February 19, 1908, Addresses and Articles, IX, 2, Taft MSS.

106. W. H. Taft to Harrison Gray Otis, April 14, 1900, Taft MSS.

all the constitutional guarantees contained in the state and federal constitutions in the United States. Taft believed these conditions essential to the restoration of peace and to the establishment of a government—tasks which would not be the work "of a day, or a week, or a month, or indeed a year," but of several years.[107]

As a matter of fact, the commission's instructions, which had been drafted principally by Elihu Root,[108] were specific on the question of guarantees of individual liberty and the conditions under which the Filipinos were to be permitted self-government.[109] All legislative power was to be transferred from the military governor to the commission on September 1, 1900. The commission was to establish provincial and municipal governments, and prepare the central government for complete transfer to civilian authority. The government created by the commission should be designed for the happiness, peace, and prosperity of the Filipinos; their customs, habits, and even prejudices should be conformed to as far as possible, consonant with just and effective government.[110] Nevertheless, the United States adhered to certain principles of government, essential to the rule of law and the maintenance of liberty. If local patterns interfered with these principles, then local patterns would have to give way. The instructions included a bill of rights similar to that in the United States Constitution. As the outline and the framework within which the civil government of the Philippines was to be formed and develop, the instructions were "thick with paternalism"; but, considering the general outlook of the McKinley administration and the expansionist sentiment in the United States, they were surprisingly liberal.[111] After more than half a century, during which the issues, conflicts, and

107. W. H. Taft to E. B. McCagg, April 16, 1900, Taft MSS.
108. Philip C. Jessup, *Elihu Root* (New York, 1938), I, 354.
109. *Papers Relating to the Foreign Relations of the United States, with the Annual Message of the President, House Documents,* U.S. 56 Cong., 1 Sess., No. 1 (1900), pp. xxxiv–xxxix.
110. Jessup, *Root,* I, 354.
111. David Bernstein, *The Philippine Story,* 85.

passions of the time have become more clearly understood, they still stand critical examination well.

While Taft's thought had moved from an original anticolonialism to where he subscribed to the paternalistic doctrine of the commission's instructions, he was quite aware that considerable anticolonial sentiment persisted in the United States.[112] Surely he was forcibly reminded of it by a chance meeting with William Jennings Bryan.[113] Shortly before the commission sailed, Taft had gone to San Diego to visit his sister, Mrs. Fanny Edwards. Bryan happened to be on the same train, and the two men talked on the way from Los Angeles to San Diego. Presumably, Bryan wanted to obtain Taft's views on policy in the Philippines; actually, he spent much of the trip lecturing Taft—on a variety of subjects. He told Taft that "the divine right of kings was still the moving force in the British form of government, and that there were a great many people in this country who wished we had a king." [114] He added, irrelevantly, that Great Britain, by means of the gold standard, was robbing India of hundreds of millions of pounds a year and producing famine in that unhappy country. Taft took exception to these and other arguments, whereupon Bryan said that he could not expect to convince a man who believed in the divine rights of kings. This misrepresentation angered Taft, and before their conversation ended the two men had "got down to some pretty plain talk." [115] Taft confessed in a letter that his respect for Bryan was "measurably decreased by the exhibition which he gave of himself," and went on: "His knowledge of history is defective; his style is that of the veriest demagogue, and while he is a handsome fellow, and has a good voice, I should be sorry to think of him as President of the

112. Pringle, *Taft*, I, 188; W. H. Taft to Annie G. Roelker, April 16, 1900; W. H. Taft to Louise Taft, April 17, 1900, Taft MSS.
113. Pringle, *Taft*, I, 188; W. H. Taft to Annie G. Roelker, April 16, 1900; W. H. Taft to Louise Taft, April 17, 1900, Taft MSS.
114. W. H. Taft to Annie G. Roelker, April 16, 1900, *ibid.*
115. W. H. Taft to Louise Taft, April 17, 1900, *ibid.*

United States, even if I agreed with his peculiar views." [116]
Taft's opinion that the work of the commission would take
years must have made the thought of a Democratic administration under Bryan doubly unwelcome.

But he had accepted the summons to public service and
was prepared for the great adventure when the commission
took ship for the Philippines in the summer of 1900. His once
placid star began its ascent in the political sky. For the great
part of two decades William Howard Taft was to devote much
of his time, energy, and thought to the problems created by
the growing participation of America in world affairs.

116. W. H. Taft to Annie G. Roelker, April 16, 1900, *ibid.*

CHAPTER II

The Judge and the General: The Establishment of Civil Government in the Philippines

ON APRIL 17, 1900, a brilliant, golden, sunny day, the United States Army transport *Hancock* with the Second Philippine Commission on board pulled away from the crowded dock at San Francisco, California, while whistles shrieked a shrill farewell and the air rang with enthusiastic cheers.[1] The boat had barely passed through San Francisco harbor when the commissioners began to hold their first meeting. All of them realized the stern nature of their task. The physical character of the Philippine Islands, the nature of its people, the prevalent uncertain social and political conditions, and a host of other factors made the work of pacifying the islands and creating a civil government complex. William Howard Taft, the "first American viceroy," was perfectly attuned to the exacting, strenuous duties which lay before him as he began the long journey to the Philippines: "He was as patient as he was large in frame. He was tolerant. He could be stubborn when stubbornness was a virtue. Above all, he had a vast capacity for affection and before very long he had become very fond, indeed, of the little men who had become, sometimes gladly and sometimes resentfully, the wards of Uncle Sam."[2]

1. Duffy, *Taft*, 86.
2. Pringle, *Taft*, I, 164–165.

During the voyage to the Philippines, the *Hancock* made stops at Honolulu, Yokohama, and Hong Kong.[3] The Philippine Commission arrived at Honolulu just before Congress passed an organic act for the Hawaiian Islands.[4] Taft wrote directly to President McKinley of his impressions, based on a three-day visit.[5] Taft believed that the changes contemplated by the "new annexation act" would be radical, and that patience and a conservative approach would be mandatory if friction were to be avoided.[6] He felt that the largely native Monarchical party would give the most trouble, because it was the party most prone to engage in intrigue and the least stable of all the factions. The question of who should become governor was of intense interest, and Taft recommended Sanford B. Dole. After citing his knowledge of the Hawaiian Islands and their peoples, his conservatism and his high personal character, Taft added significantly: "It is the custom to decry the missionary element here, but it is that which gave us these pearls of the Pacific and which has really made them what they are—I do not think a Missionary Governor would be a bad balance wheel for a probably native majority in the legislature." [7]

The impressions of three days were obviously naive. Had Taft spent more time in the islands he might have realized that when it came to intrigue the coalition which made the Hawaiian Revolution, deposed Liliuokalani, and arranged annexation could give the native party aces and spades, and win—as they had done. He might also have come to admit that Sanford Dole and his associates represented the busi-

3. Duffy, *Taft*, 86.
4. On April 30, 1900, Congress enacted an organic act for the Territory of Hawaii, which was to take effect forty-five days after the date of approval. The effect of this organic act was to make Hawaii an incorporated territory. Julius W. Pratt, *America's Colonial Experiment: How the United States Gained, Governed, and in Part Gave Away a Colonial Empire* (New York, 1950), 179 (hereinafter referred to as Pratt, *America's Colonial Experiment*).
5. W. H. Taft to William McKinley, April 27, 1900, McKinley MSS.
6. *Ibid.*
7. *Ibid.* President McKinley for the same reasons nominated Sanford B. Dole for the governorship on May 4, 1900. The United States Senate confirmed the appointment. William McKinley to W. H. Taft, May 21, 1900, McKinley MSS.

ness community at least as much as the "missionary element." But the letter shows Taft to be a much more convinced expansionist than he was when he first talked to President McKinley about the Philippines. And one might be excused for wondering whether Taft did not feel his own future role to be that of a "missionary governor" preaching the doctrine of "liberty in law."

His experiences in Hawaii, and the discouraging reports on the Philippines which he received at every port *en voyage,* strengthened Taft's conviction that McKinley's re-election was essential to the eventual success of the commission.[8] The re-election would convince the Filipinos that the United States would continue its sovereignty in the islands; this, in turn, would increase their confidence in the continuity of the commission, and possibly encourage their support of it. The progress which he hoped the commission would be able to make in projected reforms should further conciliate the islanders and gain their support. On the other hand, the election of Bryan, on which, he noted, the insurgent Filipinos were counting, would produce "turmoil and anarchy in the Islands, with the subsequent annexation of the Islands to the United States just as Hawaii has been annexed under the succeeding Republican Administration, after the failure of the Cleveland Administration to restore the status quo ante." [9] It is interesting to speculate as to why Taft had come to view the annexation of the Hawaiian Islands with equanimity, but was unwilling to see the outright annexation of the Philippines. Possibly he felt that the Hawaiian culture and government were already substantially American in tone and would become increasingly so, while he did not feel that this would happen in the Philippines.

But even if McKinley were re-elected, there would be difficult problems in the Philippines: it became more and more obvious to the commission that the American authorities had

8. W. H. Taft to Charles P. Taft, June 2, 1900, Taft MSS.
9. *Ibid.*

woefully mismanaged public affairs to the point where any hope of speedily pacifying the islands was remote. Taft was particularly disturbed by what he heard about the conduct of the army. Apparently, frustrated by the effective bush warfare of the insurgents, and (quite normally) looking for an alibi, the American soldiers decided that Filipino tactics were "uncivilized." [10] The alibi only reinforced whatever racial feeling was latent in the soldiers, who began to regard and treat all Filipinos as "niggers." [11] Social and racial prejudice appeared to be especially strong among the "Ladies of the Army." The commission proposed to end this situation as quickly as possible. Taft, himself, felt quite strongly about it. He concluded that the conduct of the United States Army toward the natives had not been as conciliatory as it should have been.

There was one ray of hope in an otherwise depressing situation. On arriving at Hong Kong, Taft sent a cable to Major General Arthur MacArthur, the military governor in the Philippines.[12] Taft and his fellow commissioners received a reassuring response: "Cordial greeting and warm welcome await the commission." [13] The members of the commission were very glad to receive this cable because, as Taft reasoned, "it argues strongly that MacArthur intends to cooperate as fully as he can with the commission, and that he does not intend to pursue the policy which Otis pursued of ignoring the old commission, and making light of its efforts." [14] The solicitude

10. W. H. Taft to Helen H. Taft, May 30, 1900; W. H. Taft to Charles P. Taft, June 2, 1900, *ibid.*
11. *Ibid.*
12. *Ibid.*
13. W. H. Taft to Helen H. Taft, May 31, 1900, *ibid.*
14. W. H. Taft to Charles P. Taft, June 2, 1900, *ibid.* The reference is to Major General Elwell S. Otis, who was designated military governor of the Philippine Islands on August 29, 1898. On May 5, 1900, General Otis was relieved at his own request and returned to the United States. General MacArthur was selected to succeed him. Forbes, *The Philippine Islands*, I, 74, 102. General Otis was famed for his inefficiency and indecision. As General MacArthur once put it: "Otis is a locomotive bottom side up, with the wheels revolving at full speed." Clark Lee and Richard Henschel, *Douglas MacArthur* (New York, 1952), 19.

and warmth of General MacArthur seemed to augur well for a spirit of cooperation and compromise between the commission and the military regime.

On June 3, 1900, a blistering, hot, tropical Sunday, the *Hancock* anchored in Manila Bay and the commissioners retired to the ship's cabin to await the arrival of Major General MacArthur.[15] Instead, however, the general sent his launch to bring the five commissioners ashore and an artillery battalion escorted them to the Ayuntamiento, the civil building of the city of Manila, where General MacArthur had his headquarters.[16] General MacArthur extended a formal but most cordial welcome to the members of the commission and an hour later he came out to the *Hancock* to return their call.[17] Taft thought him "a pleasant looking man, very self-contained." [18] The next day Taft and MacArthur had lunch informally at Malacanan Palace.[19] Although he suggested that the commission find offices elsewhere than in the Ayuntamiento, the general did not press the point and soon arranged separate offices for each commissioner in that building which was "pleasant and cool." [20] He even helped Taft find a suitable residence. Twelve days after his arrival, Taft wrote to McKinley that MacArthur had been "most courteous and anxious in every way to cooperate with us to bring about the end we both have in view." [21] On so short an acquaintance, he could hardly have said less in what was, after all, an official communication. But a slightly earlier letter to his brother

15. Pringle, *Taft*, I, 167–169.
16 Rowland T. Berthoff, "Taft and MacArthur, 1900–1901: A Study in Civil-Military Relations," *World Politics*, V (Jan., 1953), 197; W. H. Taft to Charles P. Taft, June 12, 1900, Taft MSS. Professor Berthoff sent me a copy of his splendid article recently. Although I had finished my work on Taft in the Philippines, it was beneficial—even stimulating—to read the writings of another scholar in the same subject area. I found that we had differing approaches to the subject, that I was more concerned with the role of William Howard Taft as was to be expected, and that I was and still am more critical of the actions of General Arthur MacArthur than Professor Berthoff.
17. W. H. Taft to Helen H. Taft, June 3, 1900, Taft MSS.
18. *Ibid.*
19. *Ibid.*, June 5, 1900.
20. *Ibid.*, June 13, 1900.
21. W. H. Taft to William McKinley, June 15, 1900, McKinley MSS.

Charles, in which he speaks of MacArthur as "exceedingly cordial . . . a very satisfactory man to do business with," shows no awareness of the jockeying for position which had begun with MacArthur's manner of welcoming Taft.[22] This letter is of further interest in that it gives Taft's sober, optimistic, and firm first estimate of the Philippine situation:

> The situation in Manila is perplexing. You meet men who are completely discouraged at it; you meet men who are conservative but very hopeful of good results; and you meet men who have roseate views of the situation. My own impression is that the back of the rebellion is broken, and that the state of robbery and anarchy which exists in the islands where the soldiers are not in control has induced a number of leading generals, quite a number of whom have been captured, to take the view that surrender is the best course. . . . I am very anxious that civil government shall be established. The Army is a necessary evil, but it is not an agent to encourage the establishment of a well-ordered civil government, and the Filipinos are anxious to be rid of policing by shoulder straps. . . . We shall be here two months at least before we assume the powers that are given us, and in that time we shall have occasion to make many investigations.[23]

As noted already, the Philippine Commission came to Manila armed with a lengthy set of instructions.[24] Basically, these instructions established the principle that the Filipinos were to have the widest possible control over their own affairs. At the same time, the Filipinos were reminded that their experience in government was meager. As was to be expected, many Filipinos were not satisfied. The heart of their argument was stated succinctly by one of their greatest statesmen, Ramon Magsaysay, when he wrote, "There is no substitute for complete self-government." [25]

22. W. H. Taft to Charles P. Taft, June 12, 1900, Taft MSS.
23. *Ibid.*
24. *Papers Relating to the Foreign Relations of the United States, with the Annual Message of the President*, U.S. 56 Cong., 1st Sess., No. 1 (1900), pp. xxxiv–xxxix.
25. Ramon Magsaysay, "Roots of Philippine Policy," *Foreign Affairs*, XXXV (Oct., 1956), 31.

Spain had governed the Philippines with her customary ineptitude.[26] Underpaid officials had been dishonest officials, and to the exactions of officialdom were added those of the Catholic religious orders, especially the Franciscans, Dominicans, Augustinians, and Recollects. Thus, Philippine discontent manifested itself chiefly in a determined opposition to the friars and to the existing political administration which the friars controlled.[27] These representatives of the Roman Catholic church performed many functions presently considered governmental and with the passage of time came to own over 400,000,000 acres of valuable land. They were harsh landlords and monopolized education.[28] The important posts in both state and church were reserved for Spaniards. The Filipinos—dismissed as "Indios" by the Spanish—were consistently treated as inferiors. These agents of the Roman Catholic church had become reactionary and venal by the nineteenth century.[29] All proposals of economic, political, and religious reforms were opposed rigorously.

Misgovernment and racial discrimination bred sporadic local rebellions over a period of years—notably the Cavite revolt of 1872.[30] In 1892 the Filipinos found a powerful leader in Jose Rizal, an able writer and extraordinary pro-

26. Pratt, *America's Colonial Experiment*, 193. Leon Wolff has written harshly but accurately: "Whatever Spain gave the Philippines in the form of decent human relations and modern institutions was incidental. Since the system was designed to nurture graft and racism, and to save souls for the Catholic Church, no attempt was made to develop economic factors or the free play of native culture. Occasional reformers who emanated from Madrid were murdered or otherwise rendered impotent. The country was really an enormous mission, rather than colony operated for commercial ends. Spanish law was paternal but autocratic; despite meaningless decrees, slavery was perpetuated. The people were thrust into a medieval mold, their initiative paralyzed, their education throttled. Taxation kept them poor. Except for a few middle-class pro-Spaniards, the natives were given no chance for advancement." Leon Wolff, *Little Brown Brother: How the United States Purchased and Pacified the Philippine Islands at the Century's Turn* (New York, 1961), 17 (hereinafter referred to as Wolff, *Little Brown Brother*).

27. Pratt, *America's Colonial Experiment*, 193; Grunder and Livezey, *The Philippines*, 12.

28. *Ibid.*

29. *Ibid.*

30. Pratt, *America's Colonial Experiment*, 193.

pagandist.[31] Rizal focused attention on the abuses of the Spanish authorities and on the even greater ones perpetuated by the Spanish priests. He did not advocate revolution or independence, but asked that reforms be instituted gradually from within. He organized the younger intellectuals and inaugurated the "Liga Filipina," a reform society composed of the less literate classes and devoted to economic development.[32] To the Spanish rulers he was a dangerous individual, and finally on the morning of December 30, 1896, after inquisitorial proceedings, Rizal was executed. His execution increased the problems that Spain faced, and more violent proposals took form and quickly gained strength among the Filipinos.

Another outbreak, aimed at reform but not independence, occurred in 1896 and was terminated the following year by the Treaty of Biac-na-bato.[33] By the terms of this treaty, the Filipino leaders agreed to turn over their arms and leave the islands, accepting in return amnesty for their followers, money for themselves, and a vague promise from Captain General Primo de Rivera to recommend reforms to the Spanish government. Emilio Aguinaldo was the most prominent among the leaders who went into voluntary exile.[34] A young man of twenty-seven, he had assumed leadership with the development of military activities. At Singapore, when the United States went to war with Spain, Aguinaldo received through the American consul general an invitation from Admiral George Dewey to return to the Philippines. Here he organized a native military force which was useful in breaking down Spanish authority in Luzon. Aguinaldo contended

31. Pringle, *Taft*, I, 157–158; Grunder and Livezey, *The Philippines*, 12–13; Wolff, *Little Brown Brother*, 23–24.

32. Pringle, *Taft*, I, 157–158; Grunder and Livezey, *The Philippines*, 12–13.

33. Pratt, *America's Colonial Experiment*, 193; Grunder and Livezey, *The Philippines*, 13–14.

34. Pratt, *America's Colonial Experiment*, 194–197; Grunder and Livezey, *The Philippines*, 13–14; Pringle, *Taft*, I, 158–159. For a work that treats these issues at great length and gives a detailed account of Emilio Aguinaldo's activities, the reader should consult Leon Wolff's book, *Little Brown Brother*.

that he had been promised independence in return for this aid. His assertions were flatly denied by Consul General E. Spencer Pratt at Singapore and by Admiral Dewey. Hostilities between Aguinaldo's forces and those of the United States began on February 4, 1899, and a long, bloody, and costly war followed. This was the state of the white man's burden when the Second United States Philippine Commission arrived at the island of Luzon.

The independence issue overshadowed all others that Taft was to face in the Philippines. Before the end of his first month in the islands he had formed some tentative conclusions on this question. While Taft felt that the rebellion had petered out, and that civil government could be established, he was convinced that independence was impossible and that the Filipinos were incapable of self-government. As he wrote to John M. Harlan, they were "nothing but grown up children" who would need the training of "fifty or a hundred years" before they could realize what Anglo-Saxon liberty was.[35] Of the educated ones among them, most were "profound Constitutional lawyers," who could discuss "with eloquence and volume" American constitutional questions and were "most glib in running off the Phrases." [36] Unfortunately, however, they had not the slightest conception of practical questions and how to solve them.

By the middle of July, 1900, Taft was sufficiently sure of his conclusions to write directly to the secretary of war, Elihu Root, about his wards:

> The population of the Islands is made up of a vast mass of ignorant, superstitious people, well intentioned, light-hearted, temperate, somewhat cruel, domestic and fond of their families, and deeply wedded to the Catholic Church. They are easily influenced by speeches from a small class of educated meztizos, who have acquired a good deal of superficial knowledge of the general principles of free government, who are able to mouth sentences supposed to embody constitutional law, and

35. W. H. Taft to John M. Harlan, June 30, 1900, Taft MSS.
36. *Ibid.*

who like to give the appearance of profound analytical knowledge of the science of government. They are generally lacking in moral character; are with some notable exceptions prone to yield to any pecuniary consideration, and are difficult persons out of whom to make an honest government. We shall have to do the best we can with them. They are born politicians; are as ambitious as Satan, and as jealous as possible of each other's preferment. I think that we can make a popular assembly out of them for the Islands provided we restrain their action by a legislative council to be appointed by the Governor, and a qualified veto for the Governor, if we can take 18 months or 2 years as a preliminary period during which the Commission, with some representative Filipinos, shall legislate for the Islands.[37]

Even before the arrival of the commission in the islands Taft had hoped that the United States Senate would pass the Spooner bill, which in essence provided for the establishment of civilian control in the Philippines, and that the House of Representatives would concur.[38] He felt that the passage of this measure would give the commission the additional sanction of congressional action, which would prove to

37. W. H. Taft to Elihu Root, July 14, 1900, *ibid.*
38. W. H. Taft to Charles P. Taft, April 23, 1900, *ibid.* In January, 1900, Senator John C. Spooner of Wisconsin had introduced a bill which provided that, after the Philippine insurrection had been suppressed, the president, until the Congress provided otherwise, should have "all military, civil, and judicial powers necessary to govern the said islands," with the powers being "vested in such persons and . . . exercised in such manner as the President . . . shall direct for maintaining and protecting the inhabitants of said islands in the free enjoyment of their liberty, property, and religion." Grunder and Livezey, *The Philippines,* 73. This bill met stiff resistance in the United States Senate. Many senators, led by George F. Hoar of Massachusetts, opposed any bill which by implication indicated our intention of remaining in the Philippines. *Ibid.* In addition, many congressmen were perfectly content to let the president administer the islands under his powers as commander-in-chief of the army. Finally, the bill was redrafted as an amendment to an army appropriation bill by Secretary Root and Senators Lodge and Spooner, and it became law on March 2, 1901. John A. Garraty, *Henry Cabot Lodge: A Biography* (New York, 1953), 207. This amendment transferred the government from a military to a civilian basis. Thereafter, the president was to govern the Philippines by authority of Congress, and not in his capacity as commander-in-chief of the military forces. Maximo M. Kalaw, *Philippine Government* (Manila, 1948), 68–69. The Spooner Amendment thus "ended the military regime in the Philippines." Arturo M. Tolentino, *The Government of the Philippines* (Manila, 1950), 156.

be important in its work. Subsequent events were to vindicate Taft in the importance that he attached to this measure.

It is interesting to compare Taft's views of a suitable government for the Philippine Islands with his view of one for the Hawaiian Islands. He saw the latter as having been made what they were by "missionary"—that is, American—influence; and he felt that enough progress had been made that an American governor would be sufficient counterbalance to a probably native-controlled legislature. It is pertinent to observe that he did not identify Sanford Dole with the business interests in the Hawaiian Islands as he should have. It was a serious misconception to use the phrase "missionary governor" in describing Sanford Dole; either Taft's knowledge was limited or he was misled.

In the Philippines, on the other hand, there would have to be a period of direct government by the commission before any form of representative government could be considered; and even then the elected assembly would have to be restrained by an appointive council as well as by the governor's veto. The idea of representative government according to Anglo-Saxon tradition was the same in both cases. But Taft approached its accomplishment pragmatically. Hawaii was ready, as he saw it, for an American type of government, with liberties secured by the checks and balances inherent in the separation of powers; but not the Philippines. Here the overriding question was not what government would be ultimately desirable, but what government would be immediately viable, in a given state of civilization, culture, and political tradition.

It is also interesting that Taft's projected frame of government for the Philippines, including an elected assembly, a legislative council, and a qualified veto for the governor, recapitulates the form of government of the American colonies under the British. It is impossible to say to what degree Taft drew consciously on this historical precedent, and to what degree he reacted directly to the situation before him in drawing his plans. In any event, they were a new variation on the form previously applied in the government of American territories.

In realizing their plans for progress toward an at least partially representative government, however, Taft and the commission were to encounter an obstacle they had not expected, in the person of General Arthur MacArthur. From military government, where the law is essentially the will of the commander, to civil government, where the will of every official is circumscribed by law, is a difficult transition under any circumstances. In a land still turbulent with rebellion, where combat as well as police forces remain necessary, the transition is doubly difficult. The difficulties inherent in such a situation were, in this instance, intensified by the personality and the convictions of the commanding general, the military governor, Arthur MacArthur. It is difficult to imagine two more contrasting personalities than Taft and MacArthur. In Taft, the scholarly and analytical temperament which had led him to the law had been reinforced by that profession. In MacArthur, valor and a talent for leadership had brought him to high rank in the profession of arms; that profession, in turn, led him into the arbitrariness which is one of the chief temptations of command.

Arthur MacArthur's military career encompassed the life of the United States Army from Fort Sumter through the Spanish American War.[39] Born in New England, raised in Wisconsin, MacArthur had enlisted at seventeen in the Union Army in 1862.[40] His ability, no less than his courage, were conspicuous; he rose rapidly. Conducting himself with distinction in some of the key battles of the Civil War, he had achieved the rank of colonel of volunteers at the age of twenty.[41] For valor at Missionary Ridge, the major commanding the Twenty-

39. Richard H. Rovere and Arthur M. Schlesinger, Jr., *The General and the President: And the Future of American Foreign Policy* (New York, 1951), 24.

40. Francis Trevelyan Miller, *General Douglas MacArthur: Fighter for Freedom* (Philadelphia, 1942), 23–25.

41. Lee and Henschel, *Douglas MacArthur*, 15; Frazier Hunt, *The Untold Story of Douglas MacArthur* (New York, 1954), 6.

Fourth Wisconsin Volunteers recommended the Medal of Honor for Arthur MacArthur, but it was not awarded to him until June 30, 1890.[42] He remained in the regular army as a career officer after the Civil War, at a time when most ambitious men found greater rewards in industry or finance.[43] He was made brigadier general at the outbreak of the Spanish American War, and shortly thereafter was promoted to major general. After active service against the Spaniards in the Philippines, he led most of the big campaigns against Aguinaldo's insurrectors.[44] He finally emerged, acclaimed as a hero, as the pacifier of the Philippines. He had commanded everything from a company to an army with distinction and courage; but note that from the end of his adolescence he had done nothing but command. Command was his education as well as his profession.

The self-confidence which had led him to command was only increased by his success. He approached large questions grandly, and would justify a point of view rather by mystical rhetoric than by realistic argument. This trait is beautifully illustrated in his testimony before the Senate Committee on the Philippines, in the spring of 1902. The general was justifying "the idea of developing our material interests in the East":

> Many thousand years ago our Aryan ancestors raised cattle, made a language, multiplied in numbers and overflowed. By due process of expansion to the west they occupied Europe, developed arts and sciences, and created a great civilization, which, separating into innumerable currents, inundated and fertilized the globe with blood and ideas, the primary bases of all human progress, incidentally crossing the Atlantic and thereby reclaiming, populating, and civilizing a hemisphere.

42. Lee and Henschel, *Douglas MacArthur*, 15. Apparently the recommendation for a medal of honor was buried and lost in the whirl of events. In a review of Civil War medals almost three decades later, the oversight was corrected. Hunt, *The Untold Story of Douglas MacArthur*, 5.

43. Rovere and Schlesinger, Jr., *The General and the President and the Future of American Foreign Policy*, 24.

44. *New York Times*, Sept. 6, 1912, 1; Miller, *General Douglas MacArthur*, 67–68; Rovere and Schlesinger, Jr., *The General and the President*, 24–25.

The broad actuating laws which underlie all these wonderful phenomena are still operating with relentless vigor and have recently forced one of the currents of this magnificent Aryan people across the Pacific—that is to say, back almost to the cradle of its race—thus initiating a stage of progressive social evolution which may reasonably be expected to result in substantial contributions in behalf of the unity of the race and the brotherhood of man. . . .

At the time I returned to Manila to assume the supreme command it seemed to me that we had been committed to a position by process of spontaneous evolution. . . . It seemed to me that our conception of rights, justice, freedom, and personal liberty was the precious fruit of centuries of strife; that we had inherited much in these respects from our ancestors, and in our own behalf have added much to the happiness of the world, and as beneficiaries of the past and as the instruments of future progressive social development we must regard ourselves simply as the custodians of imperishable ideas held in trust for the general benefit of mankind. . . . I felt that we had attained a moral and intellectual height from which we were bound to proclaim to all as the occasion arose the true message of humanity as embodied in the principles of our own institutions.[45]

Long before 1902 Taft had seen in MacArthur the qualities which led to this curious passage, in which half-baked Darwinism is expressed in phrases borrowed from law and inaccurately applied ("due process") and confused, rather than combined, with political idealism. He dryly remarked of a much earlier pronouncement by the general, that "the obscurity of the language is its safety." [46]

Two days after the arrival of the Philippine commission in Manila, MacArthur suggested to the War Department that an offer of "complete immunity for past and liberty for future" be made to all those Filipinos who had not violated the laws of war and who would renounce insurrection and accept the sovereignty of the United States.[47] President McKinley

45. *Affairs in the Philippine Islands*, U.S. 57 Cong., 1st Sess., S. Doc. 331, Pt. II (1902), 867–868.
46. W. H. Taft to Elihu Root, Sept. 26, 1901, Taft MSS.
47. Grunder and Livezey, *The Philippines*, 65.

agreed with this suggestion after expanding the proposal by providing a ninety-day period for acceptance of these terms and authorizing the payment of thirty pesos to each Filipino who presented to the military authorities a rifle in good condition. General MacArthur issued this amnesty proclamation on June 21, 1900.[48] Taft was not sure how much good it would do but remained hopeful. However, as he watched MacArthur negotiate with the various Filipino factions, he began to have misgivings. Although he made allowances for the fact that the general had been ill, Taft did not believe him "as keen witted" and "clear-headed" as was mandatory in dealing with such political matters.[49] As for MacArthur's censoring of a reporter's dispatch which was critical of his role in these negotiations, Taft found such action "revolting" and "utterly un-American."[50] And when it appeared that MacArthur resented the commission's efforts to investigate other matters, Taft predicted trouble for the future.[51] He was certain of it upon learning that the military governor was asking the War Department to diminish the commission's power of appointment, for such action contained "the seeds of a controversy" between the civil and military authorities.[52]

Taft's critical view of General MacArthur's abilities and actions soon received ample confirmation in the latter's handling of an important insurgent leader, Pedro A. Paterno.[53] After being released on parole in early July, 1900, on the strict understanding that he was not to engage in any activities hostile to the United States, Paterno had written an article in the Philippine newspaper *El Progreso* advocating in-

48. W. H. Taft to Helen H. Taft, June 21, 1900, Taft MSS.
49. *Ibid.*, June 27, 1900.
50. *Ibid.*, July 5, 1900.
51. *Ibid.*, July 8, 1900.
52. *Ibid.*, July 18, 1900.
53. Pedro A. Paterno had served in the cabinet of Emilio Aguinaldo during the short-lived Philippine Republic of 1897, was second in authority to Aguinaldo, and had acted as the representative of the insurrectos in negotiating the Pact of Biac-na-bato of December 14, 1897, which ended the insurrection of 1896. W. H. Taft to Charles P. Taft, July 7, 1900; W. H. Taft to Charles P. Taft, July 25, 1900, Taft MSS; Kalaw, *Philippine Government*, 43–44.

dependence under an American protectorate.[54] Clapped in jail again for this indiscretion, Paterno quickly repented and was once again put at liberty.[55] Resourceful and infinitely imaginative, he now proposed a three-day grand fiesta, which in the Philippine tradition would be replete with music, speeches, fireworks, marching, and dancing.[56] This fiesta, intended as a celebration of the amnesty granted by General MacArthur and designed to eclipse any previous festival in Philippine history, was suggested as an event of pure entertainment and good will.[57] Since the proclaimed purpose of the festival was the promotion of the cause of peace and because "if there is one thing more than another that a Filipino likes, it is a fiesta," Taft gave his approval.[58] As he wrote to Secretary Root: "The *fiesta* which is coming off, if it does not result in a *fiasco*, as I hope it may not, will be quite an important event, in that it brings home to the people the fact that peace is near at hand, and is a recognition by them that they would like to have peace." [59]

The fiesta was scheduled to begin on July 28, 1900. That morning Taft learned that Paterno and others among the Philippine leaders had written speeches advocating the cause of independence and at the very least a protectorate relationship between the United States and the Philippines.[60] Accordingly, he declined to attend a banquet prepared for the first evening and by way of a rebuke wrote the following to Paterno:

> We are advised that a number of speeches which have been submitted to you for delivery this evening in express terms support the view that an independent government should be

54. W. H. Taft to Charles P. Taft, June 30, 1900; W. H. Taft to Elihu Root, July 26, 1900; W. H. Taft to Charles P. Taft, July 30, 1900, Taft MSS.
55. W. H. Taft to Elihu Root, July 26, 1900, *ibid.*
56. W. H. Taft to Charles P. Taft, July 25, 1900; W. H. Taft to Elihu Root, July 26, 1900, *ibid.*
57. *Ibid.*; Duffy, *Taft,* 97–98.
58. W. H. Taft to Elihu Root, July 26, 1900, Taft MSS.
59. *Ibid.*
60. W. H. Taft to Charles P. Taft, July 30, 1900, *ibid.*

established in these Islands under the protectorate of the United States. . . . In other words, that the United States should assume responsibility to the world for a government in which it could exercise no direct influence.

No one having any authority to speak for the United States has ever said one word justifying the belief that such a protectorate will be established. It is impossible. We of the Commission who are sent here with instructions to establish a civil government have no authority whatever to consider or discuss such a proposal.

By destroying the power of Spain in these Islands, and accepting the sovereignty thereof, the United States assumed a responsibility to the world to establish here a civilized government of law and order, which should duly respect the rights of all, whether foreigners or natives. It proposes to meet this responsibility by making a government in which the citizens of the Islands shall exercise as large a measure of self-government as is consistent with the establishment of law and order. . . . Further than this the government of the United States will not go.[61]

Taft finally went to the banquet after Paterno appeared at his house and entreated him to come, but it was held under such restricted conditions, no speeches being allowed, that the affair turned out to be a fiasco.[62] Although Taft's position in this matter was arbitrary, it was a reflection of a basic conviction—that the Filipinos would have to go through a period of tutelage before they could assume fully the responsibilities entailed in complete self-government. The outcome of the banquet measurably lessened his respect for MacArthur. Taft felt that MacArthur, who bore the official responsibility, had bungled in not keeping firm control over the affair, especially in regard to the political content of projected speeches.[63] He came to hold a diminished regard for the gen-

---

61. W. H. Taft to Pedro A. Paterno, July 28, 1900, *ibid.*
62. W. H. Taft to Charles P. Taft, July 30, 1900, *ibid.*
63. W. H. Taft to Elihu Root, July 30, 1900; W. H. Taft to Charles P. Taft, July 30, 1900, *ibid.*

eral's political astuteness and his grip on the situation.

To Mrs. Taft he poured out his discouragement with Mac-Arthur and particularly the problems their relationship would pose for the success of his mission.[64] The more he had to do with the general, "the smaller man of affairs" he thought him. "I have no doubt that he is a good soldier but his experience and his ability as a statesman or politician are nothing," he wrote. In a caustic comment he noted that Mac-Arthur had "all the angularity of military etiquette and discipline and he takes himself with the greatest seriousness." In this instance Taft appeared to have been less liberal than the general, but MacArthur, once roused to the political implications of the fiesta, proposed measures which appeared to Taft to be "almost brutal in their severity." MacArthur felt that the banquet should be suppressed unless Taft was willing to attend, and proposed to arrest any Filipino who made speeches offensive to American officials.[65] Finally, Taft attended the banquet in order to "let the matter down easy." [66] This was indicative of his deeply entrenched conservatism, his avoidance of extremes—on the one hand, he would not hold out false hopes of immediate independence and democracy, nor would he, on the other hand, impose a policy of brutal repression.

But the central disagreement between the two men came over the fundamental question of how soon civil rule should be established. While Taft and the other members of the commission hoped that many towns and provinces might soon be given civil governments, American soldiers, engaged in a grim and thankless jungle war, were deeply skeptical.[67] Taft had characterized the Filipinos as our "little brown

64. W. H. Taft to Helen H. Taft, July 29, 1900, *ibid.*
65. *Ibid.*; W. H. Taft to Charles P. Taft, July 30, 1900, *ibid.*
66. W. H. Taft to Helen H. Taft, July 29, 1900, *ibid.*
67. W. H. Taft to Elihu Root, July 26, 1900, and July 30, 1900, *ibid.*; Forbes, *The Philippine Islands*, I, 125; Worcester, *The Philippines Past and Present*, 273; Ernest L. Klein, *Our Appointment with Destiny: America's Role on the World Stage* (New York, 1952), 119; John Holladay Latané, *America as a World Power, 1897–1907* (New York, 1907), 82–99; Lee and Henschel, *Douglas MacArthur*, 18–23.

brothers," but Robert F. Morrison, writing in the Manila *Sunday Sun,* countered with a piece of doggerel that mirrored the sentiments of many American soldiers:

I'm only a common soldier-man in the blasted Philippines;
They say I've got Brown Brothers here, but I dunno what it means.
I like the word Fraternity, but still I draw the line;
He *may* be a brother of William H. Taft, but he ain't no friend of mine.[68]

Alarmed by what he viewed as widespread Filipino disaffection, MacArthur took a dim view of the commission's optimistic proposal that a native constabulary would inspire popular support for the military campaign against the insurrectos.[69] The general, Taft informed Secretary Root, "regards all the people as opposed to the American forces and looks at his task as one of conquering eight millions of recalcitrant, treacherous and sullen people." [70] Despite verbal allegiance to the theory of civil control, MacArthur appeared to trust only "the strong hand of the military." [71] Taft believed that the proper exercise of police powers was an integral part of the preparation needed by the Filipinos toward the ultimate goal of self-government.[72] And in this respect he did not seem to fear the possibilities of sabotage in the actual operations of the force. In 1901 the commission organized the Philippine constabulary and in due course the constabulary was to justify the confidence placed in it by the commission.[73]

As the first of September, 1900, drew near, the date on which the commission was to take up its legislative functions, the members of the commission formally expressed their de-

68. James P. Warburg, *The United States in a Changing World: An Historical Analysis of American Foreign Policy* (New York, 1954), 201; Wolff, *Little Brown Brother,* 313.
69. W. H. Taft to Elihu Root, July 30, 1900, and Nov. 30, 1900; W. H. Taft to J. B. Bishop, Nov. 30, 1900, Taft MSS.
70. W. H. Taft to Elihu Root, Aug. 18, 1900, *ibid.*
71. *Ibid.*
72. *Ibid.,* July 30, 1900.
73. Forbes, *The Philippine Islands,* 203–207; Joseph Ralston Hayden, *The Philippines: A Study in National Development* (New York, 1942), 733–734.

sire for harmony with the military government.[74] MacArthur was receptive to an invitation to attend commission meetings and even proposed a conference to resolve points of friction in their relationship.[75] At this juncture Secretary Root stepped into the picture to clarify the boundaries of authority between the military and the commission. His explanation that the commission's power of appointment included the power of removal, while helpful, was counterbalanced by his confirmation of the military governor's full control over civil officials.[76] Actually Root did not clarify the important question of where ultimate authority lay. Thus mutually reassured, Taft and MacArthur conferred on August 30, 1900, and as Taft reported to Root: "the General expressed himself as disliking much the cutting down of the power of the military Governor and transferring it to the Commission, but he said that he was very anxious to assist in every way the Administration and to carry out its purposes, but that the Commission was an anomalous body and that the plan was likely to result in discord unless there was hearty co-operation, which he proposed to give and that he was willing to abide any construction put upon the instructions." [77]

Nevertheless, on a basic issue of policy like the constabulary question, MacArthur was still "very, very sensitive." [78] For his part, Taft was scornful of MacArthur for being "weak enough to express great personal humiliation in having his power as Military Governor cut down in this wise and to give us the opportunity to know how anxious he has been to avoid the transfer." [79]

It was apparent to Taft that MacArthur was exceedingly jealous of his prerogatives as military governor. In fact as Taft reported to Elihu Root, MacArthur now felt that the office of

74. W. H. Taft to Arthur MacArthur, Aug. 23, 1900, Root MSS.
75. Arthur MacArthur to W. H. Taft, Aug. 24, 1900, ibid.
76. Elihu Root to W. H. Taft, Aug. 28, 1900, ibid.
77. W. H. Taft to Elihu Root, Aug. 31, 1900, Taft MSS.
78. Ibid.
79. W. H. Taft to Charles P. Taft, ibid.

military governor had been "mediatized." [80] By way of explanation, Taft said that MacArthur felt he had suffered a deep and painful personal humiliation in the loss of power and authority he had been accustomed to exercising and which he had felt to be his due. In a letter to his brother Charles, William Howard related the growing estrangement between the two men, which he attributed to the "formality and military etiquette" which MacArthur insisted upon observing with the commission, coupled with "certain sensitive points" by the general on matters of policy.[81] Taft was convinced that the vast majority of Filipinos were desirous of ending military control because of its "abrupt and unconciliatory character," and confessed that he himself felt "impatient at it." [82] Nor were relations helped by the fact that General MacArthur gave "no social recognition of the presence of the Commission here." [83]

In the uncertain stalemate that existed between general and judge, the latter enjoyed one supreme advantage, which a more authoritarian personality might have employed with deadly effect. After all, it was Taft who could write at any time to Secretary Root explaining his side of the case.[84] Such communication was apparently foreclosed to MacArthur, whose channel was limited to his military superiors in Washington. And it should be noted that Taft was a voluminous correspondent, who left no phase of the Philippine situation untouched in his letters to the secretary of war. Had he been bent upon the destruction of General MacArthur, he certainly had every opportunity to accomplish this purpose. Yet, as he

80. W. H. Taft to Elihu Root, Sept. 18, 1900, *ibid.*
81. W. H. Taft to Charles P. Taft, Aug. 31, 1900, *ibid.*
82. *Ibid.*
83. *Ibid.*, Sept. 12, 1900.
84. One writer described the enormous powers exercised by Secretary Root in the following manner: "The power of the Secretary of War in the new possessions was unlimited. His brief cable was law; his verbal utterance to an Army officer about to take charge of a province or an island was as binding as a sealed and signed decree. Through the governors-general or the military commanders the Secretary was the legislature, the executive, and the judiciary for the millions of people in the Philippines and in Cuba." Dunn, *From Harrison to Harding,* I, 256.

stated to Secretary Root, he wished to do MacArthur "full justice," and within the limitations of human frailty he appears actually to have attempted to do exactly that.[85]

Why did Taft not urge the secretary of war to transfer immediately all powers in the Philippines to civilian hands—thus, in effect, abolishing MacArthur's governmental powers? The probable answer lies in Taft's innate caution, for he felt that "the change to a civil government should be made with care and deliberation." [86] At this time, it must be remembered, he was in the process of formulating his conceptions of administrative policy and wanted to avoid a premature transfer of authority. He was feeling his way in an area in which there were no precedents as guideposts—and as was characteristic of the conservative jurist, he was not going to take precipitate action.

For all of his reservations about the general, Taft did indicate in his correspondence some of the positive features of the military governor. Thus he pointed out that MacArthur was strongly in favor of cultivating the good will of the Filipinos, and the failure of other military officers to take such a course met with strong opposition from the general.[87] In addition, Taft credited MacArthur with being hostile to the tendency of many military officers and their wives "to draw the color line" in dealings with the Filipinos. As for MacArthur's general military abilities, his bearing, his devotion to duty, and his personal qualities, Taft had the highest praise.[88]

But the basic difference between the two men was continuous and profound. Taft summed up his attitude in one highly concentrated sentence:

> General MacArthur is a very courtly, kindly man; lacking somewhat in a sense of humor; rather fond of profound generalizations on the psychological conditions of the people; politely incredulous, and politely lacking in any great consider-

85. W. H. Taft to Elihu Root, Aug. 18, 1900, Taft MSS.
86. W. H. Taft to Gustavus H. Wald, Sept. 7, 1900, *ibid.*
87. W. H. Taft to Elihu Root, Aug. 18, 1900, *ibid.*
88. *Ibid.* and Nov. 14, 1900.

ation for the views of any one as to the real situation who is a civilian and who has been here only a comparatively short time, and firmly convinced of the necessity for maintaining military etiquette in civil matters and civil government.[89]

An uncertain stalemate was the significant aspect of the status of the military governor and the Philippine Commission at the end of 1900.[90] The basic problem—one of jurisdiction, the age-old problem of where the ultimate power lay—was finally clarified by the enactment of the Spooner Amendment on March 2, 1901.[91] Up to this time the legal basis for the government of the Philippines had found its sanction in the president's constitutional power as commander in chief. Now the president's actions were confirmed by Congress, and the president was given full authority to proceed with the establishment of civil government. Actually the president had already been exercising this authority, but Congress wanted to put the matter on a longer range basis and remove any areas of doubt.

The significance of this change was not lost upon General MacArthur, who now informed Taft that the new status reduced their dispute of the previous months to "an academic question." [92] This was so because now there was definitely to be a civil government and the role of the military would perforce be subordinate. More astonishing to Taft was the revelation that MacArthur had never really accepted the underlying basis for their past relationship, for MacArthur indicated frankly that he had viewed the president's instructions to the commission as "an unconstitutional interference with his prerogative as Military Commander in these islands." In short, MacArthur felt that these instructions were *"ultra vires*

89. *Ibid.*, Aug. 18, 1900. On another occasion, Taft remarked about one of General MacArthur's pronouncements: "The obscurity of the language is its safety." *Ibid.*, Sept. 26, 1901.

90. Berthoff, "Taft and MacArthur, 1900–1901," 205.

91. Grunder and Livezey, *The Philippines*, 73–74.

92. W. H. Taft to Elihu Root, March 17, 1901, Taft MSS. The quotations in the remainder of this paragraph are taken from this letter.

under the constitutional limitations upon the powers of the President as a commander-in-chief."

This extraordinary language, with its even more astounding conclusion, was mystifying to Taft, a man who had spent most of his life in the pursuits of law. He tried hard to comprehend what it was that MacArthur was saying. In effect, if MacArthur's *ipse dixit* meant anything, it meant that the president of the United States had acted unconstitutionally in issuing instructions which impaired the military powers of a commander in the field. Taft wondered how anyone could stray so far afield—was it not obvious that the powers of a commander in the field could derive only from the war powers or the powers as commander in chief of the man who was his superior? As Taft put it:

> It has always been a curious phase of political human nature to me to observe that men who have not had the slightest knowledge of legal principles and who do not claim to have had any legal education feel entirely at home in the construction of the constitution and in using its limitations to support their views and to nullify action, the wisdom of which they dispute. The constitution has not often been used to maintain undiminished the absolute legislative, executive, and judicial power of a subordinate military commander as against the express orders of his constitutional commander in chief.[93]

The constitutional question was not the key issue, as MacArthur clearly indicated. What was at stake was the very real and apparently very painful diminution of his authority which was implicit in the Spooner Amendment. MacArthur frankly told Taft that the "strain" to which he had been subjected by the cutting down of some of his powers and the transferring of others was "so great that he could not endure it much longer." Normally, an increase in responsibility produces strain, but in this case the opposite seemed to prevail. Perhaps the answer lay in what MacArthur termed his "ex-

---

93. *Ibid.* The two quotations in the next paragraph are drawn from this informative letter.

treme humiliation," for according to Taft, as MacArthur saw it, "it was the cutting down of his power and the interference with his efficiency by the cutting down of his power that had the element of humiliation in it." Although he did not desire to leave the Philippines until a civil governor was appointed, MacArthur felt the transfer should now be made as quickly as possible. The statement of humiliation was astounding to Taft, who felt that MacArthur, far from occupying an insignificant position, in fact held the most important position that the United States could assign to a soldier—he was in command of 65,000 men and exercised, in addition, a large civil authority. MacArthur's position was comprehensible to Taft only on the basis that the general no longer regarded himself as a soldier, but looked upon himself as a kind of proconsul, the first American to occupy that position in United States history.

Within a few months a civil governor would assume the commanding general's civil functions, for Secretary Root had already decided to make a surgical separation of the military and civilian authority. Up to this time Secretary Root had not clarified in explicit terms what the boundaries of authority were in the Philippines. But the situation had now changed; in the opinion of the secretary of war the establishment of civil government would hasten the pacification of the Philippines, would end the evils inherent in an unduly long continuance of military government, and would "get the army out of the governing business and get its officers back to the performance of their proper function as soldiers." [94] However, Root delayed changing the command until Taft became governor.[95] The foregoing principles he enunciated in clear and explicit language in his instructions to Major General Adna R. Chaffee, the successor to General MacArthur.[96] He reaffirmed a basic historical principle when he stated: "We in-

94. Elihu Root to Adna R. Chaffee, Feb. 26, 1901, Root MSS.
95. W. H. Taft to Charles P. Taft, May 17, 1901, Taft MSS.
96. Elihu Root to Adna R. Chaffee, Feb. 26, 1901, Root MSS.

tend to discontinue the military government of the Philippine Islands and to establish a civil government which will be supreme there, subject only to review by the executive and legislative branches of the United States Government here, and to which the Army will bear substantially the same relation that the Army bears to the civil government here." [97]

On the fourth of July, 1901, William Howard Taft at last became civil governor of the Philippines with unchallenged authority.[98] Symbolically, General MacArthur departed on the same day that Taft assumed his new position. The departure was on a friendly basis.[99] Taft held a reception in MacArthur's honor and accompanied the general to the dock.[100] Upon his arrival in San Francisco, General MacArthur declared that the new civil administration was welcome both to the Filipinos and to the military, "to whom the civil task was hard and tedious," and expressed the view that "the two departments are well set apart." [101]

Taft was clearly the victor, and in his inaugural address as civil governor of the Philippines he made it clear where the ultimate authority lay, although he did not exult in his triumph.[102] His speech is especially meaningful to one familiar with the developments which had preceded it. Taft reviewed the events of the past as significant stages in the eventual road to permanent civil government on a more or less popular basis. This speech also provides a basic insight into Taft's subsequent success as a great colonial administrator, for, as he put it, "government is a practical, not a theoretical, problem and the successful application of a new system to a people like this must be brought about by observing

97. *Ibid.*
98. *New York Times,* July 5, 1901, p. 1.
99. Helen Taft, *Recollections,* 210.
100. Berthoff, "Taft and MacArthur, 1900–1901," 210.
101. *New York Times,* Aug. 19, 1901, p. 1.
102. William Howard Taft, *Present Day Problems: A Collection of Addresses Delivered on Various Occasions* (New York, 1908), 1, 4–5.

closely the operation of simple laws and making changes or additions as experience shows their necessity." [103]

Inferentially he alluded to the controversy with General MacArthur, although, of course, he did not do so directly. He contented himself with the truism that there would be "the same cooperation in the future" that there had been in the past and that "the possible friction which may arise" between the civil and the military in the future would have no encouragement from "those in whom is the ultimate responsibility." [104] There was work enough and more for all who were truly concerned with the regeneration of these islands.

In his peroration Taft invoked divine blessings upon the cause of the United States, a cause which he conceived in profoundly paternalistic terms. The goals to strive for were the attainment of liberty, order, and prosperity for the Filipinos, but always within the context of American guidance and tutelage. No instinct was more basic in the man than an inherent paternalism characteristic of an American aristocrat who conceived of duty and responsibility in terms that might be expressed in the words, government for the people, but by no means by them.

One final but basic dispute between MacArthur and Taft should be noted. Fundamental to the entire struggle for power was the ideological couching of the difference between them. General MacArthur's thinking was almost entirely along tactical and strategic lines. To a Senate committee on the Philippines in the spring of 1902 he elaborated his philosophy when he stated:

> The archipelago, I think, perhaps is the finest group of islands in the world. Its strategic position is unexcelled by that of any other position on the globe. The China Sea, which separates it by something like 750 miles from the continent, is nothing more or less than a safety moat. It lies on the flank of what

103. *Ibid.*, 3–4. Lord Curzon provided another basic insight when he said: "Taft was the first Saxon to love the Malay—and the Malay returned it." Edward H. Cotton, *William Howard Taft: A Character Study* (Boston, 1932), 53–54.
104. *Ibid.*, 9.

might be called a position of several thousand miles of coast line; it is in the center of that position. It is therefore relatively better placed strategically than Japan, which is on a flank, and therefore remote from the other extremity; likewise, India, on another flank. The Philippines are in the center of that position. It affords a means of protecting American interests which, with the very least output of physical power, has the effect of a commanding position in itself to retard hostile action.[105]

It is significant that such considerations played no part in the thinking of William Howard Taft.[106] Rather Taft was concerned with the political relationship between the islands and the United States. His thoughts on this subject found their fullest expression in a letter written early in 1904, when the question of Philippine independence arose again. It was not true, he wrote, "that any independent self-government of a people is better than the best government by any other people." [107] And he summed up his thoughts in this concluding paragraph:

> We have a definite, practical problem in the Philippines, and it serves no useful purpose to hinder its solution by discussing what we are going to do fifty or a hundred or one hundred and fifty years hence, or by binding ourselves to a fixed course so far in advance. . . . When we shall have made a successful government; when we shall have developed and educated the people; when we shall have created an independent public opinion—then the question what shall be done may well be left to both countries; for if America follows her duty, as I am sure she will ultimately, I do not think that the Filipino people will desire to sever the bond between us and them.[108]

When the immediate and urgent problems were solved, as Taft saw it, the way would be paved for the assumption of larger responsibilities. But in the meantime it was idle and

---

105. *Affairs in the Philippine Islands*, U.S. 57th Cong., 1st Sess., S. Doc. 331, Pt. II (1902), p. 867.

106. In my study of Taft's correspondence, I found no allusions to the tactical or strategic importance of the Philippines for the United States.

107. W. H. Taft to William Lawrence, Feb. 16, 1904, Taft MSS.

108. *Ibid.*

mischievous to hold out false hopes as a delusive torment to those who were not likely to realize them. In a growing mutual trust and confidence, the future would bring its own solutions.

After he became civil governor, Taft labored arduously in solving the complex problems concerning colonial administration in the Philippines. Under his administration enormous improvements in the government and economy were effected: municipal and provincial governments were established; a civil service system was created; courts with a simplified procedure, civil and criminal, were established, and fair-minded judges were appointed to the bench; the first insular bureaus (health, agriculture, and forestry) commenced operations; an educational system was established, designed to provide every Filipino child with a free public education; a postal savings bank was founded to encourage habits of industry and thrift; a public land act was passed which enabled and encouraged every Filipino to acquire a free homestead; church and state were divorced and the large agricultural estates of the friar orders were purchased by the government; public buildings, docks, harbors, and roads were constructed; and a native constabulary was organized which suppressed brigandage and lawlessness.[109] William Howard Taft had done an excellent job and in accomplishing these feats displayed the necessary qualities of patience, diligence, extreme thoroughness, honesty, and reliability.

109. Primo L. Tongko, *The Government of the Republic of the Philippines* (rev. ed., Manila, 1953), 14; D. R. Williams, *The United States and the Philippines* (New York, 1926), 121–131; Cotton, *William Howard Taft*, pp. 54–55.

CHAPTER III

Colonial Administrator and Colonial Diplomat: Godfather to a New Nation

A MERE LISTING of the impressive accomplishments of the civil government in the Philippines does not provide a complete explanation for the real progress that was made there in the years between 1900 and 1904. What is needed is a detailed examination of William Howard Taft, functioning as a colonial administrator and colonial diplomat. Certain questions provide a framework for inquiry. How did Taft approach the peoples of the Philippines and how did he get along with them, was he sympathetic with them? How did Taft see the issues of the day? What principles and ideals governed his actions in the Philippines? Finally, what objectives did he hope to achieve in the Philippines? Before seeking the answers to these probing questions, it is necessary to offer a few, brief explanatory and interpretative comments in order to provide a proper setting.

Greatest of the problems thrust upon or assumed by the United States from the outcome of the war with Spain was the Philippines, what to do with the islands and the peoples. Very few Americans comprehended it then, many did not comprehend it in subsequent years. Here and there in the United States there were men who saw the real obligation which the "unavoidable course of events" had thrust upon the United States government. Nearly all of these gentlemen were opposed to taking permanent possession of the Philippines and were regretful that it had been necessary. Few, very few, believed that the United States would ever see the responsibility laid upon it, or thought that the William McKinley administration could rise to the duty of meeting it fully and fairly. It is to President McKinley's credit that he not only saw this obligation with clarity from almost the very beginning, but that he determined at the same time, with increasing firmness, to meet it with all the power of the United States government so long as he could shape its course.

What President McKinley saw thus in the beginning was that by our intervention in the Philippines we had contracted an obligation toward the Filipinos which we could not in honor or decency fail to discharge. It was the most difficult obligation that a nation could incur, for it was violently opposed by the very people for whose benefit it was undertaken. It put the United States in the position of compelling the Filipinos by armed force to accept what we knew for certain would be to their enduring benefit and which would lead to their ultimate freedom, but which they regarded only as another form of oppression. To leave the islands to themselves, upon the cessation of the Spanish-American War, William McKinley saw "would be only to abandon the Filipinos first to bloody internecine strife, and then to the domination and control of some other power which would never be actuated toward its wards by the altruistic interest which he recognized as the true attitude of the United States." [1] This was an already sufficiently difficult position, rendered infinitely more so by the demand of the Filipino leaders for immediate independence.

The Philippine Insurrection, which cost the United States a thousand lives and $170,000,000, was an embarrassing aftermath to the acceptance of title to that archipelago in the Treaty of Paris which concluded the Spanish-American War

1. Wolff, *Little Brown Brother*, 288.

in 1898. An unexpected consequence of the new venture in manifest destiny, the task of subduing Aguinaldo's nationalist army, put the United States in the place of the Spaniards, whose regime in Cuba had provoked the war in the first place. A display of force, and the re-election of President McKinley in 1900 on a Republican platform of avowed imperialism, served to convince the Filipinos that the Americans were in the islands to stay indefinitely; but force might have been required upon an even larger scale, and the testing of American determination carried much farther, had it not become American policy to accommodate the Filipino politicians by such concessions as would enable them to accept American sovereignty as a desirable alternative to guerrilla warfare. The concessions amounted to a practical recognition of earlier native grievances against Spanish rule, and a promise to eschew any course reminiscent of that era.[2]

As it was, the suppression of the Philippine Insurrection was very difficult. One supreme blunder had been made by all United States military commanders in the Philippines. They had permitted Émilio Aguinaldo to issue repeated proclamations to the Filipinos that the United States had come to the islands to give the people their independence. Not once did an American commander protest that Aguinaldo had no right to make such a pledge on behalf of the United States, although his proclamations were issued from camps so near their own that it must unavoidably have appeared to the trusting Filipinos that their leader was acting with the knowledge and assurance of the Americans. It gave to Aguinaldo's proclamations the effect of an implied promise on our part. The immediate result was to make the Filipinos welcome the Americans as their saviors. The ultimate impact was quite different. The Filipinos had expected independence, and when instead the islands were annexed by the United States, many of their "liberated" people, far from welcoming American rule, soon came to dislike the new masters as much as the

---

2. Oscar King Davis, *William Howard Taft: The Man of the Hour* (Philadelphia, 1908), 108 (hereinafter cited as Davis, *Taft*).

old ones. Unlike some Americans, they did not view annexation as an act of humanity toward an ignorant, downtrodden, and backward people. So, on February 4, 1899, two days before the United States Senate ratified the annexation treaty, the Treaty of Paris signed on December 10, 1898, Filipino insurgents attacked the American expeditionary force stationed in and around Manila.

At first it seemed an easy matter to put down the insurrection, for in battle after battle the Americans beat back the disorganized and poorly equipped rebel army. But before disappearing into northern Luzon in December, 1899, Emilio Aguinaldo abrogated open warfare and issued orders to conduct the war along guerrilla lines.[3] Henceforth, his hideouts became secret even to his own commanders. The troops returned to their various home provinces. The archipelago was divided into guerrilla districts, each under a general officer, and into subzones commanded by majors or colonels. Everything now depended upon whether the people at large would support and supply the resistance movement.

The resistance movement was given ample support. Realizing now that they could not win by conventional means of warfare, thousands of Filipinos resorted to guerrilla tactics, and "the struggle became a grim series of sudden ambuscades, brutal reprisals, and small patrol actions in the jungle—a type of combat for which the harassed Americans were totally unprepared." [4] "Once the rebels discarded their uniforms, the transformation from soldier to civilian was simply a matter of hiding rifle and bolo in the brush. Villagers who turned out of their thatched huts to wave flags and shout 'amigo' at passing American columns became insurrectors again the moment the troops faded from sight." [5] This plan of resistance did have an Achilles' heel, however, for it was predicated on the guiding spirit and indispensable impor-

3. John T. Farrell, "Background of the 1902 Taft Mission to Rome. I," *The Catholic Historical Review*, XXXVI (April, 1950), 1–2.
4. William F. Zornow, "Funston Captures *Aguinaldo*," *American Heritage*, IX (Feb., 1958), 25.
5. *Ibid.*, 25.

tance of one man, Emilio Aguinaldo, who led the insurgent army and who had proclaimed himself president of the Philippine Republic. A wiry, boyish-looking little man who weighed only 115 pounds, Aguinaldo was a seasoned veteran of revolutionary activity in the cause of Philippine independence. "To the superstitious natives—and to the Americans as well—he seemed to possess 'antinganting,' a mystical power to resist bullets and capture." [6] In March, 1901, by a daring, elaborate ruse, General Frederick Funston captured Emilio Aguinaldo. Since the Filipinos had no other leader of Aguinaldo's stature and prowess, the small but exasperating war, which for two years had engaged an American expeditionary force of 70,000, producing 6,000 United States casualties and many more Philippine casualties, was virtually over.[7]

By the early part of 1900, after a year and a quarter of vexatious and strenuous campaigning, which had produced victories over the insurgent forces and had scattered the guerrillas, the most optimistic began to talk of the "dawn of peace." It was then that President McKinley prepared to inaugurate his real policy for the Philippines, to "lay the foundations of a superior civilization, with specific reference to the needs of the people to be governed, and with definite reference to the welfare of the islands, both material and moral." [8] McKinley had made a trial effort in the previous year with the Schurman Commission, but the time was not yet ripe. Now he prepared for another effort, and again selected a civilian commission as the medium. He needed a man in thorough accord with his conception of "the American obligation to the Filipinos." Where was he to be found? In all the United States there were few men who shared his views

6. *Ibid.*
7. *Ibid.* The reader should consult also Wolff, *Little Brown Brother*, 288–292, 333–347.
8. As quoted in Davis, *Taft*, 109. For more detailed policy statements by William McKinley, the reader should consult *William McKinley 1843–1901: Chronology-Documents-Bibliographical Aids*, ed. Harry J. Sievers, S.J. (Dobbs Ferry, N.Y., 1970).

of what was to be done. With the American people generally the glamour that had surrounded the Philippines was wearing off, and they were growing tired of all the problems presented by them. Even among men of influence and importance, the men in high station in public life, there was a growing opposition to our remaining in the islands. The man needed by President McKinley was very, very hard to find.

"I want a man to head the commission," he said to Secretary of State William R. Day one morning when they were discussing the situation, "who is strong, honest and tactful; a man of education and executive ability; a man who is fearless, but conservative, and who will get along with the army people." [9]

"That sounds like Bill Taft," replied Mr. Day.[10] Caught in a storm center, under renewed vilification, his conscience stirring, President McKinley turned to Judge William Howard Taft. "Here was the man—huge, wise, and benign—to wrest civil control from the horny hands of the generals and to restore mercy and enlightenment to the great crusade." [11]

A stubborn, conservative, middle-class Ohioan well known as a federal circuit judge, Taft accepted the chairmanship of the commission, and sailed for Manila. He knew next to nothing about Philippine geography or sociology, nor even about the recent Filipino revolutions against Spain and America. "From start to finish, the history of the insurrection follows this remarkable pattern. Anderson, Otis, Dewey, Merritt, Schurman, Root McKinley, Greene, Lawton, MacArthur, and Taft drift across the scene like ghosts, as unfamiliar with the Philippines as with the differential calculus. Their education began on the day they reached Manila, and some of them never did learn." [12]

Yet William Howard Taft sailed with as humanitarian a set of instructions as ever were handed to a colonial potentate.

9. Davis, *Taft*, 110.
10. *Ibid.*
11. Wolff, *Little Brown Brothers*, 307.
12. *Ibid.*, 308.

Unlike Schurman's investigative commission, his was a legislative and executive organ with orders to take over civil control of the islands no later than September 1, 1900. "It came with the law in its hands, and this law was progressive." [13] Its fundamental principle was that the Filipinos should control their own affairs insofar as possible. They were given all the guarantees of the American Bill of Rights except trial by jury and the right to bear arms. There would be a civil service system staffed by natives. Elementary education would be free and compulsory, with English the official language. All local government officers were to be elected by the people, and natives would be preferred for higher positions. The land problem—especially in reference to tracts formerly owned by Spain and the Roman Catholic church—would be equitably resolved by redistribution. Local customs were to be left inviolate. Only certain unpleasant habits of the lower tribes, such as headhunting, were to be abolished. In all these matters the United States would intervene "only when its superior civilization made such intervention advisable, as well as at the highest level of policy, law, commercial regulation, and taxation." [14]

But the Philippine people viewed this humanitarian, progressive code without enthusiasm. "Its rolling phrases could not feed the hungry, house the homeless or restore the dead; and—above all—the independence they craved was denied them." [15] To some Japanese interviewers who had once asked President Ulysses S. Grant how to learn the art of self-government, he had replied simply, "Govern yourselves." This was the Filipino philosophy, and no amount of enlightened suzerainty could nullify it. In addition, the commission said nothing to allay Filipino fears of economic exploitation. Finally, almost every native thought that Mr. Taft was lying, just as all Spaniards down to Primo de Rivera had lied, and just as they thought Dewey had lied.

13. *Ibid.*
14. *Ibid.*, 309.
15. *Ibid.*

Then Taft came. His first order of business was conciliation, but almost before the official calls were over he issued a statement which was a knockdown blow to the Filipinos. The statement declared the definite purpose of the United States to maintain their sovereignty over the islands. This was the first authoritative announcement on that subject, and it was a crusher for the islanders. The statement said also that the commission would not negotiate with men in arms, with whom it was the function of the army to deal; that the military government would continue indefinitely; and that the commissioners were prepared to stay in Manila three years to see civil government "well begun." Thus, ironically, the first step in the "policy of attraction" was the destruction of every hope the Filipinos had cherished. Their only comfort and hope was in the broad promise that they should participate as far as possible in the government to be established.

William Howard Taft rubbed out the barrier between East and West—he destroyed even its imaginary existence. "He showed those Orientals that there was one Occidental, at least, whom race difference could not keep out of their hearts. Here was a man of the West to whom the East was as open as his own land, who read their desires and purposes, and fathomed their minds as easily as he towered above their bodies. And they capitulated. He won them by the power of the most persuasive personality they had ever known." [16] The "policy of attraction" soon became a great success, but it puzzled the Filipinos at the start. Mr. Taft showed them from the beginning that there was to be no fooling with him, that nothing was to be gained by attempting to trick or deceive him.

This was entirely characteristic of William Howard Taft. He had come out to the Philippine Islands on a mission, the fulfillment of which the first step was necessarily the conciliation of the Filipinos. If he could not win their good will he had no hope of success in anything else. Nothing could be ac-

16. Davis, *Taft*, 118.

complished without that. Taft began by clearing away entirely all the underbrush, so that everybody could have a clear view of the field. There was to be no concealment or deception. He told them the very worst the first time he spoke to them. After that he was unhampered in his efforts to secure their friendship.

The only experience the Filipinos had had was that of dishonesty and deceit. Their history was of tyranny and oppression. Their tradition taught them hatred of foreign domination.[17] Their struggle with the Americans had left them suspicious and sullen. This was the situation with which Mr. Taft had to work. He took three months to study the condition and situation of the Filipinos before he began to put into operation the governmental policy which he intended to pursue. During that time he went to the bottom of the causes of Filipino discontent. He set out to comprehend the Filipino, and he succeeded. He penetrated the mask of Orientalism. He began by treating all exactly alike. High or low, any one could come to Mr. Taft at any time and say all that was on his mind and in his heart. Taft never ran out of patience. He met the Filipinos with absolute frankness, which was a new experience for them. In the past they had been accustomed to indirection and concealment. Taft met them on their own level and spoke to them on any subject with an openness and freedom that was amazing. His good humor was unfailing, and his hearty, infectious laugh caught the Filipinos and put them at once at ease with him. His quick understanding of their complaints and desires, his boundless sympathy with all their troubles and difficulties, made them recognize him at once as a forceful factor in their destiny. No barrier of reserve, concealment, or open hostility could withstand such an appeal. This was the crowning achievement of his career in the islands. It was crucial that he should see into the hearts

17. The reader who is interested in examining this important subject in depth should consult the following splendid scholarly article: Vincente R. Pilapil, "The Cause of the Philippine Revolution," *Pacific Historical Review*, 34 (Aug., 1965), 249–264.

and minds of the people, for failure there meant failure for his entire mission.

When in due course Mr. Taft was ready to begin the establishment of civil government in accordance with the policy proclaimed on his arrival, he made again an announcement that brought conflicting emotions to the Filipinos and Americans in the islands. His aim—and it was the aim of the United States government, too—was "the Philippines for the Filipinos," the development of the islands in such a manner that the natives should reap the first benefit, and have the first consideration. The government to be established should be devised primarily for the welfare of the Filipinos, and again he promised that as rapidly as they would demonstrate fitness for participation in it they should be permitted to enjoy that participation.[18]

This declaration produced a prompt effect among both the Filipinos and the Americans, and other foreigners in the islands. The Filipinos saw in it, quite properly, a definite and authoritative promise as to their future treatment by the United States. The Americans and foreigners saw what they properly interpreted to be the death blow to their schemes of exploitation and mistakenly took to be a serious obstacle to their commercial development. The Filipinos were happy; the Americans and foreigners were angry.[19]

Mr. Taft was not diverted in the least from his course by the bitter protests that went up from the Americans and foreign businessmen. It was a bitter, virulent campaign against him. They assailed him with angry invective and bitter denunciation. They started a campaign against him in the United States, and sent letters and memorials to congressmen and senators about his "betrayal" of American interests in the Philippines. They roared in the newspapers and in public

18. Duffy, *Taft*, 101–102, 117–121; Pringle, *Taft*, I, 182–184, 193–195, 201–202; Davis, *Taft*, 121–122.

19. *Ibid.*, 122. Later, Taft was even more explicit: "We hold the Philippines for the benefit of the Filipinos and we are not entitled to pass a single act or to approve a single measure that has not that as its chief purpose." Pringle, *Taft*, I, 171, 213.

speeches, and it took them over two years to see that they were in fact helping Mr. Taft to accomplish his objectives with the Filipinos. Nothing could have been a stronger proof to the Filipinos of the genuineness of Mr. Taft's labors on their behalf than this violent opposition on the part of the exploiters. And just as soon as the peoples of the Philippines saw that the United States government was behind Mr. Taft and supporting him in all he did, that the wails and yelps of the exploiters were not availing to make the least alteration in his course, they realized that the program he had announced was in fact definitely laid down by the American government and would be carried out. Thus, ironically, the American and foreign opposition in the end furnished the last, convincing argument for the defeat of its own purpose.[20]

As scheduled, Mr. Taft and his aides assumed administrative control over the Philippine Islands on September 1, 1900, and with swiftness began to prove that benevolent assimilation was no smoke screen.[21] The power of the military was undermined, except for its conduct of the war. Highways and harbors were improved, schools were built and amply staffed, sanitation measures were instituted, eminently fair modes of taxation came into being, civil graft was almost extinguished, Filipinos were brought into the Philippine Commission, and a Filipino assembly was authorized as the lower house of the legislature relative to the upper house, which was the commission itself. "It was and remains a novelty in the colonial history of the Western World." [22] Could it be that the United States had been sincere all along? Many Americans and Europeans watched and pondered. "Of course the islands were being intensively utilized for commercial advantage, but that was to be taken for granted, and meanwhile most legal and social rights common to French, German, English, and American citizens were being thrust upon the Fili-

20. Davis, *Taft*, I, 122–123.
21. Wolff, *Little Brown Brother*, 314.
22. *Ibid.*

pinos, whether they liked it or not. Such a process had never occurred in the course of empire." [23] What devious game was America playing? To make matters more confusing—and perhaps more suspicious—she had not even annexed Cuba. "It was unfathomable because it was indeed altruism, if in a somewhat limited sense." [24]

While this was going on, Mr. Taft had entered upon a systematic campaign to win the sympathy and confidence of the Filipinos.[25] In his study of the causes of their discontent he made it generally known that he desired to talk with any and every man or woman who had any grievance to submit or suggestion to make. And he really talked with them. He was always interested, and never betrayed the smallest symptoms of weariness. All alike were welcome at Mr. Taft's home or office, and each had an opportunity to say all that he wished.

In the entire history of the Philippines there had never been anything like this. Here was a governor who was willing to stop and talk with a coachman or a grass cutter in the fields. For once the Filipinos were all absolutely on the same level with the government. There was no more of the gold lace and gaudy uniforms that emphasized distance and separation. Governor Taft wore the same kind of clothes that the Filipinos did. He went to them and they could come to him freely, openly, and on terms of frank equality. Nor was there the least mystery about him wherever he went. He told them the absolute truth, and he showed them that he expected just the same from them. He did not hesitate or mince words in order to conceal something that was disagreeable. When he had an unpleasant decision to give or a disappointing announcement to make, he did it in a manner that convinced the Filipinos of his sincerity and sympathy. He took the time and pains to explain in detail, to make perfectly clear and simple the reasons for his action, to indicate the convincing arguments that had compelled his conclusion.

23. *Ibid.*
24. *Ibid.*, 315.
25. Davis, *Taft*, 123–124; Pringle, *Taft*, I, 180.

There is testimony from a prominent newspaperman, Juan de Juan, who wrote an editorial entitled "Senor Taft" in a prominent Manila newspaper, *El Progresso*, one month after the second Philippine Commission had assumed power:

> The most uncompromising jingoes; the rabid partisans of militarism, as well as the men of democratic sentiments who consider the occupation of the Philippines as an odious Caesarism, respect and venerate the President of the Civil Commission, whose surname serves as the caption of these lines. Uprightness and *bonhommie* always demand recognition.
>
> Before the *Hancock*, bearing this statesman, had anchored in Manila Bay, the echo of his reputation and the radiations of the brilliant aureole which his success in the judiciary of his country had *imposed* upon him—and we underline the word imposed because the characteristic trait of Mr. Taft is his modesty—had reached the Philippines. The Filipinos awaited him with the same pleasing curiosity with which a child opens a toy with a concealed surprise, and the foreigners as the incarnation of those American patriarchal, democratic ideas with which Castelar portrayed to his followers the country of Lincoln.
>
> Behind that spacious brow of the thinker, between his liberal tendencies and the incomparable exactions of the enormous burdens which his country undertook in Paris, fierce struggles are waging. The President of the American Civil Commission has broad shoulders, but the weight of a people whom patriotism endows with the strength of a colossus is very great.
>
> We must concede to all the leading authorities whom America has sent to the Philippines the trait of being industrious. We know that General Otis worked more than twelve hours a day; MacArthur, that Daban of the American Army through the rapidity of his advancement, follows the same course as his predecessor, and Mr. Taft leaves his house every morning at eight and, as unostentatiously as a clerk, proceeds to become a part of his chair in the Ayuntamiento. There his first occupation is glancing over the American press, and what is of interest in the Spanish papers.
>
> Then the show begins. Paterno, Macabulos, Montenegro,

some envoy from Cebu, for example, who come to sound him, as the slang saying goes, arrive. Mr. Taft has the same respectful smile for all, the same courtesy, and addresses them all in the same terms, which his athletic Secretary, Mr. Fergusson, repeats in Spanish with the gravity of a Sphinx and the fidelity of a phonograph. When the matter warrants it, Mr. Pepperman, the chief stenographer of the Commission, enters the office and proceeds to take notes of the interview.

In this way the Americans are forming a luminous record which, united to what were our archives, which they preserve through the terms of the Treaty of Paris, will guide them well in the administration of the Philippines.

Later Mr. Taft becomes engulfed in the examination of the bills which the other members of the Commission present for him to study; he discusses their text with his colleagues, listening to all their observations, and judging them by a standard most favorable to the interests of the Philippines, the most liberal within the instructions from Washington—it is proper to say that Mr. Taft is the most democratic element of the Commission—he expresses his opinion, generous, calm and noble, which assuredly, in view of his personal prestige, must carry great weight in the framing of the bills, whose execution is entrusted to the Military governor.

To dissipate the gloomy smoke of the conflagration, to still the groans of those who fall in this immense *expoliarium* into which fatality has converted the Philippine fields, is the mission which the men composing the American Commission desire to bring to a successful issue. To make peace. For this they came, and if fortune does not reserve for them the happy chance of accomplishing so beautiful an ideal, they will retire, and the factor they represent in the problem to be solved, with its distinguishing traits of civil moderation, will be substituted as a system that has failed, by another, wherein the martial power will prevail over political wisdom.

As General MacArthur undoubtedly spends many hours over maps of the Philippines, Mr. Taft also often rests his gaze on a map covering one of the walls of his office, tracing, *in mente*, a railroad which, crossing the island, shall down with the cheery whistle of the locomotive the moans of the victims of war. Thus would Mr. Taft like to pacify the Philippines.

It is now one o'clock P.M. and Mr. Taft is at home, where this personage stands out more boldly before us, since the trials through which the country is passing do not permit us yet to judge him politically.

The president of the Commission, in his private life, has many points of similarity with Count de Caspe, that stainless gentleman the Filipinos still recall with veneration. Excepting the brilliancy of those splendid entertainments with which he endeavoured to blot out all racial differences by mingling in fraternal embrace Filipinos and Spaniards at the Malacanan villa, there ordinarily reigned in the governor's mansion the placid silence of the home of a well-to-do retired merchant. The Countess, who on Thursdays did the honours of her *salon* with exquisite tact, was during the other days of the week a housekeeper who did not disdain to go to a grocery store to make purchases, or to look over the laundry list.

The same thing happens in the elegant *chalet* at Malate where Mr. Taft lives. This is a quiet and peaceful home, a temple erected to the affections, under whose roof Mr. Taft rests some hours after the efforts which his political work demands.

His table reflects his modest character. Four courses, two kinds of fruit, a dessert and sauterne compose the menu of the luncheon where Mr. Taft is always accompanied by some guest, either Filipino, American or Spanish. During the meal politics are banished; if the guest is a Filipino who speaks French Mrs. Taft interrogates him on the customs of the archipelago; if he is Spanish, as to the toilettes worn in Manila by the ladies at the most brilliant receptions held here; as to the favourite musical composer of the Hispano-Filipino society; and this conversation increases in attraction when Miss Herron, sister-in-law of Mr. Taft and the incarnation of the modern woman's education, takes part therein. Miss Herron speaks French correctly, has travelled much, and journeyed through Spain like an intelligent tourist. The architectural lace-work of the Alhambra charmed her, and she went into ecstasies over the orange blossoms growing along the banks of the Guadalquivir. With what Miss Herron was not in harmony, and she berates them like an unsubsidised journalist, were the Spanish railroads. Miss Herron is right.

The children, Robert, about eleven years old; Helen, a girl of nine, and Charles, a baby of three, who is the king of the household:—the McKinley, as it were, of this patriarchal republic—do not come to the table; they eat with the governess.

After the meal, in the fine gallery overlooking the sea, sipping the coffee, Mr. Taft talks of the education of his children, of the difficulties met in the Philippines in the solution of so interesting a problem; and his wife converses of the charitable work she expects to undertake when she shall have assumed a more permanent place in the Archipelago, which Magellan discovered for Spain, and which, through a horrible fatality, is no longer ours. Politics are also eschewed on the gallery.[26]

Thus, full scope was given to the personal element in the "policy of attraction," and with immediate and far-reaching effect. After September 1, 1900, the Second Philippine Commission held both the purse strings and the power of appointment to civil positions; and on July 4, 1901, executive power passed from the United States Army to William Howard Taft as first civil governor of the Philippines.[27] Taft's responsibility was great and the work was unending. Now he had to provide a form of government which, "without giving independence or too much native participation, would be satisfactory to the majority of the people." [28] The executive branch of the government was organized in four departments—commerce and police, finance and justice, interior, and public instruction—with a commissioner at the head of each.[29] The Second Philippine Commission continued in existence under the new arrangement. Taft, in addition to being civil governor, was its chairman. The other appointments that he made were as follows: Commissioner Luke E. Wright, secretary of commerce and police; Commissioner Henry Clay Ide, secretary of finance and justice; Commissioner Bernard

26. Helen Taft, *Recollections*, 113–117. The Tafts had entertained Juan de Juan at dinner and he proved to be a careful observer of every minute detail.
27. Pratt, *America's Colonial Experiment*, 197.
28. Pringle, *Taft*, I, 204.
29. Pratt, *America's Colonial Experiment*, 197; Pringle, *Taft*, I, 204.

Moses, secretary of public instruction; and Commissioner Dean C. Worcester, secretary of the interior.[30]

An important, constructive step was the addition of three Filipinos to the commission.[31] They were Benito Legarda, Jose R. de Luzuriaga, and T. H. Pardo de Tavera. All three were gentlemen of education and moderate wealth, but not one was an advocate of independence. Indeed, not one of them was even an outspoken proponent of a greater degree of self-government. Taft "remained unshaken in his conviction that the Filipinos would not for decades be capable of ruling themselves." [32] Yet Taft was much more liberal than his fellow commissioners regarding representation of the Filipino people on the board which would govern the islands under the new arrangement—he thought that five native leaders should be named! He even considered—but rejected—the wisdom of offering one of the places to Emilio Aguinaldo. He was overruled by his colleagues, however, and the number of Filipinos was reduced to three.[33]

"Some of us," Taft complained, "have not as much confidence in the Filipino as others." It was important, he added, to avoid the charge that a small group of Americans were running the Philippines without consulting the people, who were their wards. Besides, he assured the secretary of war, there was no possible danger that the Filipino members of the commission would be a radical influence. "We can elect the men who will be as orthodox in matters of importance as we are and by the vote of the Chief Executive, the majority will be American at any rate." [34] Senores Legarda, de Luzuriaga, and de Tavera proved to be quite orthodox. The meetings of the commission were almost always harmonious.

30. *Ibid.*
31. *Ibid.*, 204–205. They headed no departments but gave the American members useful advice in both legislative and executive matters. Pratt, *America's Colonial Experiment*, 197–198.
32. Pringle, *Taft*, I, 205.
33. *Ibid.*
34. W. H. Taft to Elihu Root, April 3, 1901, Taft MSS.

Disagreements "were rarely based on racial differences and the view of the majority was accepted without rancor." [35]

Governor Taft "was not entirely astute, however, in dealing with political issues among the Filipinos; his lifelong ineptitude in the complicated art of politics created resentment among certain factions in the islands." [36] To educate further the Filipinos for active participation in their own government, Taft had helped prominent leaders such as Senores Legarda, de Luzuriaga, and de Tavera to organize late in 1900 the first Philippine political party, the Federal party.[37] The objectives of the Federal party were peace, a speedy restoration of civil authority, perpetual fealty to the United States, and ultimately not independence, but admission to the federal union as a state.[38] The Federal party, composed as it was of leading citizens of the archipelago, made its influence strongly felt. Branches of this party were established throughout the islands to hasten the surrender of the insurrection leaders and to convince the Philippine people that the United States government wished them well.[39]

"I really think that there is a great deal of hope to be placed in the growth of this party," Taft wrote in January, 1901, "for people are seizing it with avidity as a means of relieving themselves from oppressive inaction." Shortly afterward, he stated that it had 25,000 members in Manila alone. The party, he asserted, was a definite force for peace.[40]

The leaders of the Federal party worked zealously to end the Philippine Insurrection. "It was natural and proper for Taft to give its program his sanction. But Taft went a good deal further." [41] In 1902, some distinguished Filipinos, men of education, standing, and influence, suggested the formation of a political party which, while it called for law and

35. Pringle, *Taft*, I, 205.
36. *Ibid.*
37. Duffy, *Taft*, 114; Pringle, *Taft*, I, 205.
38. *Ibid.*
39. Duffy, *Taft*, 114.
40. W. H. Taft to Elihu Root, Jan. 9, 13, Taft MSS.
41. Pringle, *Taft*, I, 206.

order, "declined to admit eternal subservience to the United States." [42] Taft, acting in his capacity as civil governor, refused to give permission. In fact, he made matters much worse by selecting most of his important officeholders from the ranks of the Federal party. In 1907, when the first general elections were held, it was found that a large majority of the Philippine voters wanted their independence. It was necessary for all the parties to insert a nationalistic plank into their platforms. Even W. Cameron Forbes, who served as governor general of the Philippines when Taft became president of the United States, felt that a mistake had been made. Unfortunately, Taft played into the hands of the radicals who demanded immediate independence.[43]

William Howard Taft took a certain solid pleasure in contemplating the problems that faced him in the Philippines.[44] The Philippines were to be turned into a great experimental laboratory of practical government. Political, social, and industrial tests were to be conducted at the offices of the commissioners until a formula, in the shape of laws, was evolved to meet the needs of the Filipinos. The application of these laws would then be always in harmony with the basic policies of the United States toward the Philippine Islands.

Among the first and most important acts made law by the Second Philippine Commission was the Civil Service bill, drafted by Taft.[45] In presenting this bill to the commissioners for consideration, Taft explained that he had sought to make it malleable, so that it might expand with the growth, progress, and requirements of the Philippine government, and exclude all possibility of favoritism and politics. The commissioners read the bill with growing amazement. It included every official and employee of the government from the heads of departments down to the lowest grade of laborers. It provided for the creation of a civil service board, whose sole

42. *Ibid.*
43. Forbes, *The Philippine Islands,* I, 146; II, 102.
44. Duffy, *Taft,* 92.
45. *Ibid.,* 103.

function would be to handle the details of its administration. Entrance to the civil service was restricted to those individuals between the ages of eighteen and forty who were citizens of the United States, natives of the archipelago, and persons who, by reason of the Treaty of Paris, had acquired the political rights of natives. The bill established an efficient civil service which had as its basis a merit system with competitive examinations as the only reason for promotion.

Other early legislative enactments were bills appropriating sums of money to improve the means of communication.[46] When the Second Civil Commission first arrived, transportation facilities were extraordinarily primitive. There was but one railroad, the Manila Railway Company Limited, which operated about 120 miles of "Oriental gauge" track from Manila to Dagupan, and the public roads were nothing more than footpaths, impassible during much of the year. Difficult to construct and even more difficult to maintain, the roads presented a very serious problem to the commission. Labor was unskilled and scarce. Road-building machinery had to be transported from the United States. The topography of the country necessitated abstruse engineering investigations and calculations. And after the roads were built, the torrential rains all too often would wash out the bridges, wreck the surface, and destroy the roadbeds. Taft and his associates determined to leave the problem of the railroads to private persons or corporations, and to devote themselves exclusively to the building and maintenance of highways. And their first bill for expenditure was one appropriating $2,000,000 (Mexican) for just that purpose. Other acts passed during early September, 1900, established three government bureaus—forestry, mining, and statistics.[47]

Another major necessity confronting the Second Philippine Commission was the revision of the civil and criminal codes.[48] The Filipinos who came before the commission to

46. *Ibid.*, 103–104.
47. *Ibid.*, 104.
48. *Ibid.*, 109–110.

register complaints revealed a maladministration of justice which astonished and outraged its members. "The administration of justice through the native judges in Manila stinks to Heaven," Taft informed Elihu Root in January, 1901.[49] Outraged by the knowledge of flagrant abuse under the old Spanish code in iniquitous persecutions, Taft proposed to make sweeping changes in the personnel of the judiciary.[50] He decided to substitute experienced, capable, and honest American judges for the Filipino, bribe-loving jurists.[51] Taft wrote to Judge Erskine M. Ross as follows about the difficulties involved:

> One of the most difficult problems we have is the establishment of a satisfactory judicial system. Such Filipino lawyers as there are have been trained in the Spanish school and under a Spanish judiciary which was as venal as the executive administration, so it is that it is impossible for us to find, with one or two notable exceptions, any Filipino lawyers capable and honest enough to administer justice as we understand that term in an Anglo-Saxon country.
>
> We cannot, therefore, make satisfactory courts unless we appoint American judges in most cases in order that by example these people may be shown what Anglo-Saxon justice means. I write to ask you whether you can recommend to me good, upright lawyers with at least ten years of experience, who would make good judges, who have the moral courage and the sense of fairness necessary to make a good judge, and who have sufficient knowledge of Spanish to enable them by one or two months practice to carry on a court in that language.[52]

As soon as he could obtain them, Taft summoned judges from the United States and put them on the bench.[53] In the meantime, the courts presided over by Filipinos and Spanish judges, trying valiantly to interpret both the Spanish code

---

49. W. H. Taft to Elihu Root, Jan. 9, 1901, Taft MSS.
50. Duffy, *Taft*, 110.
51. *Ibid.*; Pringle, *Taft*, I, 206.
52. As quoted in Duffy, *Taft*, 110–111.
53. Pringle, *Taft*, I, 206.

and the legislative enactments of the commission, were grinding out a confused body of law.[54]

For eight months the commissioners conducted open hearings on both the Judiciary Act and the Code of Procedure.[55] The civil commission urged the College of Advocates (the name for the Filipino Bar) and the American lawyers practicing in the Philippines to attend these sessions and cooperate with them in the framing of these acts, but "these overtures were received with passive, if not active, opposition." [56] The apathy and hostility of the American lawyers was due to Taft's unwillingness to substitute English for Spanish as the official court language. The American lawyers had proposed this change. Taft pointed out, in rejecting this proposed amendment, that if Spanish were replaced by English as the official court language, "every Filipino attorney, by reason of his inability to understand and speak English, would be eliminated from the practice of law." [57]

As matters stood, the judicial machinery was practically paralyzed, and the commission finally passed the Judiciary Act and the Code of Procedure, without assistance from the native and American attorneys.[58] These new rules in the Code of Procedure, governing the commencement of actions, process, trial, and judgment, displaced the archaic Spanish Procedural Code. By the Judiciary Act, the islands were divided into fourteen judicial districts and, in each district, courts of first instance, municipal courts, and justice of the peace courts were established. There was no provision for a jury system because Taft and the other commissioners, knowing that so many of the natives were illiterate, believed them as a whole unfit for such service. The commissioners believed that the installation of a jury system would imperil rather than aid the efforts they were making to remove corruption from the administration of justice. The act did pro-

54. Duffy, *Taft*, 111.
55. *Ibid.*, 112.
56. *Ibid.*
57. *Ibid.*
58. *Ibid.*, 112–113.

vide for the appointment of assessors, upon application of either party to a litigation, who would sit with the court and render a finding of fact.

Besides setting up trial courts in each judicial district, the new law created a Supreme Court of the archipelago, to consist of seven members, a chief justice to be a Filipino, and six associate justices, three of whom were to be Americans and three of whom were to be Filipinos.[59] The judges were to be appointed by the governor general of the islands, subject to confirmation by the commission, and to hold office during good behavior. Power of removal of any judge was vested in the governor general, with the consent of the civil commission.

The Second Philippine Commission divided the islands into provinces and municipalities, and they proposed to test the qualifications of the Filipinos for self-government through these governmental units.[60] The relation of each province to the insular government was much like that of each American state to the United States; and the Filipino municipalities were to the provinces what the American cities were to the states. In point of fact, the commissioners had modeled the Provincial Government Law and the Municipal Government Act upon the constitutions of the American states and the charters of American cities and villages. There were, however, conspicuous and crucial differences due to the nature, background, and training of the people in the Philippines.[61] Eager as they were to grant the Filipinos a degree of popular control that really meant independence, the commission had been constrained, "by the natives' lack of experience in self-government and consequent disregard of the significance and responsibility of governmental duties," to draft laws containing many checks and restrictions.[62] These two monumental acts, the Provincial Government Law

59. *Ibid.*, 113.
60. *Ibid.*, 115–116.
61. *Ibid.*, 116.
62. *Ibid.*

and the Municipal Government Act, were passed finally in early January, 1901, after months of labor.

Under the Municipal Government Act, the Filipinos were for the first time granted an opportunity to control their own affairs.[63] Believing that the exercise of suffrage would be a valuable first step toward political education, Taft included a provision for the election, by the people, of all municipal officials except the treasurer. And the suffrage was confined to persons possessing prescribed qualifications. The offices of president and vice-president were created, as well as a council, and the duties of each were carefully defined. These were to be filled by Filipinos. A secretary and treasurer, both Americans, were to be appointed by the president, with the consent and approval of the council. The councillors were to be elected on the theory of ward representation, their numbers to be decided by the size of the village population. Following an ancient Spanish custom, the commission specified that the municipal officers should carry canes as badges of office.

Under the Provincial Government Law, each province, corresponding roughly to a state in the United States, was governed by five officials—governor, secretary, fiscal, treasurer, and supervisor.[64] The provincial government functioned not only as an independent unit, but also exercised supervision over the municipal authorities, with power to suspend any officer charged with malfeasance or nonfeasance in the duties of his office. The legislative body of the province was "the provincial board," composed of governor, treasurer, and supervisor. Temporarily, the commission intended to appoint the governors of each province, but eventually these were to be selected by the councillors of the municipalities when they met at the provincial capitals.

The fiscal was the legal official of the province, while the supervisor had the duties of an engineer, including the construction, repair, and maintenance of roads and bridges.

63. *Ibid.*, 116–117.
64. *Ibid.*, 117.

"Realizing that the Filipinos, owing to their training under the Spaniards, had not grasped the sacredness of public funds, the Commissioners concluded it best to appoint only Americans to the office of Provincial Treasurer." [65] The provincial treasurer was to collect all taxes, municipal as well as provincial, except the morro fees accruing to local governments, which were to be collected by respective local financial officials. A shameful number of these American officials "went wrong." [66] But the disgrace of these humiliating experiences was not wholly without its beneficial lesson to the Filipinos, "for in the swift prosecution of these malefactors, and the sternness of their punishment, the island people saw the readiness of Mr. Taft to mete out justice to his own people." [67] It was an important example of good faith on his part. In contrast, never in all their history had a corrupt Spanish official been punished when only Filipinos were his victims.

When it came time to establish provincial governments the commission made a grand tour of the provinces, visiting more than thirty of them, some of them two or three times.[68] The commissioners wanted to give the first application of the Provincial Government Law their personal supervision, and to establish direct and friendly contact with the people of the provinces by making a tour of all the islands.[69] The tours were made by train and carriage, boat, horseback, in fact, by any conveyance suitable to the surroundings. The same ceremony was repeated at each village along the route.[70] A few leading citizens stepped forward from the group, and one of them made a welcoming address. Taft responded, and the train started on again, amid a musical clamor played by the native bands in which strains of "A Hot Time" mingled with those of "The Star-Spangled Banner." To add to the sound, there were swelling shouts of "Vivas" for "La Comision

65. *Ibid.*
66. Davis, *Taft*, 137.
67. *Ibid.*, 137–138.
68. *Ibid.*, 132.
69. Duffy, *Taft*, 118.
70. *Ibid.*

Civil." As the railroad cars had no facilities for platform speaking, the members of the commission had to lean out of the car windows in order to be heard. The cars were small, the windows even smaller, and Taft was a very large man, "so that it was something of an achievement to get even part of his upper portion through the inadequate aperture." Although Taft himself and the other commissioners thought it funny, "the grave, always polite Filipinos gave no sign of amusement. Plainly, they liked Taft, his directness, his chuckle, his expansive, disarming smile." [71]

In each province a public meeting was held for the discussion of the new Provincial Government Law.[72] Mr. Taft began by reading the law and explaining each of its provisions simply and directly, so that all could understand. He took special care to show them how many matters were left to the determination of the province itself, and how largely they would share in the functioning of their government. Then he invited general discussion. This procedure was new to the Filipinos, and quite often it happened that although many of them had suggestions which they wanted to make, they were abashed and timid in the presence of the governor. Simply stated, they had never before been invited to this sort of a conference with the man at the head of the government of all the islands. But Mr. Taft had a way of getting them started, a plan that never failed. It was to have someone of his party propose that the location of the provincial capital be changed. Such a proposal always precipitated a lively discussion. The champions of the existing provincial capital forgot their embarrassment under such a stimulus, and once they were started, Mr. Taft could question them generally as to local conditions and shift the discussion into the desired areas where he needed or wanted information. Thus was the "school for self-government" set working.

Mr. Taft's geniality and hearty good nature, "with his ready, sunshiny roar of laughter," was a great agent for the

71. *Ibid.*
72. Davis, *Taft*, 132–133.

"policy of attraction" with the Filipinos.[73] His democracy was an added element of strength. The Filipinos were impressed because Taft received their suggestions thoughtfully and graciously. Many of these proposals had to be considered by the commissioners in private session but they were, whenever possible, put into effect. "He met them on the level and acted on the square, and they understood and loved him. They felt his sincerity and sympathy in his hearty handclasp." [74] The news of his coming always preceded him and the fiesta-loving Filipinos received him invariably with displays of arches and decorations. Some of the Americans grew weary of these celebrations, and at times were inclined to sneer at them, but Taft always entered enthusiastically into the entertainments. He was not deceived into thinking that they meant a sudden conversion of enemies into friends, but he knew how to make them serve his ends in bringing about an era of good feelings. The lavish entertainment and hospitality shown to the Second Philippine Commission by the Filipinos made almost as much impression upon the guests as the new Provincial Government Law did upon the natives.[75] Upon his return to Manila, Taft wrote to Secretary of War Elihu Root that "some sort of pension should be provided for the widows and orphans of the men who fell in action before the powerful onslaughts of native hospitality." [76]

When business matters were concluded on the tour, there was always a *banquete* and a *baile*.[77] Governor Taft made it a point always to take one of the leading native women in at the banquet. And he went religiously through the banquet courses, which were always formidable. At a typical *banquete*, one at Cebu, the following courses were served: (1) oyster soup, (2) roast turkey, (3) roast beef, (4) roast pork, (5) boiled ham in jelly, (6) chicken, French-style, (7) oyster pie, (8) baked fish, (9) boiled tongue, (10) veal pot pie, (11) beef

73. *Ibid.*, 133.
74. *Ibid.*
75. Duffy, *Taft*, 121.
76. *Ibid.*
77. Davis, *Taft*, 133.

steak, (12) pork chops, (13) veal cutlet, (14) fried chicken, (15) roast chicken, (16) chipped ham, (17) fried pigeons, (18) cream pie, (19) apple pie, (20) peach pie, (21) pineapple pie, (22) chocolate cake, (23) raisin cake, (24) jelly roll cake, (25) apple pudding, (26) minced potato, (27) fried potato, (28) shoestring potatoes, (29) sweet corn, (30) stewed beans, (31) asparagus, (32) raw tomatoes, (33) green onions, and (34) radishes.[78]

At the *baile* which followed the *banquete*, the first dance was the old Spanish quadrille, which the Filipinos called the *rigodon*, an extremely complicated dance requiring great skill.[79] At the first bars of the *rigodon* music, Taft rose, gallantly led the wife of the local *presidente* out on the floor, and to the evident astonishment of his fellow commissioners and the delight of the Filipinos, went through the intricate steps with perfect ease. Anticipating just this social emergency, he had taken the time and trouble to learn the dance before starting out from Manila—he had had a young Filipino make a diagram of the figures of the *rigodon*, which he had studied until he was letter perfect.[80] Throughout the tours of the commission, Taft kept up this practice. When he was describing it to the House committee, during the Congressional hearings of 1902, he commented wryly: "That entailed, I may say, a considerable effort, when the number of 'bailes' reached twenty or more in forty days." [81]

The personal influence of this man was irresistible. "He found the Filipinos sullen, suspicious and resentful, every man our enemy. He made them all his friends, and gradually the friends of the Americans." [82] Some things about them touched him very deeply—the eager desire, especially of the lower classes, for even-handed justice, and the quickness with which they recognized it at the hands of Taft and his fellow commissioners; also, the deep longing of the whole

78. Duffy, *Taft*, 125–126.
79. *Ibid.*, 126; Davis, *Taft*, 133–134.
80. Duffy, *Taft*, 126; Davis, *Taft*, 134.
81. *Ibid.*
82. *Ibid.*

people for education.[83] The chance to go to school was first of all their wants. Gray-haired old men and women craved the opportunity to learn, and when the way was opened they went cheerfully to sit on the benches with little children of five and six, their children, and their grandchildren, to learn the rudiments, the simplest matters of the elemental branches, and were glad and proud to go.

Taft had given attention to an educational system even before leaving the United States.[84] He needed an outstanding man to take charge in the islands. After a careful search, the position went to Frederick W. Atkinson. In tendering the position of general superintendent of education, Taft indicated that a large number of men and women teachers, to be paid from $600 to $1,500 a year, would be needed and asked that he conduct a search of the colleges and universities of the United States for prospects.[85] "The young people who came, and scores of them did, were real pioneers of the blackboard." [86] The Filipinos came flocking to the schoolhouses. "Their quick, imitative minds, peculiarly sensitive to sound, enabled them to acquire large English vocabularies in short order. But they repeated whole sentences like parrots. The teachers often discovered that they did this without the slightest idea of what they were talking about." [87] As a consequence of such results, the benefits of the educational program were, at least for a while, limited and indirect. Nevertheless, a large amount of friendly sentiment for the United States and the American authorities sprang up among the people.

From his conversations and interviews with the Philippine people and the testimony they gave before the Second Philippine Commission, Taft learned that the principal factor in the disaffection of the Filipinos was the domination of the friars who had been in charge of their churches and who had

83. *Ibid.*
84. Pringle, *Taft,* I, 191.
85. W. H. Taft to Frederick W. Atkinson, May 8, 1900, Taft MSS.
86. Pringle, *Taft,* I, 191–192.
87. *Ibid.,* 192.

been active participants in the oppression and tyranny of an unjust and arbitrary government.[88] Excluded from any participation in the government, except from such subordinate and unimportant places as they could purchase, and repressed in their yearning for education, most Filipinos found that they could not secure title and peaceable possession of their homes. Instead, they were held largely as unwilling tenants on lands owned by the same friars who ruled their churches, ran the government, and dominated their lives. It was a curious and tangled situation. The Filipinos are nearly all members of the Roman Catholic church, and to an exceptional degree loyal and faithful to it. "It had been the instrument of their civilization, the means of bringing them from the same state of barbarism which still holds certain of the island tribes. But its administration had been corrupted by too great use of power. The friars had become in fact the arbiters of the lives and destinies of the Filipinos, and their rule had been accompanied by grinding oppression, injustice, corruption and immorality." [89] Driven to desperation, the Filipinos had revolted, and the Americans were confronted by the anomalous spectacle of a race of loyal churchmen in armed rebellion against the administration of their own church. This was an extremely delicate condition for an American to try to settle.

"In the assignment of subjects," Taft noted in a family letter, "the most delicate matter of the whole lot—the friar question—has fallen to me. I made the assignment myself so that I have no reason to complain of it." [90] His mother, Louise Taft, was amused "that you should be the one to identify yourself with the religious contests of the people . . . not being theological in your tastes, or fitted for it by education." Mrs. Taft was pessimistic about the "friar question." "You will have the whole Catholic world down on you," she warned. "They

88. Davis, *Taft*, 124; Pringle, *Taft*, I, 220–225.

89. Davis, *Taft*, 124, 127. The reader who wishes to read detailed accounts of the friars' activities should consult Duffy, *Taft*, 105–109, and Pringle, *Taft*, I, 220–225.

90. W. H. Taft to Horace Taft, Sept. 8, 1900, Taft MSS.

quarrel among themselves, but like the Democratic party, they stand together against outsiders." [91]

After hearing voluminous testimony before the Second Philippine Commission in Manila on the friar question, William Howard Taft wrote as follows in December, 1900: "The truth is that the friars ceased to be religious ministers altogether and became political bosses, losing sight of the beneficent purpose of their organizations. They unfrocked themselves in maintaining their political control of this beautiful country. Distance from Rome and freedom from supervision made them an independent quantity and enabled them to gratify their earthly desires for money and power and other things and they cut themselves off from any right to consideration by the church, by those who are in the church, or by those who being out of it, respect it. It is said that all the civilization these islands have is due to the friars. In the first place, the civilization is not a great deal, and in the second place the obligation was contracted many years ago and the condition of things was much better in the early days of the islands than it had been during the present and last generation." [92]

The Philippine Commission quickly reached two conclusions. [93] The first was that the lands should be purchased from the friars, whose legal title was clear. The second was that the Roman Catholic church must send other priests in place of the Spanish friars. Chairman Taft favored American priests: "These Philippine people are yearning for the church to send them ministers whom they can respect and love, and the influence of the church can be restored and increased beyond what it ever was, if only an effort is made to send enlightened priests here." [94]

Taft came to realize more and more that unless the friar question was adjusted to the satisfaction of the Filipinos,

91. Louise Taft to W. H. Taft, Jan. 30, 1901, *ibid.*
92. W. H. Taft to Mrs. Bellamy Storer, Dec. 4, 1900, Taft MSS.
93. Pringle, *Taft*, I, 223.
94. W. H. Taft to Mrs. Bellamy Storer, Dec. 4, 1900, Taft MSS.

armed resistance was inevitable.[95] So deep-seated was the hostility of the natives toward the clerics of those four orders (the Recoletos, the Augustinians, the Franciscans, and the Dominicans) that, as Taft well knew, if they were allowed to return to their parishes the Filipinos would believe the United States government was following in the footsteps of its predecessor. On the other hand, all property rights had been expressly guaranteed by the United States under the Treaty of Paris that brought an end to the Spanish-American War.

It simply could not be disputed that these religious orders possessed valid titles to the land, which promised them protection in the enjoyment of their property. It was equally evident that the friars were patiently awaiting the re-establishment of order and the reorganization of the civil courts before enforcing their rights.[96]

The real, sensitive problem lay in the necessity of dispossessing the friars without offending or infringing upon the rights of a religious body.[97] The disposal of the clergy was a matter of church policy and one over which the United States government could not exercise any control. Failing to understand the impossibility of any immediate solution of the issue, the people were flooding Taft and the Second Philippine Commission with letters and petitions protesting the return of the churchmen, and demanding that the new government prohibit the restoration of their civil rights. The matter of the friars' lands thus became a question of policy rather than one of law, for, as the commission had reported, the return of the friars to the Philippines would have had the same effect as "the return of General Weyler under an American Commission as Governor of Cuba would have had on the people of that island." [98]

What Taft hoped to do was to purchase the vast estates of

95. Duffy, Taft, 108.
96. Ibid.
97. Ibid.
98. Ibid., 108–109.

the religious orders and then sell the land back to the natives on easy terms.[99] In this way, he believed strongly, the friction between the people and the friars could be eliminated. Accordingly, in order to acquaint himself further with the situation, he interviewed heads of the various religious orders and prominent Filipinos.[100] He conferred also with Archbishop Chappelle of New Orleans, who, by direction of the Vatican, had come to Manila to assist the United States in working out the friar problem.[101] It was much later that he finally solved and closed it.[102]

Meanwhile, delay followed delay. Most Reverend P. L. Chapelle, Archbishop of New Orleans and charge d'affaires on behalf of the Vatican in the Philippine Islands, proved to be a most difficult, exasperating prelate. Taft complained that his evidence on either side of the friar question was "altogether worthless, and the sooner Rome finds out how utterly useless he is for bringing about a solution of these difficulties here . . . the better." [103] For his part, Archbishop Chapelle declared that the Philippine Commission "has taken, unconsciously perhaps, indirectly surely, a hostile attitude towards the Catholic Church and her interests." [104] The charge was baseless. Baseless also were the rumors that the opposition to the friars was an opening wedge in a massive drive to substitute Protestant missionaries for the Roman Catholics who had been in the island for so long. Taft was very firm on this point: "As to the schools I can assure you that we do not expect or wish to make them proselytizing instruments." [105]

---

99. *Ibid.*, 109.
100. *Ibid.*
101. Davis, *Taft*, 109; Pringle, *Taft*, 178, 221–222, 224.
102. The reader who desires a complete account of the background to Taft's 1902 mission to Rome should consult the following two excellent scholarly articles: John T. Farrell, "Background of the 1902 Taft Mission to Rome. I," 1–32, and also "Background of the Taft Mission to Rome, II," *The Catholic Historical Review*, XXXVII (April, 1951), 1–22.
103. W. H. Taft to Elihu Root, June 23, 1901, Taft MSS.
104. P. L. Chapelle to W. H. Taft, April 13, 1901, *ibid.*
105. W. H. Taft to Mrs. Bellamy Storer, June 22, 1900, *ibid.*

Meanwhile, Taft was finding it very difficult to fix a price at which the lands could be bought and then resold to the natives. "The promoters whom the friars have employed," he reported, "desire to hold up the price as much as possible." [106] Such was the sad situation as Taft, in the late fall of 1901, prepared to return to the United States to regain his health. Before leaving Manila he suggested that it would be wise to send a representative directly to Rome: "It would need, of course, a very clearheaded man to carry on the negotiations. . . . Now have we a man competent to do this business?" [107]

The Tafts sailed from Manila for San Francisco on Christmas Eve, 1901.[108] After a brief stop in Cincinnati, Taft hurried on to Washington, D.C., to testify before the United States Senate Committee on the Philippines. For three weeks he remained, as guest of Secretary and Mrs. Root, while in a Senate committee room he was subjected to searching examination and cross-examination as to affairs in the archipelago. In testifying, Taft said it was the duty of the United States to establish in the Philippines "a government suited to the present possibilities of the people, which shall gradually change, conferring more and more right upon the people to govern themselves, thus educating them in self-government, until their knowledge of government, their knowledge of liberty, shall be such that further action may be taken either by giving them statehood or by making them a quasi-independent government like Canada or Australia or, if they desire it, independence." [109]

The problem of the friars' lands especially engaged the United States Senate Committee. In response to many questions, Taft told the Senators:

I think it may be said generally that the title of the friars to those lands is, as a legal proposition, indisputable. . . . The

106. W. H. Taft to Carmi Thompson, April 12, 1902, *ibid.*
107. W. H. Taft to Elihu Root, Sept. 26, Oct. 14, 1901, *ibid.*
108. Duffy, *Taft,* 141.
109. *Ibid.*

most distinguished lawyer who is engaged in opposition to the friars, Senor Don Felip Calderon, admitted that under any law of Prescription or statute of limitations of which he knew, the title to the friars' lands, speaking generally, of course making allowances for special cases, was unimpeachable. . . . If we can buy those lands and make them government property, and in that way separate in the minds of the tenants the relation of the friar to the lands and say to the tenants, "We shall sell you these lands on long payments, so that they will become yours," I believe that we can satisfy the people and avoid the agrarian question which will arise when our government is appealed to to put into possession of those lands the people who own them. . . .[110]

On February 18, 1902, a conference was held at the White House at which Theodore Roosevelt, Elihu Root, Archbishop John Ireland of St. Paul, Minnesota, and William Howard Taft discussed the situation.[111] The presidential order to Taft was "You'll have to go to Rome yourself." [112] Taft went to Cincinnati for a third abscess operation and then prepared for his first assignment as the troubleshooter of the Theodore Roosevelt administration. Taft was to receive·many more such assignments before Roosevelt left the presidential chair.

The mission to the Vatican was of a delicate nature. In the instructions handed to Taft, Secretary of War Root specified that the journey "will not be in any sense or degree diplomatic in its nature, but will be purely a business matter of negotiation by you as governor of the Philippines for the purchase of property from the owners thereof, and the settlement of land titles, in such a manner as to contribute to the best interests of the people of the islands." [113] This was vital. If the United States were to send a diplomatic mission to the Vatican, it would mean in the view of anti-Catholic voters recognition of the Pope as a sovereign. This, in turn, would mean defeat for Theodore Roosevelt or any other Republican can-

110. *Ibid.*, 142.
111. Farrell, "Background of the Taft Mission to Rome, II," 1–22.
112. W. H. Taft to Helen H. Taft, Feb. 24, 1902, Taft MSS.
113. Elihu Root to W. H. Taft, May 9, 1902, *ibid.*

didate in the 1904 presidential campaign. But the Vatican, in contrast, greatly desired that a diplomatic flavor surround the American mission, as this would increase its prestige in the courts of Europe. A battle of wits was expected among the hills of imperial Rome.

To assist Taft in his negotiations with the Vatican, President Roosevelt appointed the Right Reverend Thomas O'Gorman, Bishop of Sioux Falls, South Dakota, Judge James F. Smith, a Roman Catholic and a member of the Philippine judiciary, and Major John Biddle Porter, to accompany the group as secretary and interpreter.[114] Major Porter was from the judge advocate's department. Bishop O'Gorman was very possibly the most valuable aide.[115] He was an Irish-American with an innate distrust of Italians, even when they were high prelates of his own church. Taft reported that he had "a keen sense of humour and . . . an imperturbability under attacks which it is pleasant to see." [116] A sense of humor would be needed for this trip.

A storm of denunciation greeted confirmation of this mission. The *Boston Watchman* (a Baptist publication) said: "However defensible the measure taken by the President may be, it indicates in a most unmistakable way the new influence which Rome is acquiring in the United States." [117] Other denominational papers were opposed to Governor Taft's going to Rome, contending that the Vatican should send a mission to Manila. Still others suggested that Taft, by going to Rome, would sacrifice his personal dignity and destroy the prestige he enjoyed in the Orient. The Catholic newspapers rather made light of the matter, one of them declaring "It is the lands that we are interested in, and the question has nothing to do with church and state." [118]

Shortly before they sailed, the commission to the Vatican was instructed to remember that there was a complete sepa-

114. Pringle, *Taft*, I, 226–227; Duffy, *Taft*, 143.
115. Pringle, *Taft*, I, 227.
116. W. H. Taft to Elihu Root, July 5, 1902, Taft MSS.
117. Duffy, *Taft*, 143.
118. *Ibid.*

ration of church and state in the United States; that there must be a readjustment of the old order in the Philippines; that the landed proprietorship of the religious orders in the archipelago should cease; that provision should be made for the ascertaining of rental to be changed for the convents and the church property occupied by the American forces on the islands during the Philippine Insurrection, and that the errand undertaken by the commission was in no sense to be construed as diplomatic, but purely a business endeavor, for the purpose of negotiating and purchasing the friars' lands and settling the land titles.[119]

It was about the middle of May that the Italian steamer *Trave* bore the American representatives out of New York City toward Naples and Rome. "No fault of preparation indicated that they were a diplomatic group undertaking a mission to a sovereign power." [120]

Elihu Root's official instructions to William Howard Taft summarized the friars' land situation in the Philippines.[121] The civil governor was directed to learn which church authorities had power to negotiate the sale of the lands so that Congress could act in the matter. The secretary of war pointed out firmly that the monastic orders which had incurred the hostility of the Filipinos could not remain at their posts. Other spiritual leaders should and must be sent in their place.

"It is the wish of our government," Root wrote, "that the titles of the religious orders to the large tracts of agricultural lands which they now hold shall be extinguished, but that full and fair compensation should be made therefor." [122]

Thus, the expedition to Rome had two main objectives: consent of the Vatican to recall the friars and sale of their holdings at a fair price.[123] Prior to leaving for Rome, Taft thought that $5,000,000 in gold would probably be an accept-

119. *Ibid.*, 143–144.
120. Farrell, "Background of the Taft Mission to Rome, II," 22.
121. Elihu Root to W. H. Taft, May 9, 1902, Taft MSS.
122. *Ibid.*
123. *Ibid.*

able figure; however, he was willing apparently to bid up to $8,000,000.[124] As it turned out, the negotiations at Rome did not progress to the point of bidding. Lyman Abbott, famed editor of the *Outlook* then on a grand tour of Europe, sent a warning from Florence: "The Vatican appears to me to be ruled by politicians who are not overscrupulous, and whose ideal of diplomacy like their ideals of theology belong to the age of Machiavelli." [125]

The *Trave* arrived at Naples on May 29, 1901, and two days later Taft and his colleagues reached Rome.[126] On June 2, 1901, they called on Cardinal Rampolla, the papal secretary of state. It was done in the grand manner; letters were presented from the American president and from Secretary of State John Hay. As a present to Pope Leo XIII, Theodore Roosevelt sent eight volumes of his own writings—"what better gift could a literary chief executive make?" [127] On June 5, 1901, at twelve-thirty, garbed in full evening dress, the Americans were received at the Vatican. Governor Taft was impressed by the pomp and color and was entertained too. Pope Leo XIII, by now extremely old, was as friendly as it was possible to be.[128]

"The old boy is quite bubbling with humor," Taft wrote to his wife. "He was as lively as a cricket."

> We were ushered through I know not how many rooms between guards of all uniforms including the Swiss and the Noble Guards and were finally met by the master of ceremonies. We waited not more than two minutes when we were taken to a small audience chamber where we found the Pope seated on a little throne and saying something in French in the way of welcome. He told us to be seated, but I stood up and

124. W. H. Taft to Henry Cabot Lodge, March 26, 1902, *ibid.*
125. Lyman Abbott to W. H. Taft, June 1, 1902, *ibid.*
126. Pringle, *Taft,* I, 228.
127. *Ibid.*
128. W. H. Taft to Helen H. Taft, June 7, 1902, Taft MSS. Judge James F. Smith wrote later as follows: "My recollection of the Holy Father is that his face was like transparent parchment, that he had brilliant eyes of a young man, and that he was wonderfully alert in his mind although bent over by the weight of years." As quoted in Duffy, *Taft,* 144.

fired a speech at him which Major Porter read in French. The Pope followed closely and when something was said he liked he bowed and waved his hand at me. He surprised me very much by his vigor and the resonance of his voice. . . . After that he sat down and we had fifteen minutes' conversation. . . . He said that he had heard of my illness but that my appearance didn't justify any such inference. . . . He expressed the most emphatic interest in my success and my good health. When the audience was at an end, he got up, gave the bell rope behind him a jerk, asked me to give him the pleasure of shaking hands with him and then escorted us to the door. . . . I understand from persons coming from the Vatican that the old gentleman was very much pleased with the interview and spoke of it a number of times. I have no doubt that it will attract some criticism from our Methodist and supersensitive Protestant friends, but if we can succeed in our purpose, that will, I believe, pass away in the excellence of the result.[129]

William Howard Taft's address to Pope Leo XIII outlined the changes necessitated by the transfer of the Philippines from Spain, a nation closely allied to the Roman Catholic church, to the United States where no church alliance of any kind was possible.[130] The "justice or injustice" of the hatreds incurred by the monastic orders, he stated, had no relation to the problem of their lands and their recall. The Philippine government, he added, proposed to purchase and to bring about, thereby, the substitution of priests "whose presence would not be dangerous to public order." [131] The price should be fixed by arbitration. Taft concluded by reiterating that the United States was in every conceivable way friendly to the Roman Catholic church; that it treated all churches and all creeds alike.[132]

Pope Leo XIII bobbed and bowed his approval as Major John Biddle Porter read the French translation of Taft's speech.[133] The Pope said that he could not go into the details

129. W. H. Taft to Helen H. Taft, June 7, 1902, Taft MSS.
130. Pringle, *Taft*, I, 229; Duffy, *Taft*, 144.
131. W. H. Taft to Horace Taft, June 10, 1902, Taft MSS.
132. *Ibid.*
133. Pringle, *Taft*, I, 229.

of the proposals made by the United States. A commission of cardinals would be appointed and would have charge of the matter.[134] These cardinals, including Vives y Tuto, reputed to be the most liberal of the Spanish prelates, Vannutelli, Gotti, the Carmelite monk, the Jesuit Steinhuber, and Rampolla, were appointed to consider the American proposals, and instructed by the Pope that he desired an amicable understanding with the representatives of the United States.[135]

Bishop Thomas O'Gorman was hopeful during the next few days that an agreement would be reached. The Bishop kept a day-to-day record of the proceedings and noted that "the United States government is giving the Holy Father the chance of his life and he is going to use it to the fullest extent. The religious orders, so recalcitrant to his policies most everywhere, are to be brought under his thumb. Washington asks him to exercise his supreme power over them." [136] Bishop O'Gorman assured Taft that success would crown the visit; any delay would be due only to anxiety on the part of the Pope to appoint cardinals who would do as they were told. Bishop O'Gorman fell back on a phrase familiar to American politics to describe what was going on in the Vatican. "Boys," he said, "the Pope had already declared to the cardinals 'this thing goes through.' " [137]

It did not, regrettably, go through. A week after the audience with the Pope, Taft was beginning to have misgivings. "These Italians are such liars," he wrote, "that I do not wish to express confidence until my ground is black and white." [138] On June 21, 1902, an answer to the American proposals was delivered to Taft, an answer, which, as he said, "agreed generally with all the proposals stated in the letter of instructions, including among other things the purchase of

134. *Ibid.* The Pope informed the governor that "the issues would be presented in a most anxious spirit to reach a settlement satisfactory to all parties." Duffy, *Taft*, 144.

135. *Ibid.*, 145.

136. Memorandum, Bishop Thomas O'Gorman, June 9, 1910, Taft MSS.

137. W. H. Taft to Helen H. Taft, June 11, 1902, *ibid.*

138. *Ibid.*, June 12, 1902.

the friars' lands by our government. . . . The answer further proposed that further negotiations be had between the Apostolic Delegate and myself in Manila." [139]

Conciliatory in tone, the reply assured the American government, "The Vatican is aware of the entire separation of church and state in the United States, but hopes that the Washington Government will take into consideration the contrary conditions in the new territory now under their jurisdiction." [140]

Governor Taft in reply suggested that the Pope agree to submit the questions at issue to an arbitration tribunal, which should consist of two American representatives, two ecclesiastics appointed by the Vatican, and a fifth member to be selected by the Viceroy of India, this tribunal to meet in the city of Manila not later than the first of January, 1903, to consider and examine the land and the witnesses, the conclusions of a majority of its members to constitute the finding of the tribunal. Taft further promised that any damages assessed against the American government by this group would be paid by the United States in Mexican dollars, one-third down, one-third in nine months, and the balance in eighteen months. The proposed contract also provided for the withdrawal of the four religious orders, the Dominicans, the Recoletos, the Augustinians, and the Franciscans, from the Philippines within two years' time, and that only secular and non-Spanish members of the regular clergy should act as parish priests.[141]

Shortly afterward Taft received the Vatican's answer to his detailed note. The cardinals composing the Vatican committee agreed to sign the contract, provided the stipulation for withdrawal of the friars be stricken out. Cardinal Rampolla said that otherwise the Vatican would offend Spain, and that since the withdrawal of the friars related solely to the administration of religious matters, it could not be made a mat-

139. Duffy, *Taft*, 145.
140. *Ibid.*, 145.
141. *Ibid.*, 145–146.

ter of commercial contract. He agreed, however, to recognize the church government in the archipelago and promised to devote the money realized from the sale of the lands to the development and welfare of the church in the Philippines.[142]

There the matter rested for the moment. "I wonder," noted Bishop O'Gorman in his diary, "if the Vatican realizes what it has lost in material profits and in diplomatic prestige." [143] Secretary of War Elihu Root cabled Taft to stand by the original instructions.[144] Further delays were caused by further debates. Finally, Root ordered Taft to end the negotiations as well as to cancel the proposals made by the United States.[145] Because the Vatican was unwilling to guarantee the removal of the friars from the islands, Secretary Root, for the United States government, declined to enter into a contract obligating the Philippine government and the government of the United States to pay an indefinite sum, the amount of which had to be determined later.[146] Taft delivered Root's message to Cardinal Rampolla, who agreed with Taft that further negotiations should be suspended until an apostolic delegate should arrive in Manila.

Taft then requested a farewell audience with Pope Leo XIII which Cardinal Rampolla set for July 21, 1902.[147] Outward harmony was preserved. The Americans were received by the Pope again and he was "full of honeyed expressions," according to Taft.[148] Taft felt that the Pope, himself, had been anxious to accede to the American demands but "the influence of the monastic orders at Rome is now all-powerful. The Pope does not dare antagonize them and they have beaten us." [149] Taft thought, however, that the visit had been valuable even if the main objective had not been gained. "We

142. *Ibid.*, 146.
143. Memorandum, Bishop Thomas O'Gorman, June, 1910, Taft MSS.
144. Pringle, *Taft*, I, 230.
145. *Ibid.*
146. Duffy, *Taft*, 146–147.
147. *Ibid.*, 147.
148. W. H. Taft to Delia Torrey, July 27, 1902, Taft MSS.
149. W. H. Taft to Horace D. Taft, July 10, 1902, *ibid.*

have told the Vatican the plain truth, and while it is not disposed to make written admission of it," he wrote, "we shall have considerably less difficulty hereafter in making Rome understand the situation." [150]

At this audience the Pope presented Taft with a golden goose quill of exquisite workmanship with Leo's coat of arms on the feather. The Pope told Taft, "I will see that orders be given the Apostolic Delegate as to his work over which I will personally watch." [151] Later that day, Taft, accompanied by Judge James F. Smith, left Rome for Naples, whence they sailed for Manila.

It was reported in the United States almost immediately after Governor Taft's departure from Rome that the Pope was dissatisfied with the results of the negotiations. Archbishop John Ireland of St. Paul, Minnesota, refuted these reports when he said in an important address: "The Pope was greatly satisfied with the Taft Mission. He said that he had the highest esteem for the American methods of treating church matters." [152]

Certain of the American Roman Catholic newspapers then attacked Governor Taft as being prejudiced against the Roman Catholic church. Once again, Archbishop Ireland defended the governor of the Philippines, disproving the allegations made by publishing a letter written by the Reverend Father W. D. McKinnon, a Roman Catholic priest then residing in Manila: "I can assure you that nothing can be more unjust than the criticism of Governor Taft in some of the Roman Catholic papers. Governor Taft has not a particle of bigotry in his makeup. In all his acts here I defy anyone to say that he has shown himself prejudiced in the least." [153]

The exact status of Taft during these negotiations raised interesting questions both inside and outside the Vatican during his stay in Rome and after his departure for Manila. His

150. *Ibid.*, July 15, 1902.
151. Duffy, *Taft*, 147.
152. *Ibid.*
153. *Ibid.*, 147–148.

position was, and to some extent still is, anomalous. His credentials gave him powers as great as those of a diplomat, if not greater. He followed diplomatic precedent and called upon the accredited ambassadors to the Vatican from Austria, Spain, France, and Portugal, just as any newly appointed representative might have done. He dined and entertained in the manner of a diplomat and by these actions placed himself in equality with foreign ministers and yet, at the same time, he scrupulously followed the tenor of his instructions and conducted himself in a tactful, unobtrusive way. It was a delicate situation, and he handled it superbly.

The venerable, beloved Leo XIII was to die before the difficult issue of the friars and their lands had been settled. "The matter assumed all the aspects of a New England horse trade." [154] Monseigneur Guidi, archbishop of Staurpoli, a far more reasonable man than Archbishop Chapelle in Taft's judgment, became the apostolic delegate for the Roman Catholic church in the Philippines in the summer of 1902. [155] In September, 1903, Guidi informed the civil governor that $10,700,000 in gold was the lowest possible figure; this figure, he stated, had been approved in Rome. [156] But $10,700,000 was a very steep figure, far more than the Second Philippine Commission was willing to pay. [157] Governor Taft again employed experts who repeated the estimate that $5,000,000 was a fair price. It soon became evident that a compromise purchase figure would have to be set.

"For the sake of peace and to accomplish our purposes," Taft reported to Elihu Root, "I should be willing to increase the estimate of our surveyor by fifty per cent, making the offer seven and one half millions. I think this is too great probably by a million or a million and a half, but I am willing to recommend the offer with a view of closing the matter up." [158]

The real difficulty lay in the fact that the monastic orders

154. Pringle, *Taft*, I, 230.
155. *Ibid.*; Duffy, *Taft*, 148.
156. Pringle, *Taft*, I, 230.
157. *Ibid.*
158. W. H. Taft to Elihu Root, April 26, 1903, Taft MSS.

knew that the Pope intended to assign the funds to general church work in the Philippines and that they would not, themselves, benefit. As the months went by, Taft grew impatient and wondered whether it would not be better to let the "owners of the friars' lands, whoever they are, 'stew in their own juice.' " [159] "We are still very far apart and the attitude . . . of my colleagues on the Commission is that of hostility to the purchase of the lands," he told Secretary Root in September, 1903. "They think that the time is past and that it would be assuming a great burden. Still, if we can buy the lands anywhere near my figure, I think it will be a good thing. . . . I should judge from what I hear that the new Pope is quite as liberally inclined toward a settlement as was Leo." [160]

An agreement was finally reached in November, 1903. Approximately 10,000 out of the 400,000 acres owned by the friars were withdrawn from the sale, and $7,543,000 was paid from the remaining acres.[161] Under authorization by the United States Congress, the insular government raised the cash through the issue of bonds. Then the lands were gradually sold, in small parcels and on easy terms to the natives. By 1912, some 50,000 new landowners were a stabilizing force in the archipelago. Meanwhile, although Rome never formally recalled the Spanish clerics, their influence waned. American and Filipino bishops were appointed in their places. Only 200 remained in the islands by the end of 1903 and they had no political power whatever.[162] The Vatican went farther than the agreement called for in sending American bishops to the islands. One of those whose work in the Philippines was most successful and conciliatory, Bishop Dougherty of Jaro, was promoted to the archbishopric of Philadelphia and created cardinal.[163]

William Howard Taft was congratulated heartily on his

---

159. *Ibid.*
160. W. H. Taft to Charles P. Taft, Sept. 24, 1903, Taft MSS.
161. *Report, Philippine Commission,* U.S. 58th Cong., 2nd Sess., H. Doc. 2 (1903), pp. 38–44.
162. Forbes, *The Philippine Islands,* II, 58–60.
163. Duffy, *Taft,* 150.

successful settlement of the friar lands question. The praise came not only from the Filipinos, but also from members of the Roman Catholic hierarchy. Archbishop John Ireland of St. Paul, Minnesota, wrote to him:

> I have obtained from Bishop O'Gorman fullest news about your visit to Rome. I cannot but admire the dignity and tactful diplomacy which marked your course during the negotiations. . . . What advices I had had from Rome give me the conviction that the Holy Father and Cardinal Rampolla were delighted with you and are in the best possible sentiments in your regard. . . .
>
> I was very much gratified with the announcement in the papers that in your address on your arrival in Manila you were able to state that the money derived from the sale of the Friar's lands was to be held in the Philippines for the use and benefit of the Catholic Church in the Islands. In my opinion this is one of the most important results that could have come from your negotiations with the Vatican.[164]

The amount paid to the Vatican attracted considerable criticism. But, as Governor Taft said, the government had not "entered upon the purchase of these lands with a view to a profitable investment, but it is knowingly paying a considerable sum of money merely for the purpose of ridding the administration of the government of the islands of an issue dangerous to the peace and prosperity of the people." [165] And its payment solved a problem which had harassed the Philippines for decades.

Meanwhile a new series of crises had arisen to plague Taft. On two occasions beginning in October, 1902, President Roosevelt offered him "the kingly crown of appointment to the Supreme Court." [166] Twice Taft refused this, his heart's desire, because he would not desert the people of the Philippines. Then came a virtual order, arriving March 27, 1903, to report to Washington and accept the portfolio of secretary of

164. *Ibid.*, 149–150.
165. *Ibid.*, 149.
166. Pringle, *Taft*, I, 236.

war.[167] Taft did not want the post. In 1903, as throughout his life, Taft was a stubborn advocate of peace. "I find it hard myself, to subscribe to the Monroe Doctrine," he had written nine months before, "and to deem it of sufficient importance to warrant, as Bismarck said with respect to the Turkish question, the loss of the bones of one Pomeranian grenadier!" [168] "I have no particular aptitude for managing an army," he wrote on another occasion, "nor do I know anything about it." [169] As always, Taft doubted his qualifications. As always, "he shrank from an assignment which led, inevitably, into the confused and swirling waters of active politics. But this time he could not decline." [170] "It seems strange," he wrote, "that with an effort to keep out of politics and with my real dislike for it, I should thus be pitched into the middle of it." [171]

William Howard Taft left the Philippine Islands with a unique and an enviable record of achievement. Supplanting the military government with a civil administration, he had created, out of confusion and chaos, a well-organized, efficiently functioning government, a government well endowed with progressive and liberal laws executed by competent and well-trained officials. His crowning achievement may well have been this work of lofty altruism on behalf of the poor and helpless, the ignorant and downtrodden Filipinos. Not often is it given to one man to bring a nation into being.

167. *Ibid.*
168. W. H. Taft to Bellamy Storer, March 23, 1903, Taft MSS.
169. W. H. Taft to Mrs. Bellamy Storer, Oct. 26, 1903, *ibid.*
170. Pringle, *Taft*, I, 236.
171. W. H. Taft to H. C. Hollister, Sept. 21, 1903, Taft MSS.

CHAPTER IV

Panama, the Canal Zone, and Titular Sovereignty

WILLIAM HOWARD TAFT'S success in the Philippines had greatly increased his prestige—to the point where he was considered fit for cabinet rank. Elihu Root, the brilliant lawyer-statesman, Roosevelt's secretary of war, expressed the feelings of the Roosevelt administration when he wrote Taft: "The number of men is very small who combine the ability and character and the special training in public business necessary to the successful conduct of great affairs. . . . I consider you one of the most valuable assets of the United States." [1]

Upon Root's resignation, February 1, 1904, Taft became the secretary of war.[2] This new position left him with a very powerful voice in Philippine affairs, for both Roosevelt and Root had indicated that the supervision of the Philippines would remain under this office.[3] From the time of Taft's arrival in Washington in late January, 1904, a singularly intimate and confidential relationship commenced between the President and the new secretary of war. Taft soon discov-

1. Elihu Root to W. H. Taft, Aug. 11, 1903, Taft MSS.
2. Leopold, *Elihu Root and the Conservative Tradition*, 44; DAB, XVIII, 268.
3. Theodore Roosevelt to W. H. Taft, Feb. 14, 1903, Theodore Roosevelt Papers (Division of Manuscripts, Library of Congress); Elihu Root to W. H. Taft, Feb. 20 and Aug. 11, 1903, Root MSS.

ered that the administration of the war department was to be an insignificant part of his work. President Roosevelt for reasons of necessity (one being the illness of Secretary of State John Hay in the spring of 1905), and because of his increasing confidence in Taft, laid some of the administration's heaviest responsibilities on his new Cabinet officer.[4] Thus as secretary of war, Taft discharged broad responsibilities in foreign affairs, an area traditionally reserved for the secretary of state. In the course of the next five years Taft was to supervise the building of the Panama Canal, mollify a troubled Cuba, and become the president's roving ambassador for peace.

When satisfactory arrangements for the construction of the Panama Canal could not be arranged with private companies, this problem was placed under the direction of the war department.[5] By executive order on May 9, 1904, President Roosevelt informed Taft that "all the work . . . in the digging, construction and completion of the canal, and all the governmental power in and over said canal zone and its appurtenant territory . . . shall be carried on or exercised under your supervision and direction as Secretary of War." [6] Thus Taft faced great responsibilities in an area with which he was almost totally unfamiliar, and he was to discover shortly that the Panama situation presented great complexities.

Taft's knowledge of Panamanian affairs was meager indeed. Two months before Roosevelt placed the construction of the Panama Canal under his supervision, the secretary confessed to his younger brother that he had "not looked into the Panama question" because "it all took place while I was away." [7] He supposed, however, that he would "have to ex-

---

4. Pringle, *Taft*, I, 258–259; Tyler Dennett, *John Hay: From Poetry to Politics* (New York, 1934), 436–437, 439; Pringle, *Taft*, I, 268.

5. Wilfrid Hardy Callcott, *The Caribbean Policy of the United States, 1890–1920* (Baltimore, 1942), 225.

6. Executive Order, Theodore Roosevelt to W. H. Taft, May 9, 1940, Taft MSS.

7. W. H. Taft to Horace D. Taft, Feb. 6, 1904, *ibid*. During the years 1900 through 1903, William Howard Taft was in the Philippines first as president to the Second Philippine Commission and then from July 4, 1901, as civil governor of the Philippines.

amine the papers with a view to discussing the matter on the stump." [8] His lack of interest, knowledge, and understanding of the political and power factors involved in the Isthmian Canal issue is revealed graphically by the only letter he devoted to the subject, written in February, 1901, to his younger brother, Horace:

> I quite agree with you in your view that it would be a great deal better to have the Nicaraguan Canal neutral. The neutrality of the canal would prevent any necessity on our part from protecting it and it is much more of a benefit to us as a means of defense that we should be able to get from one side of our country to the other through the canal than it is a detriment to us that other countries so far from their base of supplies could do the same thing; and then the question of what is to be done in time of war does not strike me as most important. I think the canal should be a commercial measure and these political discussions hazard the passage of the bill.[9]

Taft's initial experience with the Panama question came in the presidential campaign of 1904. It was inevitable that the Panama issue would be raised during this election campaign because of the spectacular fashion in which Theodore Roosevelt had handled the question. In an address at Montpelier, Vermont, on August 26, 1904, Taft reviewed all aspects of this complex issue at great length. The speech could not have been more favorable to President Roosevelt's conduct of affairs had the president written and delivered it himself. He believed that the course of conduct pursued by the United States toward Colombia had "been characterized by the greatest patience and honor and probity" whereas, in contrast, Colombia's conduct had been "vacillating and dishonorable." [10] His presentation was an advocacy for the Roosevelt administration's position rather than a judicial estimate of the complexities involved in the situation.

8. W. H. Taft to Horace D. Taft, Feb. 6, 1904, Taft MSS.
9. *Ibid.*, Feb. 16, 1901.
10. Address by William Howard Taft at Montpelier, Vermont, on Aug. 26, 1904. *Addresses and Articles*, I, 240–266, Taft MSS.

The United States Congress, labor officials, the press, and the American public expected miracles in the completion of the Panama Canal without any comprehension of the difficulties involved. They were destined for disappointment, for the seven members of the Isthmian Canal Commission, confused as to the nature of their functions, showed irresolution and an apparent incapacity under the existing administrative arrangement to meet and solve the problems involved. To make matters even worse, the United States had barely taken formal possession of the Canal Zone when the first major dispute arose with the Republic of Panama.[11] The exercise of sovereignty by the United States government in the establishment of ports of entry, customhouses, tariffs, and post offices in the Canal Zone produced a mounting storm of protest from the government of Panama.

When it became evident that the criticism from Panama was not going to abate, President Roosevelt instructed his secretary of war to proceed to Panama to allay the hostility of the Panamanians. Taft conceived his mission as one of expediting the building of the Panama Canal within the framework of the then existing treaty structure between the United States and Panama.[12] There were innumerable technical problems connected not only with the physical construction of the canal which presented enormous difficulties from an engineering viewpoint, but also complex political problems involving relations with the Panamanian government and people. There were several extraordinarily difficult and seemingly insoluble currency, tariff, and fiscal problems which might well have tried the patience of Job. Few men were equipped with the ability and the gargantuan perseverance to tackle these problems. But Taft seemed to relish the challenges and administrative details were for him an apparently pleasurable pursuit.

11. Alfred D. Chandler, Jr., "Theodore Roosevelt and the Panama Canal: A Study in Administration," in Roosevelt, *Letters*, VI, 1548–49; William D. McCain, *The United States and the Republic of Panama* (Durham, N.C., 1937), 23.

12. Theodore Roosevelt to W. H. Taft, Oct. 18, 1904, Taft MSS; W. H. Taft to Crammond Kennedy, Nov. 11, 1904, *ibid.*

Secretary Taft had a definite attitude about Latin Americans and their governments. He frankly regarded the Latin American countries as "dirty so-called republics" unworthy of strenuous exertions on the part of the United States government unless calculated to advance the interests of the United States. In particular, he objected to the idea of pouring out American "money and treasure" to the Latin Americans.[13] But while Taft confided such sentiments to his private correspondence, he was much too politic and mature to permit any manifestation of such feeling in his official capacity. And when subordinates of his who were serving in Panama made no secret of their contempt for the Panamanians, Taft bore down hard on them. He was convinced that "the exercise of proper tact on the part of the officials representing the United States" would prevent any recurrence of hostile feeling on the part of the people of Panama toward the United States.[14]

On November 17, 1904, the day of his departure from Washington, D.C., Taft indicated that there had been "a tempest in a teapot" in the Republic of Panama. In regard to the revolutionary disturbances which he had been dispatched to quell, Taft alluded to the Hay-Bunau-Varilla Treaty of November 18, 1903, which defined America's relations with the new Republic of Panama.[15] He noted that this treaty "permits us to prevent revolutions," and added imperiously, "I shall advise that we'll have no more." As to the caliber of the republic, he referred to it in contemptuous tones as "a kind of Opera Bouffe republic and nation." For any threat posed by General Huertas and the Panamanian Army, Taft was explicit in his assessment of the power balance: "Its army is not much larger than the army on an opera stage. We have four hundred

13. W. H. Taft to Horace D. Taft, July 3, 1904, *ibid.*
14. W. H. Taft to Theodore Roosevelt, Dec. 19, 1904, *ibid.*
15. W. H. Taft to Charles P. Taft, Nov. 17, 1904, *ibid.* For the full text of this treaty, known formally as Convention with Panama for the Construction of a Canal, see William M. Malloy, ed., *Treaties, Conventions, International Acts, Protocols, and Agreements between the United States of America and Other Powers, 1776–1909* (Washington, D.C.,*), II, 1349ff.

marines and a fleet on one side and three naval vessels on the other so I think we can attend to Mr. Huertas." [16]

Underlying Taft's approach to the problem was the conviction that the Panamanian authorities were not trustworthy and had to be dealt with firmly. He wrote: "I do not propose in my dealings with the Government officials of Panama to be embarrassed by their assumption that they hold a club over me or the administration which they may use to blackmail me or it into some course I would not otherwise take." [17] He felt that Roosevelt's policy toward Panama was based on justice, but Taft would be the sole interpreter of what justice meant. Here Taft displayed a firmness and determination wholly at variance with the picture of falstaffian joviality so often ascribed to him. Taft saw as the sole purpose of his mission in Panama "to see how far within our rights under the treaty with that State we may keep for the present, and still not injure our opportunity and means of building, maintaining and protecting the Canal." [18] He was not going there to make a new treaty, but rather to find the least offensive method by which the United States government could assert its treaty rights without upsetting the economy of Panama.

What did the Hay-Bunau-Varilla Treaty stipulate with reference to American rights in Panama? Was Panama to retain any vestiges of its sovereignty? By the terms of the treaty, the United States guaranteed the independence of Panama, but there were several important qualifications. The United States obtained control over the Canal Zone and, for all practical purposes, virtual sovereignty over as much of the Isthmus as was required for the exercise of complete control over the canal.[19] But the Canal Zone was an integral part of the country, profoundly affecting its economy.[20] Thus its con-

16. W. H. Taft to Charles P. Taft, Nov. 17, 1904, Taft MSS.
17. W. H. Taft to William Nelson Cromwell, Oct. 21, 1904, *ibid.*
18. *Ibid.* and W. H. Taft to Crammond Kennedy, Nov. 11, 1904.
19. Van Alstyne, *American Diplomacy in Action*, 175; Graham H. Stuart, *Latin America and the United States* (5th ed., New York, 1955), 120–121.
20. Van Alstyne, *American Diplomacy in Action*, 175. By asserting certain powers within the Canal Zone, the United States government could injure, if indeed not destroy, the economic independence of the Republic of Panama. This was particularly

trol could direct the affairs of the entire country. The provision of the Hay-Bunau-Varilla Treaty, in effect, made Panama a "protectorate" of the United States, although the degree of independence Panama was to retain would depend upon the interpretation that the United States might place upon the treaty.

William Howard Taft sailed from Pensacola, Florida, on November 22, 1904, and arrived in Colon, Panama, on Sunday morning, November 27, 1904. He immediately boarded a special train for Panama City, and several hours later was welcomed officially by President Manuel Amador Guerrero. Taft undertook an exhaustive inquiry into Panamanian affairs, and his recommendations were presented to President Roosevelt in a confidential report dated December 19, 1904.[21] With Taft's fastidious attention to detail, the report covered every aspect of the Panamanian situation. It ranged from considerations of tariffs, fiscal policies, postal services, military and engineering matters to the larger questions of political and economic policy.

Article XIII of the Hay-Bunau-Varilla Treaty provided for the duty-free importation of all goods and materials by consignment for use by the United States in the construction of the canal. However, since the two key ports of Colon and Panama lay within the Canal Zone, there would be the real possibility of establishing a large duty-free area for all goods which might make their way into Panama proper.[22] Panamanian merchants were alarmed over this threat to their businesses and the government was concerned over a possible serious loss in customs revenue. Taft recommended that the

true for Panama's two cities, Panama and Colon, which were located inside the Canal Zone, though legally they had been declared separate from it. The terminal ports of the canal, Ancon and Cristobal, were urban areas continuous with Panama and Colon, respectively.

21. W. H. Taft to Theodore Roosevelt, Dec. 19, 1904, Taft MSS; William D. McCain, *The United States and the Republic of Panama*, 39. This was not a formal report, but a long letter from the secretary of war to the president written in the form of a report.

22. *Ibid.*,30–31; Van Alstyne, *American Diplomacy in Action*, 175.

possibility of such an enlarged tariff-free area be held as a weapon *in terrorem* over such merchants, who were bent upon a policy of gouging the workers employed in the building of the canal. He realized the importance of tariff revenues for the financial stability of the government of Panama, but firmly held the reins of control in determining precisely what those tariffs should be.[23]

Taft wanted a tariff rate that would provide sufficient revenue for the operation of the government, but one that would not burden the people with high prices. To accomplish these goals, he set the tariff rate at 10 percent *ad valorem*. As he put it: "I should say here that it may turn out that ten per centum ad valorem will not produce sufficient income for the running of the Government, and if so, I think it would be wise to permit a restoration of the fifteen per centum duty." [24] In this instance, Taft issued the orders and the government of Panama complied.

Taft indicated that the financial stability of Panama was essential to the construction of the canal. He was worried about the basic economic soundness of the country and the inevitable corollary, political unrest. He would "issue orders" covering parity problems to eliminate harmful fluctuations in exchange rates.[25] He concluded that the government would have to reduce its consular fees, revise its postage rates, and build and maintain certain roads and highways running into the Canal Zone. He felt that free trade between Panama and the Canal Zone was a wise policy, and saw to it that Panama granted to the United States the right to make quarantine regulations for the cities of Colon and Panama.

There was no doubt from Taft's recommendations to the president and their subsequent implementation, that he, and he alone, was making the decisions. Taft gave cogent expression to the true situation in these unambiguous words:

23. W. H. Taft to Theodore Roosevelt, Dec. 19, 1904, Taft MSS; McCain, *The United States and the Republic of Panama*, 32–33.
24. W. H. Taft to Theodore Roosevelt, Dec. 19, 1904, Taft MSS.
25. *Ibid.*

The truth is that while we have all the attributes of sovereignty necessary in the construction, maintenance and protection of the Canal, the very form in which these attributes are conferred in the Treaty seems to preserve the titular sovereignty over the Canal Zone in the Republic of Panama, and as we have conceded to us complete judicial and police power and control of two ports at the end of the Canal, I can see no reason for creating a resentment on the part of the people of the Isthmus by quarreling over that which is dear to them, but which to us is of no real moment whatever.[26]

With "titular sovereignty" alone remaining to Panama and with real control in the hands of the United States, how much sovereignty rested with Panama? Control of the Isthmus, an integrally vital part of the country, carried with it substantive and not symbolic control over the rest of the country.

Secretary Taft, with an amazing capacity for detail, surveyed the physical aspects of canal construction. He offered opinions about the various individuals involved in the great undertaking, evaluating their technical abilities and innate drive. Although conceding a lack of expertise in engineering problems, he offered affirmative conclusions on the scope of the project: "It seems to me that there are no great engineering problems in the construction of the Canal, that is— problems requiring engineering genius to overcome great difficulties. The problem of the Canal is a problem of the excavation of a mass greater than ever before made in the history of the world." [27]

What emerges from the pages of this report is the figure of a man possessed of enormous vitality. This appears all the more surprising considering the caricature of Taft as an amiable, pleasant, elephantine personality. In reality, he had the sure touch for issues and their resolution; he hated slothfulness and inefficiency; and he had an uncanny knack for catching defects in character and organizational snags. If any

26. *Ibid.*
27. *Ibid.*

man were capable of galvanizing the flagging project into precipitous action, it was he.

Taft devoted especial attention to the political parties of Panama. He analyzed the political situation there within his own particular frame of reference. But he was not interested in an academic discussion of the matter—his primary and exclusive concern was for such political arrangements as would consolidate the position of the United States. This purpose was best served when the Conservative party, composed of the old families which were mostly whites, held the reins of power. He noted in contrast that the Liberals looked for their support largely to the Negroes who were citizens of the republic but who were "much less trustworthy" than the Conservatives. The only danger that portended trouble would be the accession to power of the Liberal party because it would mean "the introduction of a large negro influence into the Government." [28]

Taft felt that the Negroes were less intelligent than "the colored people of the United States," and he was certain that there would be a strong tendency under a liberal government toward the establishment of a government such as in Santo Domingo or Haiti.[29] The Liberals were—although he offered no evidence to buttress his comment—at the bottom of the attempt of General Huertas to overthrow President Amador. The Liberals, according to Taft, had filled the general with the foolish notion that he was a great man, possessed of great powers, and charged with the responsibility of toppling the government which he in the revolution had set up. Then followed a terse statement that spelled finality itself: "The threat of the use of the United States forces ended the power of Huertas. His resignation was demanded and the army disbanded a few days before I reached Panama. This was done at the instance of Minister Barrett and Governor Davis by President Amador, and was made possible by the under-

28. *Ibid.*
29. *Ibid.*

standing that United States forces would be used if any attempt was made by Huertas to subvert the laws of the Republic." [30]

It would be misleading to convey the impression that all problems connected with building the canal were now solved. The canal was for some time a very real source of aggravation to President Roosevelt despite Secretary Taft's able administrative attention and competence. Gradually these difficulties were overcome, but not before the nation learned a great deal about building an American project in foreign territory.

By the spring of 1908 the political pot in Panama was boiling once again, so President Roosevelt sent his chief troubleshooter to Panama to pacify the political turmoil. Taft arrived in Panama on May 6, 1908, and examined existing relations between Panama and the Canal Zone. He feared that the United States faced the probability of an insurrection in Panama growing out of "the heat of an election controversy and the indignation felt at the threatened frauds upon the franchise." The conflict, a fierce struggle for power, was entirely within the Conservative party. In the absence of President Amador, the vice-president, Jose Domingo de Obaldia, had held the presidency for six months and administered the office in a manner "to command him to the people of the Republic." [31] Moreover, Dr. Amador had conveyed the impression to Obaldia that he would be the next president with Amador's assistance. In reality, however, Dr. Amador had pledged his support to the secretary of state, Ricardo Arias. One of the strongest, ablest, and richest men in the republic, Arias was very determined and resourceful. The Liberal party did not have a presidential candidate, so announced its support for Obaldia because of his splendid rule.

In many voting places where hundreds of voters wished to register and where the majority were for Obaldia, election boards had not assembled and lists had not been published.

30. *Ibid.*
31. *Ibid.*, May 10, 1908.

In the elections two years before, Washington received complaints of ballot fraud and there were serious disturbances in Panama. The American authorities then had not felt compelled to intervene to prevent bloodshed and to insure honest returns.[32] Interestingly enough, the same police officers who had committed fraud upon the ballot at that election were in charge of the police for the 1908 elections. The number of police had been increased, and there was strong evidence that Arias, through the secretary of the interior, proposed to carry the election against the will of the people. There was no question in Taft's mind that—if the elections were honest—Obaldia would be elected by the vote of the Liberal party and a substantial part of the Conservative party.[33]

Petitions setting forth proof of the preparations for fraud had been presented to Taft personally by a committee of the Liberal party and a committee of that wing of the Conservative party supporting Obaldia. Taft was convinced that if Arias were to carry the election, as he would "unless prevented by our interference, there would be an outbreak" which would create turmoil in the country.[34] Although he spent considerable time in investigating the background of Panamanian politics, the secretary was not concerned only with the problems that faced Panama. His primary objective was the avoidance of any situation that would militate against completion of the Panama Canal. As he wrote to the President: "it is certainly contrary to the interests of the United States to have a succession of elections in which fraud is

32. *Ibid.* Secretary of State Elihu Root explained the government's position in instructions to Minister Charles E. Magoon, dated December 4, 1905: "The Liberal party should be informed that the Government of the United States, while guaranteeing the independence of the Republic of Panama, does not propose to interfere with that independence. . . . As between the two parties, the United States stands in an attitude of perfect impartiality and will do nothing to help either the party in power or the party of opposition." *Papers Relating to the Foreign Relations of the United States, with the Annual Message of the President,* U.S. 59th Cong., 1st Sess., H. Doc. I (1905), p. 720.
33. W. H. Taft to Theodore Roosevelt, May 10, 1908, Taft MSS.
34. *Ibid.*

present, and which give rise each time to ground for insurrection by the defeated party. The thing of all others which must be avoided, if we are to construct the canal, is disturbance of any kind in Panama and Colon, and nothing is more certain to engender this than the bitterness of a party defeated by fraud at the polls." [35]

Nor was Secretary Taft sanguine about any miraculous democratization of the Republic of Panama. He was quite certain that there had been "sufficient demonstration" of the fact that at every election in Panama the United States must expect "the use of government aid to secure the fraudulent election of a government candidate." [36] He foresaw the threat of revolution as a continuing feature of Panamanian politics unless "we take some decided steps through a treaty to assume ourselves control over the elections, in case we deem it necessary to secure a fair expression of popular will." [37] One can conjecture how Taft would have reacted to a "fair expression of popular will," if that expression had manifested itself in the election of other than a Conservative government.

Taft was well aware that his views would seem undemocratic to many in the United States. But he was convinced that democracy is a form of government that requires education and precedent and, above all, an educated citizenry, literate and capable of understanding issues. Such was not the case in Panama and would not be for a long time. Taft was not prepared to see a vital interest of the United States sacrificed upon the altar of a meaningless abstraction. Accordingly, he recommended to the president that in the new treaty with Panama, the United States government "be given direct control over the elections, so as to permit us, should we desire, to intervene and determine who is fairly elected." He conceded that this would detract from the independence of the republic, but as Panama had "not shown itself competent in this

35. *Ibid.*, May 16, 1908.
36. *Ibid.*
37. *Ibid.*, May 10, 1908, and May 16, 1908.

regard," the United States was entirely justified in insisting upon greater control "to protect" its own interests which were "so closely involved with the peaceful continuance of the Panamanian Government." [38]

President Roosevelt, once apprised of the situation, responded affirmatively, and Secretary Taft presented the president's views plus his own to President Amador in a strongly worded letter. On May 15, 1908, Foreign Secretary Ricardo Arias appealed to the United States for assistance in holding fair elections. Secretary Arias pointed to the immense interests of the United States in the Canal Zone that should not be upset by election disorders, and invited the United States government to appoint members to a joint commission for investigating any complaints that might arise. For its part, the government of Panama promised to correct any abuses that might be uncovered.[39] The United States government accepted this invitation, and as events unfolded there was no need for actual intervention. Yet the harsh truth was that President Amador had been pushed into extending the invitation, a deft move to avoid the outward appearance of an overt intervention by the United States. The faction of the Conservative party headed by President Amador demonstrated its resentment by staying away from the polls, and Jose Domingo de Obaldia was elected to the presidency on October 1, 1908. Ex-President Amador and his supporters failed to attend the inauguration.[40] Taft's immediate objective, uninterrupted progress in the construction of the Panama Canal, had been fulfilled. But many thoughtful Ameri-

38. Theodore Roosevelt to W. H. Taft, May 11, 1908, and W. H. Taft to M. Amador Guerrero, May 12, 1908, Roosevelt MSS; McCain, *The United States and the Republic of Panama*, 71–72.

39. W. H. Taft to M. Amador Guerrero, May 12, 1908; W. H. Taft to Theodore Roosevelt, May 18, 1908, Roosevelt MSS; W. H. Taft to George W. Goethals, June 11, 1908, Taft MSS; McCain, *The United States and the Republic of Panama*, 72.

40. For a detailed account of the disputed election and inauguration of Jose Domingo de Obaldia see *Papers Relating to the Foreign Relations of the United States with the Annual Message of the President Transmitted to Congress December 8, 1908*, pp. 665–670.

cans entertained grave misgivings about a policy that they feared would provoke serious resentment against the United States.

Secretary Taft's efforts found fruition in the completion of a great historic project—the official opening of the Panama Canal on Saturday, August 15, 1914.[41] The first vessel which saw the joining of the waters of the Caribbean and the Pacific made the journey in nine hours and forty minutes. Two thousand persons cheered the arrival of the steamship *Ancon* which carried a distinguished passenger list, including the president of Panama and his cabinet. The next day six vessels which had been waiting at the terminals passed through the canal, three in each direction, and the linkage of the Atlantic and Pacific Oceans by way of the Panama Canal was consummated.

The completion of the Panama Canal and the new era in world commerce which it presaged was a momentous historical event. And William Howard Taft played a major role in the great undertaking. He had been concerned primarily and almost exclusively with getting the job done, with "making the dirt fly," and he was willing and determined to sacrifice almost every other consideration to the attainment of that supreme objective. He was like a military commander conscious only of the realization of his specific assignment. And again, as it is not usually the responsibility of a military commander to weigh the social and political consequences of his mission, Taft did not feel constrained in his position to evaluate the broad political and social repercussions which his determined action would produce. The job was done—enormous obstacles overcome; engineering miracles achieved; but there was no feeling of doubt or concern on Taft's part over the possible legacy of suspicion and resentment which American conduct would leave to future generations. This was Taft's strength—enabling him to concentrate all his energies on completion of the task at hand—and it was his

41. Brainerd Dyer, "Today in History," Los Angeles *Times*, Aug. 15, 1956, Pt. 3, p. 5.

weakness, too, for deep philosophical considerations were not the substance of which a practical mind such as his was made.

The progress in Panama would have done your heart good. . . . When I look back and consider the strenuous times through which we had to go in respect to the organization of that great work, when I see how helpless we would have been, had we not acquired the rights we have under that Bunau-Varilla Treaty which was negotiated by you over night, and in a hurry and in which you never builded better, it is hard to escape the belief that Providence looks after us.[42]

He went on to say that the difficulties which the French had experienced because of their "lack of complete control," and which the United States had avoided, grew on him as he studied the whole situation. Taft was convinced that the "promptness" with which Roosevelt had "seized the opportunity" and carried his purpose through against great criticism and stubborn opposition would "in history be one of the chief grounds for the gratitude of your countrymen." With reference to his own role, Taft noted only that under President Roosevelt he had taken "an interested part." [43]

42. W. H. Taft to Theodore Roosevelt, Nov. 30, 1910, Taft MSS.
43. *Ibid.* For a different assessment of the roles of Theodore Roosevelt and William Howard Taft, one that is sharply critical, see Sheldon B. Liss, *The Canal: Aspects of United States Panamanian Relations* (Notre Dame, Ind., 1967), 17–24.

CHAPTER V

Nightmare in Cuba

Cuba, "THE PEARL OF THE ANTILLES," has perhaps loomed larger on the political and economic horizon of the United States than any other compact area of territory which has not come permanently under the American flag. Ever since the presidency of Thomas Jefferson, the United States has retained an abiding interest in the fate of Cuba.[1] This was true because of obvious geographical factors of propinquity and strategic location in the Caribbean, considerations of trade and commerce, and emotional reasons interwoven with the interminable political turmoils so endemic to the island.[2] During the greater part of the nineteenth century, a kind of uneasy balance of power produced a situation in which the United States, Great Britain, and France acquiesced in the retention of Cuba by Spain. And while the United States looked forward to the day when the strategic isle would fall into its possession, domestic slave politics were followed after the Civil War by the problems of reconstruction, westward expansion, and industrialization, as well as naval limita-

1. Russell H. Fitzgibbon, *Cuba and the United States, 1900–1935* (Menasha, Wis., 1935), 1; Van Alstyne, *American Diplomacy in Action*, 98.
2. Fitzgibbon, *Cuba and the United States, 1900–1935*, 2–4; Stuart, *Latin America and the United States*, 187; Van Alstyne, *American Diplomacy in Action*, 98–99.

tions throughout most of the nineteenth century, combined to postpone this seemingly inevitable development.[3]

Relations between Spain and the people of Cuba were marked by endless clashes. The volatility of the Cuban temperament and the political clumsiness of the Spanish government combined to produce tensions which on three occasions after 1848 resulted in revolts. The third of these revolts began in 1895, and due to the indignation and unrest which it produced in the United States, this struggle between the Cuban insurgents and the Spaniards was merged eventually into a war between Spain and the United States.[4] This war, which was brief and decisive, suddenly placed the United States in military occupation of Cuba. In acquiring control of Cuba after the Spanish-American War, the United States inherited not only a strategic position in the Caribbean, but also a prostrate island with manifold social, economic, and political problems.[5]

Successive Republican administrations faced the task of assuming effective control over Cuba while, at the same time, seeking to avoid the political perils involved in the issue of imperialism. For the secretary of war, Elihu Root, there was yet another consideration—the danger of European interference. In particular, the secretary did not trust Germany.[6] Lacking any tradition, experience, or education in self-government, Cuba offered a fertile field for anarchy. Thus, the United States was faced with a dilemma—either Cuba had to be annexed outright with all the hazards such action would bring politically, or Cuba had to be cut adrift and run

3. Van Alstyne, American Diplomacy in Action, 99; Stuart, Latin America and the United States, 187–188; Fitzgibbon, Cuba and the United States, 1900–1935, 7, 8–12.

4. J. Fred Rippy, The Caribbean Danger Zone (New York, 1940), 151; Stuart, Latin America and the United States, 203, 205; Van Alstyne, American Diplomacy in Action, 621.

5. Alfred L. P. Dennis, Adventures in American Diplomacy, 1896–1906 (New York, 1928), 259; Fitzgibbon, Cuba and the United States, 28–29.

6. Dennis, Adventures in American Diplomacy, 1896–1906, 259; Van Alstyne, American Diplomacy in Action, 163–164. Elihu Root was influential in shaping United States policy toward Cuba.

the twin perils of domestic anarchy and alleged foreign intervention.

An ingenious solution was found in making Cuba a quasi-protectorate of the United States by a provision attached to the army appropriation bill of March 2, 1901.[7] Faced with the limited alternatives of accepting this amendment which was designed to regulate future relations between Cuba and the United States, or enduring a continued military occupation of their country by United States military force, the Cuban Constitutional Convention accepted the provisions of the amendment as an annex to Article Three of the Constitution for the Republic of Cuba, adopted on February 21, 1901. Cuba again acknowledged this modification of her international position when the same amendment was incorporated word for word in the treaty of permanent relations signed on May 22, 1903, by which the independence of the island was acknowledged formally.[8]

Formulated in the Congress of the United States and based on the suggestions of many individuals, the agreement became known subsequently as the Platt Amendment, because Senator O. H. Platt was the individual to attach it as a rider to the army appropriation bill of March 2, 1901. Its salient features forbade Cuba to alienate territory to any foreign power or to become entangled politically or financially with a foreign power, ratified acts of American officials during the occupation, granted the United States the right to purchase or lease two sites for naval stations, and authorized American intervention when necessary to preserve Cuban independence, to maintain a stable government, or to guarantee fulfillment of international obligations.[9]

The last act of the Cuban Constitutional Convention was

7. Chester Lloyd Jones, *Caribbean Interests of the United States* (New York, 1916), 81.

8. *Ibid.*, 82; Dana G. Munro, *The United States and the Caribbean Area* (Boston, 1934), 9–15; Latané, *America as a World Power, 1897–1907*, 177.

9. Brainerd Dyer, "Today in History," Los Angeles *Times*, June 6, 1956, Pt. 3, p. 5; William M. Malloy, *Treaties, Conventions, International Acts, Protocols and Agreements*, I, 362–364.

the adoption of an electoral law that provided for a general election on December 31, 1901, for all officers elected by popular vote, and for a second election on February 24, 1902, at which the president, vice-president, and senators should be chosen according to the constitution by the electoral colleges selected at the first election. The electors met on February 24, 1902, and selected Tomas Estrada Palma as president and Luis Esteves Romero as vice-president.[10] In March, 1902, Secretary of War Elihu Root, Major General Leonard Wood, military governor of Cuba, and President Palma conferred in Washington, D.C., and on March 24, 1902, Secretary Root sent instructions to General Wood for the transfer of the government to Cuban officials. On May 20, 1902, Tomas Estrada Palma was inaugurated as the first president of the new Republic of Cuba, the government was formally handed over to the newly constituted authorities, and Major General Leonard Wood and the American forces embarked for the United States.[11]

On the surface all was serene and democratic, but deeper down was the question of the capacity of the Cubans to operate the machinery which they had so well established.[12] It was soon apparent that the Cubans had not learned the most elementary lesson of democracy—submission to the will of the majority. Political relationships between the United States and Cuba remained uneventful until the year 1906. The election of 1905, however, portended trouble.[13]

10. Albert Edward McKinley, *Island Possessions of the United States* (Philadelphia, 1907), 86; Fitzgibbon, *Cuba and the United States*, 86.

11. Howard C. Hill, *Roosevelt and the Caribbean* (Chicago, 1927), 77.

12. By the constitution adopted on February 21, 1901, the legislative power was vested in a congress of two houses—a senate and a house of representatives; the executive power was vested in a president; and the judicial power was vested in a supreme court of justice and in such other courts as might be established by law. This constitution contained a bill of rights, which included thirty-one articles, drawn from many different sources. Latané, *America as a World Power, 1897–1907*, 177; McKinley, *Island Possessions of the United States*, 81. Thus Cuba was fitted with the trappings of democracy, but in the absence of any vestige of democratic experience, the gap between theory and actual practice was vast.

13. Latané and Wainhouse, *A History of American Foreign Policy*, 515; Charles E. Chapman, *A History of the Cuban Republic: A Study in Hispanic American Politics* (New York, 1927), 187–189.

That election produced a bitter struggle between the Moderates and the Liberals, and President Palma who had been reelected by the Moderates was accused by the Liberals of resorting to bribery, intimidation, and violence in order to keep in power. On August 16, 1906, an armed uprising against the government led by General Faustion ("Pino") Guerra started in the province of Pinar del Rio. On August 27, 1906, President Palma issued a proclamation granting amnesty to all insurgents who would lay down their arms. When this proclamation failed, President Palma secretly requested Frank Steinhart, the American consul general at Havana, to ask President Theodore Roosevelt to dispatch two vessels immediately.[14] The reason given was that the government forces were unable to quell the rebellion. On September 8, 1906, Steinhart telegraphed Palma's request to the Department of State at Washington, D.C.

On September 10, 1906, Assistant Secretary of State Robert Bacon cabled Frank Steinhart that two ships had been ordered to Cuba, but that President Roosevelt regarded it as "a very serious thing to undertake forcible intervention, and before going into it we should have to be absolutely certain of the equities of the case and of the needs of the situation." [15] President Roosevelt felt that reliance upon American intervention under the Platt Amendment would make the Cubans too dependent and would militate against the development of a real democratic tradition in Cuba. He felt that only extreme circumstances bordering upon anarchy presented sufficient justification for American intervention.[16] An astute politician with his finger constantly on the public pulse, Roosevelt was anxious to avoid the appearance of American overlordship in the Caribbean. Moreover, the election of 1906 was drawing near in the United States, the people there had

14. Stuart, *Latin America and the United States*, 216; Hill, *Roosevelt and the Caribbean*, 93.

15. David A. Lockmiller, *Magoon in Cuba: A History of the Second Intervention, 1906–1909* (Chapel Hill, N.C., 1938), 40.

16. Theodore Roosevelt to George Otto Trevelyan, Sept. 9, 1906, Roosevelt, *Letters*, V, 401; Lockmiller, *Magoon in Cuba*, 40.

shown recently a stubborn tendency to resist overseas complications, and President Roosevelt did not want his political opponents to have any unnecessary ammunition.[17] Such considerations provide the logical explanation for his reluctance to take positive action. In a letter to Don Gonzalo de Quesada, Cuban minister to the United States, he said: "Our intervention in Cuban affairs will only come if Cuba herself shows that she has fallen into the insurrectionary habit, that she lacks the self-restraint necessary to secure peaceful, self-government, and that her contending factions have plunged the country into war." [18]

The situation in Cuba grew more tense and uncertain. The revolution of 1906 was not the simple type of revolt so common in the past.[19] This time economic conditions were especially wretched and many men were idle—fertile breeding grounds for a major uprising. The rapid growth of the revolution surprised everyone; within a comparatively short time an estimated 15,000 to 20,000 rebels were engaged in active hostilities. Although the vast majority of them were poorly disciplined and inadequately armed, their numbers increased. In contrast, the Cuban government had only a few thousand incompetent and untrustworthy rural guards and militia.

A consideration highly relevant to an understanding of the Cuban problem was the vulnerability to destruction of from $75,000,000 to $100,000,000 of foreign investments in sugar—both in mills and growing cane. A large percentage of these investments were held by Americans able to bring extraordinary pressure upon Washington.[20] Moreover, except in

17. Callcott, *The Caribbean Policy of the United States, 1890–1920*, 232.
18. Theodore Roosevelt to Don Gonzalo de Quesada, Sept. 14, 1906, Roosevelt, *Letters*, V, 412.
19. Fitzgibbon, *Cuba and the United States, 1900–1935*, 115.
20. *Ibid.*, 116. The consequences resulting from any such widespread destruction would have been momentous, for sugar was then and still is "the life-blood of the Cuban economy." Myron S. Heidingsfield, "Cuba: A Sugar Economy," *Current History*, XXII (March, 1952), 151; Foster Rhea Dulles, *The Imperial Years* (New York, 1956), 263. In 1906 the total investment of American capital in Cuba was estimated at $150,000,000. Harry F. Guggenheim, *The United States and Cuba: A Study in International Relations* (New York, 1934), 113.

Matanzas, the government was "practically without sympathy or moral support." [21]

President Roosevelt had held conferences at Oyster Bay with Secretary of the Navy Bonaparte, Secretary of War Taft, and Assistant Secretary of State Bacon, and in his letter to Quesada of September 14, 1906, he announced that he was sending Taft and Bacon to Havana to do everything possible to bring about the pacification of the island. Secretary of State Elihu Root was in South America on a goodwill tour at the time, and the advanced stage of the crisis would not wait until his return. Accordingly, Taft and Bacon left Oyster Bay for Cuba on the evening of September 14, 1906.[22] They stopped first, however, in Washington, D.C., where Secretary Taft conferred with Generals J. Franklin Bell and Fred C. Ainsworth concerning "what could be done by the Army in case it was thought necessary to enforce peace in the Island." Taft found that 6,000 men were available for immediate duty, and learned that a force of 18,000 men could be assembled within a month. In conveying the information to the president, he noted: "If we have to go at all, I am in favor of going with as much force as we can command, so as to end the business at once." [23]

It was characteristic of Taft with his judicial background to be concerned about whether the president had the right to intervene without asking permission of Congress.[24] Although he felt that there was ample precedent in the treaty between the United States and Cuba, he suggested a precise question for the attorney general to decide:

Upon receipt of formal notice by the President of the Cuban Government that that Government is unable to furnish adequate security to American lives and property in the Island of Cuba, is the President Authorized, under the laws and treaties

21. Fitzgibbon, *Cuba and the United States, 1900–1935*, 116.
22. *Ibid.*, 117. Theodore Roosevelt to Don Gonzalo de Quesada, Sept. 14, 1906, Roosevelt, *Letters*, V, 412; Jessup, *Root*, I, 474; Lockmiller, *Magoon in Cuba*, 46.
23. W. H. Taft to Theodore Roosevelt, Sept. 15, 1906, Roosevelt MSS.
24. *Ibid.* and Sept. 16, 1906.

of the United States, including the treaty with Cuba, to direct the Army or any part of it to be transported to Cuba, there under his command to maintain law and order for the purpose of preserving American property and lives, without further authority from Congress? Is this making war which would require specific constitutional Congressional authority? [25]

President Roosevelt, however, did not view the question from the same frame of reference. He looked to what he deemed the larger questions of foreign policy, and especially the enlarged role of the executive in meeting those questions. The president wrote Taft that he would not submit the matter to the attorney general for a ruling, and would intervene if he felt compelled to.[26] As for asking permission of Congress, he would not "dream" of seeking this. The treaty with Cuba was "the law of the land," and, as the chief executive, constitutionally empowered to enforce treaties, he would so construe his duties. He earnestly hoped that there would be no necessity for intervention, feeling that Taft would be able to settle the problems of Cuba.

Moreover, Roosevelt believed that the Cubans would be powerfully impressed "by the notice of what will come to them if they do not quit quarrelling." If intervention should prove unavoidable, however, Roosevelt intended to establish "a precedent for good by refusing to wait for a long wrangle in Congress." The president then lectured his secretary of war on the issue. "You know as well as I do," he wrote, "that it is for the enormous interest of this Government to strengthen and give independence to the Executive in dealing with foreign powers," for a legislative body, because of its "very good qualities in domestic matters," was not well fitted "for shaping foreign policy on occasions when instant action is demanded." Therefore, the important consideration, for a president who was "willing to accept responsibility," was "to establish precedents which successors may follow

25. *Ibid.*, Sept. 15, 1906.
26. Theodore Roosevelt to W. H. Taft, Sept. 17, 1906, *ibid.*

even if they are unwilling to take the initiative themselves." [27]

Taft was reluctant to go to Cuba, for he was acutely aware of his own limited knowledge of the Cuban tangle. The day after the conference at Oyster Bay he wrote to Elihu Root to say that he wished Root could go in his place. He felt that Root knew the Cuban situation in detail and that in contrast he was "so lacking in knowledge of it," that it was "quite embarrassing" for him to go.[28] Apparently Taft had followed developments in Cuba rather casually, but this had proven no hindrance to the formation of some rather positive convictions. By May, 1901, he was convinced that "the trouble in Cuba" was just beginning, and felt that "the lack of wisdom in the Teller Resolution" was becoming increasingly apparent.[29] A month later, noting the rapid decline in General Leonard Wood's popularity among the Cubans, he remarked condescendingly that this was "so common a change among a Latin people" as to be "hardly worthy of comment." [30]

Despite his reluctance to accept the assignment, Taft was convinced that action was necessary at once, for the Cuban government had proven to be nothing but "a house of cards." Taft frankly saw the destruction of the property of foreigners as the key issue, because that factor appeared to make "intervention necessary on international grounds much as we

27. *Ibid.*

28. W. H. Taft to Elihu Root, Sept. 15, 1906, *ibid.*

29. W. H. Taft to Charles P. Taft, May 17, 1901, *ibid.* Prepared by Senator Henry M. Teller of Colorado, the Teller Amendment disavowed any intention on the part of the United States to annex or control Cuba. Instead, it affirmed the determination of the United States to free the island following the establishment of peace. It was incorporated into a joint resolution passed by Congress on April 19, 1898, and signed by the president on the following day. It was in effect a declaration of war upon Spain. Julius W. Pratt, *A History of United States Foreign Policy* (New York, 1955), 284.

30. W. H. Taft to Theodore Roosevelt, June 23, 1901, Taft MSS. Three years later, in approving the idea of the governor of Puerto Rico that an independent person should sit on an election board, Taft offered a generalization about election practices in Latin American countries, the truth of which, at least for Cuba, was soon to be demonstrated: "The Spanish American, or one educated in the Spanish political school, has no idea of impartiality, and if he is an election officer, regards it as a duty to cheat for his party." W. H. Taft to Beekman Winthrop, Sept. 16, 1904, Taft MSS.

would wish to avoid it." Although he realized that the government of Cuba had almost collapsed, Taft's plans for coping with the situation were rather indefinite.[31] Such information as had been received from Cuba was too vague and untrustworthy to make it possible for him to devise any definite plan of action.[32]

Taft and Bacon arrived in Havana, Cuba, on the U.S.S. *Des Moines* on the morning of September 19, 1906, during a truce which had been agreed to by the contestants at the request of President Roosevelt. Although the two commissioners were ostensibly coequal in authority, Taft was the actual head of the mission, for Bacon was "the live incarnation of reserve and discretion." [33] In a letter to his wife, written the day after his arrival in Havana, Taft noted that the Cuban government controlled only the towns along the coast, having been forced to relinquish the interior to the insurgents. In his judgment the government seemed to have "abused its power outrageously" in the 1905 election, and the hostility of the Cuban people was "a protest against that." He was not sure whether the matter could be resolved satisfactorily, since the government had so clearly forfeited the support of the people. The entire matter demonstrated "the utter unfitness of these people for self-government." But the transcendent consideration was that unless the United States restored peace in the embattled island, "some $200,000,000 of American property" would "go up in smoke" in less than two weeks.[34]

In a letter to President Roosevelt two days later, Taft wrote in a contradictory vein. On the one hand, he was "doubtful of the wisdom of keeping Palma in the Presidency," and on the other, he felt that Palma's continuance in office "would be valuable" because of his honesty. Besides, and this was for Taft a most important consideration, "the property holders

31. W. H. Taft to Elihu Root, Sept. 15, 1906, Taft MSS; W. H. Taft to Helen H. Taft, Sept. 14, 1906, *ibid.*

32. W. H. Taft to Theodore Roosevelt, Sept. 16, 1906, Roosevelt MSS.

33. Callcott, *The Caribbean Policy of the United States, 1890–1920*, 234; Fitzgibbon, *Cuba and the United States, 1900–1935*, 118.

34. W. H. Taft to Helen H. Taft, Sept. 20, 1906, Taft MSS.

and conservatives would be gratified by his continuance." He pointed out that the outrages had not been committed by Estrada Palma, who was, in Taft's opinion, not aware of the abuses. The secretary of war believed it would be possible to construct a mixed cabinet in order to secure a compromise, but was doubtful about the permanency of such an arrangement. The great advantage of retaining Estrada Palma in office was that it continued "the identity of the government which was established four years ago by the United States." On the other hand, the setting aside of the 1905 election results by the resignation of those who were elected to the House and Senate by that fraudulent election would impress all of the people with the importance of greater care in the matter of fair elections and the danger in the future of fraud and terror and abuse of official power in elections. There was, in his opinion, nobody in the Liberal party "fit to be President." [35]

What was needed here, as elsewhere in the tropics in dealing "with people like this," was patience. The trouble lay "in the irresponsible character of the men in arms, who although they represent the great majority of the people in their cause," were themselves "lawless persons of no particular standing in times of peace," and whose motive for continuing in arms was very strong because of the importance that they enjoyed under such conditions. Peace to "such people" meant that which they most hated—"work." [36] Taft was well aware that President Roosevelt was most anxious to avoid outright intervention. Nevertheless, by September 25, 1906, he felt that it would be necessary for the president to assume control over Cuba and establish a provisional government there. Such action was justified under the Platt Amendment, as the only constituted government in the island had abdicated, and was needed urgently in order to preserve law and order, to suppress the insurrection, and to continue the ordinary administration of the government of Cuba until "a more

35. W. H. Taft to Theodore Roosevelt, Sept. 22, 1906, Roosevelt MSS.
36. Ibid.

permanent policy" might be determined.[37] By September 28, 1906, Taft was convinced absolutely that intervention was the only way out.[38]

On the afternoon of Saturday, September 29, 1906, Taft, with Roosevelt's approval, issued a proclamation of intervention by the United States under the Platt Amendment and declared the establishment of a provisional government with himself as temporary governor. His "chief anxiety" was to secure an agreement with the rebels for their surrender "in formal form." [39] Taft was aware of the public political repercussions that might follow the actions taken in Cuba. As he observed in writing to his wife: "I suppose that there will be a great deal of criticism of us both here and in the United States and I must be prepared to meet it, but I shall not mind the hammering if I can bring about peace." [40]

On September 30, 1906, the secretary of war noted that the peace proceedings were moving forward. However, he "was dealing with rascals and fools and cranks" and thus found it very difficult "to steer between the rocks." Although uncertain how the American people would react to the provisional government, he noted that "all parties" in Cuba seemed to be "delighted" with it. He judged "from President Roosevelt's reluctance to have it occur," that there must have been great objection to the intervention "from a political standpoint" in the United States. As for the future—"we are likely to be bitterly attacked in Congress for our course." [41] Always harried by legal doubts, Taft believed that the action taken in Cuba would be much discussed as a new development in law growing out of the Platt Amendment, but he was sure that it would stand the test of legal scrutiny. "The President," he

37. Theodore Roosevelt to W. H. Taft, Sept. 17, 1906, Taft MSS; W. H. Taft to Theodore Roosevelt, Sept. 25, 1906, *ibid.*

38. *Ibid.*, Sept. 28, 1906.

39. Fitzgibbon, *Cuba and the United States, 1900–1935*, 121. Taft previously had submitted this proclamation by cablegram to President Roosevelt. Chapman, *A History of the Cuban Republic*, 210–211; W. H. Taft to Helen H. Taft, Sept. 29, 1906, Taft MSS.

40. *Ibid.*

41. *Ibid.*, Sept. 30, 1906.

wrote, "has been very anxious to avoid intervention and so have I, and some of his telegrams have been a little extreme, but on the whole he has been supporting me well." [42] Showing a growing awareness of American public opinion and in particular the power of the press, he confided to his wife: "I don't know what they are saying in the states but I feel as if I was going to have a great fall from the heights to which the compliments of the press raised me. But I cannot allow my thoughts on this subject to take possession of me for they are most depressing." [43]

In referring to the president's anxiety to avoid overt intervention unless mandatory, Taft was cognizant of the president's explicit wishes contained in a telegram, dated September 26, 1906. After praising the secretary's handling of the Cuban situation, President Roosevelt came to the point. "Avoid the use of the word 'intervention' in any proclamation or paper," he instructed, "and if possible, place the landing of our sailors and marines on the ground of conservation of American interests." [44] In addition, Taft was to emphasize the temporary character of the landing, and especially to represent any intervention of United States armed forces as being that very brief and necessary prelude to the establishment of a permanent Cuban government. A painstaking politician, the president was determined that the situation be handled in a manner that would minimize adverse criticism in the United States. The president's uncanny political shrewdness is evident in the following carefully thought out instruction: "I want to make it evident, beyond the possibility of a doubt, that we take no steps that we are not absolutely forced to by the situation, and, therefore, I should like to avoid taking possession in appearance of the entire island, if that is possible." [45] In other words, Taft was to infer from the foregoing that the "appearance" of intervention was to be

42. *Ibid.*, Sept. 28, 1906.
43. *Ibid.*
44. Theodore Roosevelt to W. H. Taft, Sept. 26, 1906, *ibid.*
45. *Ibid.*

avoided. The secretary of war was to protect American lives and property to the best of his ability without offending the sensitivity concerning intervention so rife in the United States.

The president's instructions did not fit easily into the rapidly unfolding Cuban picture. On September 25, 1906, Roosevelt had telegraphed Estrada Palma, the president of Cuba, urging him to remain in office for the stability of the island. Palma had threatened to resign rather than accept a proposed settlement in which there was to be a coalition government.[46] Under the projected settlement, which Taft and Bacon approved, fighting in Cuba would come to an end with the establishment of a broadly based government. This agreement was unacceptable to Palma, who formally rejected it on September 25, 1906. The following day the Liberals accepted the proposed solution. Taft thus was impaled on the horns of a dilemma. Could he put pressure on the Moderates, who were demonstrating an intransigent attitude? This would leave support of the Liberals as his only alternative, and he was loath to align himself with those whose political philosophy was unacceptable to him. Moreover, the Liberals had resorted to armed force, and this act he profoundly deplored.[47]

In the ensuing impasse, Taft correctly saw the impossibility of a quasi-intervention which would serve the appearances of nonintervention. His propensity for constitutional procedures made him oppose any plan which would set up a new president by a rump Congress. "Clean intervention" was to his mind more honest and workable, despite the feelings of President Roosevelt, who spurned such an approach in favor of a solution which would bring peace to the island without incurring too much displeasure in the United States.[48]

By September 28, 1906, Taft was certain that intervention

46. Callcott, *The Caribbean Policy of the United States, 1890–1920*, 234–235; Fitzgibbon, *Cuba and the United States, 1900–1935*, 119.
47. W. H. Taft to Theodore Roosevelt, Sept. 22 and Sept. 25, 1906, Roosevelt MSS; Fitzgibbon, *Cuba and the United States, 1900–1935*, 120.
48. *Ibid.*

by the United States government was inevitable. The truth, as he saw it, was that both sides favored intervention, although for vastly different reasons. The Liberals had been impressed and reassured by Taft's statesmanlike proposal that they surrender their arms and quit the fighting in exchange for the promise of a democratic solution to Cuba's difficulties and the guarantee by the United States of a full and complete amnesty for all political offenses committed during the course of the late rebellion.[49] Under such circumstances, the Liberals were not averse to a settlement that provided for holding a new election which they felt sure of winning. The Moderates also wanted intervention. If an election had to be held, they felt it was best to conduct it under the auspices of the United States government. Besides, they were in favor of annexation to the United States. However, as Taft pointed out, neither party was willing to take the responsibility "of saying so out loud."[50]

Events were now rapidly moving toward a climax. On the afternoon of September 28, 1906, Palma and his entire cabinet resigned and the vice-president likewise submitted his resignation. The Congress of Cuba was virtually paralyzed by the refusal of Moderate members to attend further sessions, thus breaking the quorum. That same evening Estrada Palma requested Taft and Bacon to relieve him of the custody of the treasury, which contained $13,625,539.65. In addition, Palma called for the immediate disbanding of the militia, the upkeep of which was now too expensive. The two peace commissioners took charge for the United States, and a small guard of United States marines was ordered to protect the treasury.[51]

On the following day Taft issued the proclamation of intervention, established a provisional government, and pro-

49. W. H. Taft to Theodore Roosevelt, Sept. 28, 1906, Taft MSS; Chapman, *A History of the Cuban Republic*, 208; Fitzgibbon, *Cuba and the United States, 1900–1935*, 119; Stuart, *Latin America and the United States*, 216.
50. W. H. Taft to Theodore Roosevelt, Sept. 28, Taft MSS.
51. Fitzgibbon, *Cuba and the United States*, 1900–1935, 121; Lockmiller, *Magoon in Cuba*, 57.

claimed himself provisional governor of Cuba. Scrupulous in its respect for Cuban sensitivity and carefully worded so as to minimize adverse political criticism, the proclamation explained that the provisional government was to be "a Cuban government, conforming, as far as may be, to the constitution of Cuba." [52] The national, provincial, and municipal governments and the courts were all to be administered as under the Cuban Republic. After this proclamation was issued, the Liberal leaders signed an agreement prepared by Taft by which they promised to disarm and disband their troops.[53]

Although never optimistic that it could last for long, Taft had tried valiantly to bring peace with a modicum of order to the affairs of Cuba. Even "peace for a time" would avoid "great disaster to the business and property interests of the Islands." [54] The longer he associated with the Cubans, the more discouraged he became over their capacity for self-government. A week before issuing the proclamation, he wrote to his wife about the basic problem: "The truth is that Cuba is no more fitted for self-government than the Philippines and the proper solution of the present difficulties would be annexation if we consulted the interest of the Cuban people alone, but the circumstances are such that the United States can not take this course now, though in the future it may have to do so." [55]

On October 2, 1906, Taft wrote to President Roosevelt, reassuring the chief executive as to the caution and delicacy with which the intervention had been accomplished. He clearly wanted to relieve the president of any apprehensions on the score of overt and unwarranted use of American troops in the island. He pointed out that it was not the purpose of the intervention "to use American soldiers to fight with Cubans except in cases of absolute necessity." The plan was to employ American troops to garrison the large towns and to

52. *Ibid.*, 58.
53. Fitzgibbon, *Cuba and the United States, 1900–1935*, 121–122.
54. W. H. Taft to Helen H. Taft, Sept. 22, 1906, Taft MSS.
55. *Ibid.*

employ the "Rural Guards for the suppression of active disorder." The American troops were present "as a background to give confidence, not to do fighting." [56]

The next day Taft sent the president a lengthy report covering many details of the Cuban situation.[57] In his characteristically thorough fashion, Taft explained the problems as he saw them. With a gift for lucid prose Taft was a faithful reporter who conveyed a full account of what had transpired. He made recommendations to the president for American generals who seemed best adapted to the Cuban problem and he cited American civilian officials who appeared best fitted for the positions of civilian administration. He described the great care being taken in supervising the surrender of the rebels, and said that he was hopeful of accomplishing a complete disbandment of the armies. In all of their actions and activities the two peace commissioners, according to Taft, were attempting to conform to the views expounded by Secretary of State Elihu Root during his trip to South America, and were trying "to show to the South Americans that we are here against our will, and only for the purpose of aiding Cuba." [58]

Taft's estimate of the caliber of Cuban President Estrada Palma was revealing. "Palma," Taft wrote, "is a good man, a man of rather limited scope, but more anxious for the prosperity of his country; very careful of expenditures and fully charged with the importance of inviting capital by giving it good security." [59] On the other hand, Estrada Palma, in Taft's view, was not skillful in managing political elements and lacked the talent which a successful administration of the Cuban government required.

The core of his philosophy relative to the new situation in which he found himself as provisional governor was expressed in the following words:

56. W. H. Taft to Theodore Roosevelt, Oct. 2, 1906, Roosevelt MSS.
57. *Ibid.*, Oct. 3, 1906.
58. *Ibid.*
59. *Ibid.*

My theory in respect to our government here, which I have attempted to carry out in every way, is that we are simply carrying on the Republic of Cuba under the 'Platt Amendment, as a receiver carries on the business of his ward; that this in its nature suspends the functions of the legislature and of the elected executive but that it leaves them in such a situation that their functions will at once revive when the receivership, or trusteeship, is at an end, so all the documents that I sign are headed "Republic of Cuba under the provisional administration of the United States" and I have signed a Decree continuing all the diplomatic functions of the government. This is of course a novel situation, but the Platt Amendment was novel in that one independent government agreed with another independent government that the latter might intervene in the former and maintain the former in law and order.[60]

Here Taft mirrored his times. The figures of the corporation in receivership operated by a temporary trusteeship was deeply symbolic of Taft's own era. And the legal allusions betray a reference frame congenial to his nature and experience. There is a note of irony in Taft's reference to the "novel situation" in which one independent government agreed with another independent government "that the latter might intervene in the former and maintain the former in law and order." But Taft did not seem to be disturbed by the incongruity of his formulation. In a somewhat pious light he felt that his effort was "exceedingly gratifying to the Cuban people and softens much the humiliation that they have suffered from the intervention." In concluding, Taft betrayed no misgivings or uncertainty about the propriety of his course. Indeed, he felt that as the situation had dictated his actions, the intervention "was really objected to by no person and seemed to come of itself and of necessity rather than at our instance." [61] And whatever Taft's personal prejudices or predilections, his utter lack of guile made it clear that he fully believed in what had been done.

Moreover, in an important address delivered at the open-

60. *Ibid.*
61. *Ibid.*

ing exercises of the National University of Havana, held on October 1, 1906, the new provisional governor presented his formula for the future development of Cuba. He began rather shrewdly by acknowledging that the "Anglo-Saxon race" had much to learn from the intellectual refinement, logical faculties, artistic temperament, poetic imagery, high ideals, and courtesty of the "Latin and Spanish races." [62] However, he felt that the Anglo-Saxon world had, due to many causes, contributed substantially to the development of popular government. The United States, for example, had achieved considerable success in the development of democratic institutions, but even here—under the most favorable auspices—the road had not always been smooth. Certainly, therefore, it was understandable why Cubans without any real tradition for self-government should be experiencing difficulties. Some of these problems he traced to the Spanish heritage which seemed to separate generally the intellectuals and men of talent from all interest about or participation in public affairs. As a consequence, the Cuban Republic which had made tremendous progress in the first four years of its existence had stumbled, and with the best intentions, the United States would assist in putting the republic back on its feet.

For the young graduates, Governor Taft counseled activities that encouraged the acquisition of material wealth. He was afraid that too many young Cubans were "not sufficiently infused with that mercantile spirit of which we have too much in America." What was needed among the Cubans was "a desire to make money, to found great enterprises, and to carry on the prosperity of this beautiful island, and the young Cubans ought most of them to begin in business." [63] The provisional governor looked forward to the day when Cubans educated in business would play a powerful role in the economic life of their own country.

In the interim, however, the proper development of Cuba

62. Address by William Howard Taft at the opening exercises of the National University of Havana, Oct. 1, 1906, contained in Taft MSS.
63. *Ibid.*

would call for foreign capital. It was in this light if in no other that Taft could find some good words for the old order in Cuba. The people of Cuba owed President Tomas Estrada Palma and his associates a profound debt of gratitude, because he had realized "the necessity" for bringing capital to Cuba and convincing the outside world of the "essentially conservative character of the Cuban government in order that foreign capitalists might depend upon the security without which capital cannot come." The arrival of foreign capital was not inconsistent with "the gradual acquirement of capital by industrious, enterprising, intelligent, energetic, patriotic Cubans." [64] In his peroration, Taft defined what were in his judgment the supreme values of life: "The right of property and the motive for accumulation, next to the right of liberty, is the basis of all modern, successful civilization, and until you have a community of political influence and control which is affected by the conserving influences of property and property ownership, successful popular government is impossible." [65] Alexander Hamilton could not have said it better.

On October 9, 1906, four days before his departure from Cuba, Taft reviewed the problems which he predicted would torment the island in the future. Among the disturbing factors that he saw were the bitterness of political rancor, the absence of patriotism and moral courage, the "aloofness and lack of political influence of the conservative and property-holding classes," the overtones of racial and class difference, the "tendency toward socialism on the part of some of the leaders," and the venality and corruption that permeated the legislatures of the municipal and national governments. The presence of such grave obstacles he felt made a man who sought to set up self-government believe that he was "making bricks without straw." [66] These discouraging realities made him long to leave the island and return to the relatively

64. *Ibid.*
65. *Ibid.*
66. W. H. Taft to Charles P. Taft, Oct. 9, 1906, Taft MSS.

quiet tribulations of domestic American politics. The alternatives as he saw them were confined to a narrow range. Had the United States supported the constituted government immediately and wholeheartedly, it would have faced a war "in which the American interest would have been the first to suffer and then all would have been involved in one conflagration." Had the United States abstained from any action he felt that the same result would have prevailed, and "years of destruction would have followed." [67] Therefore, in his judgment, the course of action taken during the intervention was the only way out.

On October 10, 1906, Governor Taft announced that active, organized warfare had ceased, and issued a proclamation of total amnesty to all who had participated in the rebellion. Three days later, he turned over the reins of the government to Charles E. Magoon, and on the same day left the island, never to return.[68] All in all, Taft had been disappointed with what he had found in Cuba. There was nothing about the "wretched Cuban business" that gave him any pleasure. The whole dreary affair had been "full of nightmares" for him. Perhaps the basic clue to his dissatisfaction lay in his estimate of the Cuban leaders. Taft, as a Hamiltonian, believed that most of them were "broken reeds" lacking manhood and patriotism.[69]

As to the long-range future of Cuba, Taft was pessimistic.[70] His ideal was a country in which the conservative and property-holding classes possessed abilities and a keen sense of public responsibility. These were qualities he hoped the Cubans would develop, but for the present he was not sanguine. Since he had little faith in the development of a sound ruling class, Taft had little faith in the development of Cuba itself.

67. *Ibid.*
68. Stuart, *Latin America and the United States*, 216; Munro, *The United States and the Caribbean Area*, 28; Fitzgibbon, *Cuba and the United States, 1900–1935*, 124.
69. W. H. Taft to Charles P. Taft, Oct. 4, 1906, Taft MSS.
70. *Ibid.*, Oct. 9, 1906.

CHAPTER VI

Two Missions to Japan

THE YEAR 1905 was crucially important in the history of United States diplomacy toward the Far East. The Russo-Japanese War thrust the entire United States position there into bold relief. With two major powers involved in armed conflict and other nations engaged in a furious struggle for power, the United States, recently in possession of the Philippines, was vitally interested in and deeply involved with the world-shaking developments then taking place. The United States government wanted to enhance the security of the Philippines, the maintenance of the Open Door in China, the expansion of a thriving trade in Manchuria, and the achievement of a balance of power that would improve its competitive position in the Far East.[1]

There was no doubt where President Roosevelt's sympathies lay vis-à-vis the Russo-Japanese War. Roosevelt had only disdain for the Russian government, which he regarded as a symbol of tyranny and oppression.[2] Moreover, he was

---

1. A. Whitney Griswold, *The Far Eastern Policy of the United States* (New York, 1938), 89; Edward H. Zabriskie, *American-Russian Rivalry in the Far East: A Study in Diplomacy and Power Politics, 1895–1914* (Philadelphia, 1946), 103; *The Shaping of American Diplomacy: Readings and Documents in American Foreign Relations, 1750–1955*, ed. William Appleman Williams (Chicago, 1956), 440–441.
2. Theodore Roosevelt to Cecil Arthur Spring Rice, March 19, 1904, Roosevelt, *Letters*, IV, 760.

convinced that if victorious in the war Russia would "organize northern China against us" and keep the United States out of all territory she controlled. In sharp contrast, Roosevelt admired the Japanese people, and believed that their government was enlightened and progressive. He viewed the initial Japanese victories in the war with pleasure because of his conviction that Japan "was playing our game." [3]

Roosevelt's sympathy for Japan and his deep suspicions about Russia coincided with public opinion throughout the United States which was strongly favorable to Japan. This was true despite the fact that Russia was a white Christian nation and had been regarded in the past as a traditional friend of the United States. Japan was believed to be engaged in a war of self-defense, and her boldness in challenging the Russian colossus aroused that inevitable admiration reserved for a smaller nation fighting for its life.[4] Moreover, Japan was thought to be defending China against an ostensible aggressive and barbaric foe, and thus appeared to be upholding commercial rights for all nations in the Far East. Finally, Japan made certain that her case against Russia was presented to the newspapers of the United States in its most favorable light.[5]

But despite this prevailing outlook, the Roosevelt administration did not view Japanese ascendancy in the Far East with unadulterated approval. However vigorous in the expression of his hostility toward the Russian government, President Roosevelt did not favor Japanese predominance in Manchuria. His purpose was to give Japan a free hand in

3. *Ibid.*, June 13, 1904. In June, 1905, the president described the Japanese as "a wonderful and civilized people" who were entitled to stand "on an absolute equality" with all of the other peoples of the civilized world. Theodore Roosevelt to David Bowman Schneder, June 19, 1905, Roosevelt, *Letters*, IV, 1240–41; Theodore Roosevelt to Theodore Roosevelt, Jr., Feb. 10, 1904, *ibid.*, 724.

4. Payson J. Treat, *Japan and the United States, 1853–1921* (Boston, 1921), 181; Thomas A. Bailey, *Theodore Roosevelt and the Japanese-American Crises: An Account of the International Complications Arising from the Race Problem on the Pacific Coast* (Stanford, 1934), 4.

5. Foster Rhea Dulles, *Forty Years of American-Japanese Relations* (New York, 1937), 70; Bailey, *Theodore Roosevelt and the Japanese-American Crises*, 5.

Korea, and to extend her both moral and financial assistance in her struggle to weaken the control of Russia over Manchuria.[6] Finally, he hoped that Russia and Japan would wear themselves out, thereby equalizing the balance of power in Manchuria and improving the economic and commercial interests of the United States in the Far East. As he wrote to an old friend in March, 1904: "It may be that the two powers will fight until both are fairly well exhausted, and that then peace will come on terms which will not mean the creation of either a yellow peril or a Slav peril."[7]

Power relationships in the Far East were in flux and the president was deeply concerned with their impact on the position already established by the United States. His major concern was for the proper protection of the Philippines and Hawaii and he gave the matter careful thought.[8] In May, 1905, he wrote his secretary of war as follows: "It seems to me this country must decide definitely whether it does or does not intend to hold its possessions in the Orient—to keep the Philippines and Hawaii. If we are not prepared to build and maintain a good-sized navy, each unit of which shall be at the highest point of efficiency, and if we are not prepared to establish a strong and suitable base for our navy in the Philippines, then we had far better give up the Philippine Islands entirely."[9]

6. Theodore Roosevelt to Cecil Arthur Spring Rice, June 16, 1905, Roosevelt, *Letters*, IV, 1234; Theodore Roosevelt to John Hay, Jan. 28, 1905 *ibid.*, 1112; Tyler Dennett, *Roosevelt and the Russo-Japanese War: A Critical Study of American Policy in Eastern Asia in 1902–1905, Based Primarily upon the Private Papers of Theodore Roosevelt* (Garden City, N.Y., 1925), 110; Zabriskie, *American-Russian Rivalry in the Far East*, 107.

7. *Ibid.*, 107–108; Theodore Roosevelt to Cecil Arthur Spring Rice, March 19, 1904, Roosevelt, *Letters*, IV, 760.

8. Theodore Roosevelt to W. H. Taft, Feb. 9, 1905, Taft MSS; Dennett, *Roosevelt and the Russo-Japanese War*, 159–160.

9. Theodore Roosevelt to W. H. Taft, May 31, 1905, Taft MSS. In the same letter the president instructed Secretary of War Taft to direct the attention of the senators and representatives accompanying him to the Philippines during the upcoming summer "to the need of fortifying Subig Bay." President Roosevelt had asked his secretary of war to draw the attention of the legislators particularly to the need for adequate defenses at Subig Bay, because Congress up to this point had been very niggardly in its appropriations for the base. William R. Braisted, "The Philippine

During the early months of 1905 President Roosevelt was concerned increasingly over the direction of world affairs. The war between Japan and Russia threatened to become the prelude to a much greater conflict. Although the president could view with equanimity little wars in which the "good civilized powers" chastised the "backward and decadent ones," he was appalled at the prospect of a showdown battle among the great civilized nations. So, he began to work through diplomatic channels to try to re-establish a balance of power between Russia and Japan.[10] Although he attempted to get Great Britain and Germany to cooperate to put pressure on the belligerents, Anglo-German rivalry was far too intense. At last, with Russia exhausted, with Germany fearful lest revolution spread to western Europe, and with Great Britain, the United States, and France unwilling to pour more money into the war, Russia and Japan welcomed an end to the long struggle.[11]

On June 8, 1905, Theodore Roosevelt invited the belligerents to a peace conference in the United States. The meeting place at Roosevelt's suggestion was at first to be Washington, D.C.; later, however, due to its cooler weather, Portsmouth, New Hampshire, was selected as the site. The peace conference opened on August 10, 1905, and on September 5, 1905, Russia and Japan signed the Treaty of Portsmouth.[12] In as-

Naval Base Problem, 1898–1909," *The Mississippi Valley Historical Review*, XLI (June, 1954), 25–30.

10. Nelson Manfred Blake, "Ambassadors at the Court of Theodore Roosevelt," *The Mississippi Valley Historical Review*, XLII (Sept., 1955), 197; Carol L. Thompson, "America in the Far East: I. The Treaty of Portsmouth," *Current History*, XIX (Sept., 1950), 150.

11. Japan realized that eventually the superior strength of Russia militarily was certain to assert itself. Hence, immediately after their victory of Tsushima they requested President Roosevelt's mediation to end the conflict. Frederick H. Cramer, "The Pacific: Sea of Decision: III. The United States Supreme (1900–1950)," *Current History*, XX (April, 1951), 194.

12. Thompson, "America in the Far East," 150; Zabriskie, *American-Russian Rivalry in the Far East*, 121, 129. By the terms of this treaty, Manchuria was divided into a southern zone which was to become part of a Japanese sphere of influence, while Russia retained her previous position in northern Manchuria. Korea once again was set aside for Japan and a few years later was annexed. Cramer, "The Pacific: Sea of Decision: III," 194. For the complete text of the treaty of peace, con-

suming the role of peacemaker, President Roosevelt had a double purpose in mind.[13] He wished to stop a war between two civilized nations which was bad for the world, and he hoped to maintain the rights of all nations in the Far East by stabilizing the balance of power there.

This background is necessary for a proper understanding of William Howard Taft's two visits to Japan to help assure the success of the Portsmouth conference and to smooth over the controversy relating to Japanese immigration. When Taft sailed from San Francisco for the Philippines on July 8, 1905, ostensibly with the sole purpose of accompanying and educating a Congressional delegation on the problems facing the United States in Philippine administration, Russia and Japan had agreed to the Portsmouth conference, but many important details remained to be settled. President Roosevelt instructed Secretary Taft to stop at Tokyo en route to the Philippines and "pay his compliments to the Japanese." [14] Apparently he was given no written instructions regarding his Japanese visit, nor is there any record of verbal instruction.[15] It would seem reasonable, however, that the president outlined his views on the Far East to his secretary of war. The timing of this visit to Japan, one month in advance of the Portsmouth conference, suggests a relationship between the events. The importance of the trip was clear to the Russians, for as President Roosevelt indicated, the Russian ambassador at Washington was "having a fit" upon learning of Taft's projected call.[16]

cluded between Russia and Japan, see *Papers Relating to the Foreign Relations of the United States, 1905* (Washington, D.C., 1905), 824–828.

13. Howard K. Beale, *Theodore Roosevelt and the Rise of America to World Power* (Baltimore, Md., 1956), 312.

14. W. H. Taft to Theodore Roosevelt, July 8, 1905, Taft MSS; Pringle, *Taft*, I, 297–298.

15. Henry F. Pringle, in his biography of Theodore Roosevelt, states flatly that Taft had received definite instructions before his visit to Japan. Pringle fails, however, to cite any evidence to sustain his position. Henry F. Pringle, *Theodore Roosevelt: A Biography* (New York, 1931), 384. Philip C. Jessup has examined this question with painstaking thoroughness, and he concludes that Taft had no previous instructions from the President. Jessup, *Root*, II, 5–6.

16. Theodore Roosevelt to John Hay, May 6, 1905, Roosevelt, *Letters*, IV, 1168.

In William Howard Taft, Roosevelt not only had a personal representative of great reliability but also one who fully shared his perspectives. Taft had set forth his views in March, 1905, to a close personal friend.[17] Writing in a strongly pro-Japanese vein he declared that "the governing classes" of the Japanese had "elevated the people" and that it was "the aim of the governing classes" that was important. He had "no fear of a yellow peril through them." He felt that their purpose was "to stand high among the nations of the earth," and that much of their ambition was "on the European ideal." He had great confidence that the Japanese were basically more friendly to the United States than they were to any other nation. But there was still a sense of uneasiness in his acceptance of the Japanese. For as he put it: "a Jap is first of all a Jap and would be glad to aggrandize himself at the expense of anybody." Moreover, because of his earlier background and the deep emotional attachment that he now felt toward the Philippines, Japanese intentions there were always uppermost in his mind. Perhaps he was trying to reassure himself when he wrote that he did not "look for any movement of Japan toward the Philippines after peace had been restored."

Taft was quite confident that Japan would look toward the United States as her friend in any negotiations that might stem from the Russo-Japanese War. Quite complacently, he added that Japan "will have her hands full peopling Korea and the Li Tung peninsula and she will be quite content to let the tropical end be on Formosa alone." Although this letter shows a lack of knowledge about the basic problems in the Far East, it is almost a perfect blueprint of the agreement that he subsequently made with Japan.

On July 27, 1905, the secretary of war conferred in Tokyo with the prime minister of Japan, Taro Katsura. Two days later he communicated to Secretary of State Elihu Root a long

17. Theodore Roosevelt to W. H. Taft, Oct. 7, 1905, *ibid.*, V, 49; W. H. Taft to Martin Egan, March 25, 1905, Taft MSS.

report on the meeting.[18] The three main topics discussed were the Philippine Islands, Korea, and the maintenance of general peace in the Far East. At the very outset Taft—in speaking of "pro-Russians" in the United States and their expressed view that victory by Japan would be "a certain prelude to her aggression in the direction of the Philippine Islands"—discounted the possibility. He observed firmly that Japan's only interest in the Philippines would be to have the islands governed by a "strong and friendly nation like the United States." Furthermore, he felt that Japan would not desire to have the Philippines "placed either under the misrule of the natives, yet unfit for self-government, or in the hands of some unfriendly European power." Count Katsura, he said, confirmed these views "in the strongest terms," and positively stated that Japan did not "harbor any aggressive designs whatever on the Philippines." In fact, Katsura, while renouncing any such expansionist aspirations, condemned any "insinuations of the yellow peril type" by cataloguing such animadversions as "malicious and clumsy slanders calculated to do mischief to Japan."

18. Pringle, *Taft*, I, 298; W. H. Taft to Elihu Root, July 29, 1905, Roosevelt MSS. This was not a formal report, but a long cablegram from the secretary of war to the secretary of state. The first public knowledge of this report, which took the form of an agreed memorandum, came in August, 1924, when Tyler Dennett, then a lecturer in history at Johns Hopkins University, presented before a meeting of the Institute of Politics at Williamstown, Massachusetts. He published it immediately afterward in photostat form—with a few deletions—together with a critical commentary. Dennett did not reveal Taft's identity but described him as "a personal representative of President Roosevelt." Tyler Dennett, "President Roosevelt's Secret Pact with Japan," *Current History*, XXI (Oct., 1924), 15–21. This agreement lacked the formality of a ratified treaty and was binding—if it was binding at all—only on the Theodore Roosevelt administration. Claude A. Buss compares it with the Yalta agreement of February 11, 1945, and states that it bound only the Theodore Roosevelt administration which made it. Claude A. Buss, *The Far East: A History of Recent and Contemporary International Relations in East Asia* (New York, 1955), 375–376. In a brilliant analysis, Raymond A. Esthus argues effectively that the Taft-Katsura conversation and accompanying memorandum was not a "secret pact" or "agreement," but rather a frank exchange of views. See Raymond A. Esthus, "The Taft-Katsura Agreement—Reality or Myth?," *Journal of Modern History*, XXXI (March, 1959), 46–51. The quotations in this and the following four paragraphs are drawn from the "agreed memorandum" as communicated by Secretary Taft to Secretary Root in the cablegram.

Then Count Taro Katsura observed that the maintenance of general peace in the Far East formed the fundamental principle of Japan's international policy. He projected an understanding among Japan, the United States, and Great Britain as the three nations possessing a "common interest in upholding the principle of eminence," and devoted to the maintenance of peace. He indicated comprehension of the traditional policy of the United States and recognition that a formal alliance was not possible. But in view of what he termed "our common interests," he saw no reason why "an alliance in practice, if not in name" should not be made by the three nations in respect to the affairs of the Far East. Such an understanding "firmly formed" would permit the maintenance of general peace in the area to the great advantage of all powers concerned.

Secretary Taft, in reply, said that it was difficult, if not impossible, for the president of the United States to enter into an understanding which, in effect, amounted to a confidential, informal agreement without the consent of the Senate. However, he was certain that even without an agreement, the people of the United States were in such full accord with the policies of Japan and Great Britain toward the maintenance of peace in the Far East that joint action by the three powers could be depended upon should the occasion and need for it arise.

The conversation then turned to the question of Korea. Count Katsura, observing that Korea was the direct cause of Japan's war with Russia, stated that it was a matter of "absolute importance to Japan that a complete solution of the peninsula question" be achieved as the "logical consequence" of the Russo-Japanese War. What did the count mean by the expression "complete solution"? He pointed out that if Korea were "left to herself" she would most certainly "draw back to her habit of improvidently entering into agreements or treaties with other powers, thus resuscitating the same international complications as existed before the war." Therefore Japan, according to Katsura, felt absolutely constrained to take some definite action toward "precluding the possibility of Korea falling back into her former condition and of placing us again under the necessity of entering upon another foreign war." In effect, in a polite but firm way, Count Katsura made it clear that Japan attached sufficient importance to the future control of Korea that she would be willing to engage in war if necessary to resolve the question.

In response Taft "fully admitted the justness" of the count's observations and remarked that the establishment by Japanese troops of a "suzerainty over Korea to the extent of requiring that Korea enter into no foreign treaties without the consent of Japan was the logical result of the present war and would directly contribute to permanent peace in the East." As if this statement alone were not encouragement enough, Taft expressed the opinion that President Roosevelt would concur in the views that he had expressed although he had no authority to provide an assurance of this. Pointing out that since he had left Washington Elihu Root had been appointed secretary of state, Taft assured the count that he would forward to Root and President Roosevelt a memorandum of the conversation. Count Katsura said that he would transmit the same conversation confidentially to Baron J. Komura.

In his cable to Root transmitting the agreed memorandum, Taft noted rather apologetically that if he had spoken too freely or unwittingly he knew, referring to Root, that "you can and will correct it." Taft stressed that the prime minister had been quite anxious for the interview and that under the circumstances it was "difficult to avoid statement and so told [the] truth as I believe it." [19] In a telegram to the president, Taft noted again that the Japanese had sought the interview, and then added significantly: "I did not because I did not wish to 'butt into' the affairs of the State Department, but they probably thought it important because I had had some relation with State Department business." If Taft went further in expressing his views than had been anticipated by

19. W. H. Taft to Elihu Root, July 29, 1905, Roosevelt MSS.

Roosevelt, it would seem that he was confident his actions would be upheld. President Roosevelt quickly telegraphed his approval of Taft's position: "Your conversation with Count Katsura absolutely correct in every respect. Wish you would state to Katsura that I confirm every word you have said." [20] Subsequently, on August 7,1905, Secretary Taft wrote to Count Katsura that he was empowered by President Roosevelt "to confirm in every respect" the statements made by him during their conversation.[21]

How did American diplomacy fare in this encounter? On balance, it is difficult to see what the United States gained from this frank exchange of views. In return for a Japanese pledge of noninterference in the Philippines, for whatever that was worth, the United States permitted Japan, in effect, a free hand in Korea. Perhaps the United States had no effective alternative in regard to Korea, but the lack of concern over the fate of China was flagrant and indefensible.[22]

The Taft-Katsura memorandum is best comprehended as part of Theodore Roosevelt's desire for a Far Eastern balance of power constructed on the friendship and mutual recognition of the interests of the United States, Great Britain, and Japan. Considered in conjunction with the second Anglo-Japanese alliance of August 12, 1905, in which Roosevelt was actively involved, it pledged the United States to the role of a

20. W. H. Taft to Theodore Roosevelt, July 31, 1905, *ibid.*
21. W. H. Taft to Count Taro Katsura, Aug. 7, 1905, Taft MSS.
22. Howard K. Beale states that Theodore Roosevelt had been convinced since 1900 that Korea could not govern itself, that the United States must not assume this task, and that it would be better for all concerned if Japan took over and governed it efficiently. The over-all pattern for Anglo-Japanese-American control of as much as possible of Eastern Asia to balance Russian strength there seemed much more important to Roosevelt than United States interests in Korea. He believes that President Roosevelt's outlook on Korea illustrates "both his conception of Japan's role as a bulwark against Russia and his concern with strategic rather than economic considerations where the two conflicted." Beale, *Theodore Roosevelt and the Rise of America to World Power*, 314, 321. William Henry Harbaugh offers another explanation for Theodore Roosevelt's Korean policy: "Events had boxed him into a situation analogous to that encountered by Franklin D. Roosevelt at Yalta when the Communists had *de facto* control of Poland." William Henry Harbaugh, *Power and Responsibility: The Life and Times of Theodore Roosevelt* (New York, 1961), 276.

silent, third partner.[23] The commitment was unofficial and not binding except as a gentleman's agreement, but its meaning was unmistakable. What Theodore Roosevelt had done, as Howard K. Beale has so aptly phrased it, "was to agree both in London and in Tokyo to join, as if we had signed a treaty, an alliance with Japan and England in which each party was committed to go to war in defense of the other if either was attacked by a third party, and in which, with Roosevelt's approval, previously independent Korea was handed over to Japan." [24]

Apparently Taft felt no apprehensions about future relations with Japan or the role that his conversations might play in whetting the Japanese appetite for further territorial and political aggrandizement in the Far East. Taking note of the "tremendous popular ovation" that he had received and the goodwill expressed, Secretary Taft was powerfully impressed by the Japanese demonstrations.[25] He described them as manifestations of sincere feeling on the part of the Japanese people. As he expressed it to President Roosevelt: "The truth is that the people have had their feelings of patriotism stirred to the depths by the war and their unexpected successes, that they are feeling the pinch of war and are most grateful to you for intervening to bring about peace and they are anxiously desirous for it. In other words, we are here at the psychological moment and that has resulted in whatever I have already described as a tremendous popular ovation." [26]

On August 5, 1905, after Taft had completed his mission to Japan and moved on to Manila, the peace conference assembled at Portsmouth, New Hampshire, and Japan was permitted to have her way in Korea. In 1910 Japan annexed Korea.[27] In retrospect, two things are surprising in Taft's out-

23. Beale, *Theodore Roosevelt and the Rise of America to World Power*, 154–158; Harbaugh, *Power and Responsibility*, 273–276.

24. Beale, *Theodore Roosevelt and the Rise of America to World Power*, 157.

25. W. H. Taft to Theodore Roosevelt, July 31, 1905, Roosevelt MSS.

26. *Ibid.*

27. On August 22, 1910, after it had been approved by the Emperor of Korea, Viscount Terauchi of Japan and Yi Wan-Yong, the Korean prime minister, signed a

look at this time. One is that he did not see any analogy between the relationship of Korea and Japan and that of Cuba and the United States. Even more striking—and disturbing—is the infinitesimal part that China played in his thinking. Was the effect of the Taft-Katsura agreement to imply that the United States would tacitly consent to further Japanese expansion? And in the process what would be left of the Open Door? Taft did not even allude to the Open Door in any of his reports to Washington or in his private correspondence at this time. Seemingly he saw no conflict between the Taft-Katsura agreement and the future of the Open Door policy for China, or he was not sympathetic to that policy.

In writing to the president, Taft had commented upon the exceptional welcome that he received in Japan. Apparently he felt that this was a happy augury for the future of Japanese-American relations. Yet the year 1905 produced the first indications of a change in public opinion on both sides of the Pacific.[28] In Japan, it arose suddenly in the anger of many of the Japanese people at the peace terms contained in the Treaty of Portsmouth, and in the firm conviction that the United States, under the leadership of President Roosevelt, had prevented the payment of an indemnity by Russia. In the United States, the Japanese immigration problem began to assume the proportions of a serious issue, and many people voiced suspicions regarding the future course of Japanese foreign policy.

The difficulties between the United States and Japan over immigration to the United States and the developing anti-Japanese sentiment on the West Coast provided the backdrop for Taft's second mission to Japan. At a conference at Oyster Bay on August 13, 1907, attended by Elihu Root, Taft, and the

treaty of annexation at Seoul. The terms involved "a complete and permanent cession of sovereignty by Korea and an acceptance and complete annexation by Japan." M. Frederick Nelson, *Korea and the Old Orders in Eastern Asia* (Baton Rouge, La., 1946), 285. The American legation in Korea had been withdrawn immediately after the convention signed on November 17, 1905, between Japan and Korea, by which Japan became "the medium for conducting the foreign relations of Korea. . . ." *Papers Relating to the Foreign Relations of the United States, 1905,* 26.

28. Payson J. Treat, *Japan and the United States, 1853–1921* (Boston, 1921), 183.

president, it was agreed that Taft should once again visit Japan on his way to the Philippines.[29] The reason for his journey to the Philippines was the opening of the Philippine General Assembly. This provided a convenient opportunity for Taft to pay yet another courtesy call to Tokyo and to take up some outstanding issues without appearing to be making a special trip to Japan for that purpose. He was instructed, however, not to initiate any discussions unless the Japanese desired them.[30]

Taft had formed clear convictions on the subject of the importation of Asiatic labor into the United States. Before leaving the United States he set forth his views in a letter to a California congressman indicating that these views were also those of the president.[31] "We agree," he wrote, "the Asiatic laborer does not amalgamate with the laborers of this country." Echoing popular prejudices of the time, he noted that "in spite of the progress that has been made both by the Chinaman and the Japanese, there is a real difference much more fundamental than between European immigrants and our American people." Because of these feelings, Taft and the president favored a treaty with Japan that would exclude Japanese labor. With regard for the sensitivity of the Japanese, Taft suggested a concession "which will satisfy the *amour propre* of the Japanese," namely, "extending to those who are lawfully in this country the right to become citizens of the United States." For Taft this appeared to be an ideal solution,

29. Bailey, *Theodore Roosevelt and the Japanese-American Crises*, 228; Jessup, *Root*, 11, 26; W. H. Taft to Charles P. Taft, Aug. 18, 1907, Taft MSS; M. A. de Wolfe Howe, *George von Lengerke Meyer: His Life and Public Services* (New York, 1920), 364–366.

30. The Philippine Bill which Congress had passed on July 1, 1902, had provided for the creation of a Philippine assembly. This body was inaugurated on October 16, 1907, at the Manila Grand Opera House. It was composed entirely of Filipinos elected by the direct popular vote of the people. Thereafter, the intelligent and educated Filipinos had both a share in the responsibilities of government and an opportunity to express officially their protests and their demands. Kalaw, *Philippine Government*, 75; Tongko, *The Government of the Republic of the Philippines*, 15; Grayson L. Kirk, *Philippine Independence: Motives, Problems, and Prospects* (New York, 1936), 37; W. H. Taft to Charles P. Taft, Aug. 18, 1907, Taft MSS.

31. W. H. Taft to E. A. Hays, Sept. 11, 1907, *ibid.* The quotations in the remainder of this paragraph are drawn from this important letter.

for as he commented, "it is quite unlikely that many will avail themselves of this privilege, and as the laborers will be excluded, those who do will not be undesirable citizens."

Taft felt that the success of his mission depended upon the attitude of the Japanese authorities, but indicated that he would proceed along the course of action already described. He arrived in Japan on September 28, 1907, and was impressed by the reception he was accorded, "not because there was so much popular demonstration, but because there was an evident desire on the part of the Japanese government to indicate that it had no desire for war." [32] Thus, Taft was able quite readily to find evidence for the view he had expressed privately in late July, 1907, that Japan was not "serious about a war" with the United States for "the next three or four years." In a press interview at Yokohama on the day of his arrival in Japan, he issued protestations of peace and goodwill which seemed to belie the true situation.[33] "So far as America and Japan is [sic] concerned," he remarked expansively but not prophetically, "they will always be friends." He could find no motive for friction and with what possibly may have held great significance in shaping his views he noted that "personally I have been subject to so much kindness here that I do not feel any great change from the United States, to Japan."

In the course of this interview he alluded once again to a favorite theme—trade, this time "the trade of the Pacific." Using language that was prosaic, he stressed an obvious fact—that the trade of the Pacific was a very important thing. Although he couched his views in diplomatic phrases, he was keenly aware of the competition among the major powers for that trade. However, he was hopeful for a friendly solution based upon reciprocity and a large volume of business transactions.

32. W. H. Taft to Louise Taft, Sept. 27, 1907, *ibid.*; W. H. Taft to Charles P. Taft, Oct. 10, 1907, *ibid.*

33. W. H. Taft to Theodore Roosevelt, July 26, 1907, Roosevelt MSS; press interview by William Howard Taft at Yokohama, Japan, Sept. 28, 1907, Taft MSS. The quotations in this and the following paragraph are drawn from this press interview.

Taft soon learned that the Japanese officials were ready to hold conversations. On the afternoon of September 28, 1907, he called upon the minister of foreign affairs, Tadasu Hayashi.[34] Hayashi asked Taft what the foundation was for a report that the United States would sell the Philippines. The Japanese foreign minister said that Shuzo Aoki, Japanese ambassador to the United States, had deemed it of sufficient importance to cable the existence of such a rumor back to Tokyo. In the light of Taft's deep affection for the Philippine people, one can only conjecture at the impact that such words surely produced. Taft quickly rejoined that "there was not the slightest foundation" for such wild rumors. Obviously worried about the agreement he had made two years ago and which he had accepted so optimistically, Taft reminded the Japanese that in the previous agreement of 1905 Count Katsura had said that "Japan did not wish the Philippines but only that the United States retain possession and maintain stable government there." For his part Hayashi responded that Japan was of the "same opinion today," but "would feel some concern if the United States were to sell the islands to a European power." Taft scotched this idea by pointing out that the United States was under an obligation to the Filipino people to retain the islands and lead them on to self-government, or to turn the islands over to the Filipinos themselves, under a protectorate which would assure stable government.

On the evening of September 28, 1907, at a dinner at Shiba Palace, Taft held a conversation with Count Tanaka, minister of the imperial household and closest personal representative of the emperor. Taft took note of the strained relations between the two countries and stated categorically that rumors of hostile intention by the United States were wholly the result of "yellow newspapers," and did not "evidence the true feelings" of the American government. Subsequently, Tanaka informed Taft that this information had been con-

34. W. H. Taft to Theodore Roosevelt, Oct. 18, 1907, Roosevelt MSS. This was a long cablegram from the secretary of war to the president written in the form of a report.

veyed to the emperor. The next morning, the Japanese minister of war called on Taft.[35] Taft related how Shuzo Aoki had requested that Taft assure the Japanese war minister that the occurrences of hostility toward the Japanese were "local and due to bitterness of feeling not shared by country at large." But for the traditional pattern of friendship between the United States and Japan, Aoki, Taft reported, would have feared the consequences of the mistreatment of the Japanese in San Francisco. Then Taft expressed his own considered views. Perhaps symbolic of the changed relations between the two countries, Taft spoke first about the question of war. He stressed the idea that the American government and people "could not believe war with Japan possible," and attributed manifestations of hostility in the United States to local disturbances which were beyond governmental control. The minister of war seemed to accept Taft's explanation without any reservations, and said that he would pass the information on to the prime minister.

On Saturday, September 28, 1907, Methodist Bishop Merriman C. Harris called upon Taft and brought a glowing account of Japanese administration in Korea.[36] After pointing out that there were 40,000 native Korean Methodists, Bishop Harris explained that the work of Japan in Korea made "for civilization and good government." Bishop Harris seemed to embody the general attitude of Americans who were in the area—one of great sympathy for Japanese policy—for he did not hesitate to state flatly that criticisms and reports detrimental to the Japanese administration of Korea "were prejudiced and grew out either of a lack of understanding or of enmity of those who had fattened on the abuses of [the] old Korean government." Other Americans confirmed these sentiments, but in all of this a new note in Japanese-American relations had been injected—the possibility of war was certainly prevalent for it hung uneasily over all of the conversations. Evidence of this is that everyone with whom Taft

35. *Ibid.*
36. *Ibid.*

spoke, Japanese or American, touched upon the subject of war if only to deny its possibility.

On September 30, 1907, Taft lunched with Foreign Minister Hayashi.[37] The latter had asked for a conference on the subject of immigration. He pointed out that only a small number of Japanese were interested in the question of immigration, and that the Japanese people would be entirely satisfied with a complete restriction of immigration by treaty. He was concerned with the acute Japanese sensitivity in the matter and desired that feelings be spared by asking that the United States apply equal restrictions to European immigrants. He observed that the chief interest in the subject inside Japan was taken by "syndicates who were engaged in the business of furnishing Japanese coolies for a commission." These syndicates, he explained, had influence politically and had carried on a campaign to rouse the people on the subject. This campaign, he thought, had been successful, not because of any popular desire on the part of the Japanese to go to America, but because of "patriotic self-conceit." It was apparent that the growing Japanese empire was experiencing a great wave of nationalism. Hayashi made this quite plain by stating that the Japanese people "bitterly resented a treaty based in inequality between Japanese and Europeans."

Taft apparently listened attentively to these remonstrances, and then expressed his view that the solution lay in a treaty giving the Japanese the right to naturalize in America and reciprocally excluding laborers of each country. This suggestion was rejected by Hayashi, who argued with considerable justification that although reciprocal exclusion was "fair on its face," it was not "reciprocity in fact," since no American laborers came to Japan. Thus while the right to naturalize would be welcome by Japan as a friendly concession, it would not be accepted as "compensation for reciprocal exclusion."

37. *Ibid.*

On the same day, September 30, 1907, Taft delivered an address before the chamber of commerce of Tokyo.[38] It was one of the most important speeches that he ever delivered abroad. He discussed the issues separating the two countries in a strong but frank bid for peace. After referring briefly to his first visit in 1905, he reviewed the gigantic achievements of Japan in the last fifty years. Noting the relationship of such Americans as Commodore Perry, Townsend Harris, and General Grant to Japan's prodigious advance to the front rank among world powers, he declared that the United States had always been sympathetic to that advance. Moreover, he compared the magnificent progress of the United States in becoming a tremendous industrial power with the parallel development of the Japanese.

At this point Taft referred bluntly to the prospects of war. While acknowledging the disturbing manifestations of discord, such as the events in San Francisco, he remarked that "there is nothing in these events of injustice" that could not be resolved through the normal channels of diplomacy, as both governments were led "by statesmen of honor, sanity and justice." Although not "one of those who hold that war is so frightful that nothing justifies a resort to it," he held that nothing but a "great and unavoidable cause" could justify anything so tragic.[39]

As to the issue of war between the United States and Japan he declared: "War between Japan and the United States would be a crime against modern civilization. It would be as wicked as it would be insane. Neither the people of Japan nor the people of the United States desire war. The governments of the two countries would strain every point to avoid such an awful catastrophe." [40]

In essence, Taft felt that neither Japan nor the United States had anything to gain from such an eventuality. What

38. Address by William Howard Taft at a banquet tendered by the Chamber of Commerce of Tokyo, Sept. 30, 1907, contained in Taft MSS.
39. *Ibid.*
40. *Ibid.*

would Japan gain from such a conflict? He pointed out that the Japanese were looking forward with confidence "to great commercial conquests" which could be achieved peaceably. With the marvelous industry, intelligence, and courage of her people "there is nothing in trade, commerce, and popular contentment and enlightenment to which the Japanese may not attain." War might stop all such developments. Then he turned to the issue of Korea. Here he reasoned that Japan had "undertaken with a legitimate intent in so close a neighbor to reform and rejuvenate an ancient kingdom that had been governed or misgoverned by fifteenth century methods." [41]

Discussing this country then little known in the United States, Taft expanded his views. He was confident, no matter what criticisms might be uttered, that the Japanese government was "pursuing a policy in Korea that would make for justice and civilization and the welfare of a backward people." [42] There was in his thinking a basic rationale to justify such situations. In words equally applicable to American policy toward Latin America, Taft gave expression to what had become dogma for the Roosevelt administration in such matters: "We are living in an age when the intervention of a stronger nation in the affairs of a people unable to maintain a government of law and order to assist the latter to better government becomes a national duty and works for the progress of the world." [43]

This, in effect, was a clear statement of the previously enunciated Roosevelt corollary. The Japanese may well have welcomed this succinctly expressed rationalization for their own course of expansion in the Far East. Nor did Taft oppose such an application. Indeed, he appeared tacitly to accept the logical extension of the doctrine to other major powers, and the Japanese did not miss the point.

Taft then extolled the material progress achieved in the United States during a decade of peace and prosperity, and

41. *Ibid.*
42. *Ibid.*
43. *Ibid.*

noted the great internal problems that the United States was seeking to resolve with her fullest attention. War would merely divert the nation into a condition "in which all the evils of society flourish and all the vultures fatten." [44] Complementary to this, there was American preoccupation with the Philippines. Here the objectives of the United States were the establishment of "a government of law and order and prosperity," and in fitting the people of these islands for the experiment of self-government. Then the secretary of war touched upon a currently explosive issue—the possibility of the sale of the islands to Japan or some other foreign power. Without insulting his hosts, he rejected such a proposal as "absurd," because Japan did not wish the Philippines, having a problem of similar nature near at home. More than this, the United States could not abandon its obligations to the people of the Philippines. American responsibilities could not be shirked for they were a matter of honor.

In the circumstances as he had stated them, Taft saw no reason for war. Why, then, had there been reports and rumors of war? These could be attributed to the "capacity of certain members of the modern press by headlines and sensational dispatches to give rise to unfounded reports," and this potential for mischief had increased proportionately to the improvements in communication in different parts of the world. Such irresponsibility on the part of the press could be laid at the door of an all-consuming desire to sell newspapers—to embarrass governments for political reasons and for other even less justifiable motives. Doubtless there were "irresponsible persons that war would aid or make prominent," and such reprehensible elements would always try to create friction and to secure a large hearing for their course of action.[45] For all of these elements he had nothing but contempt.

On the whole, Taft's speech was well received by the government, press, and people of Japan, and he felt that his address had been well-timed because of the then current

44. *Ibid.*
45. *Ibid.*

United States press campaign, which saw in the visit of the United States fleet to the Pacific an attempt "to cause war," and which was continually harping on the theme that war was inevitable.[46]

On October 1, 1907, Taft held a second conference with Hayashi. The Japanese foreign minister repeated his government's position on the immigration question and said that "it was impossible in the temper of the Japanese people to consent to a reciprocal treaty of exclusion." [47] In Hayashi's view, the only method of dealing with the situation was administratively through the foreign office. When Taft asked if the Japanese were willing to restrict immigration provided such restriction did not involve an open concession in a treaty, Hayashi replied that this was a correct statement of the Japanese position. In fact, he promised that the Japanese government would be most discreet in issuing passports and stated categorically that the danger from immigration could be met only by voluntary administrative action which would continue.

That same day, the secretary of war held yet another conference, this time with Marquis Saionzi, the premier, at the latter's request.[48] The two principals discussed substantially the same subjects already covered. But Taft apparently sought additional assurances about the Philippines. On this score, the count solemnly affirmed the promises made by Count Katsura two years earlier. The present government, he avowed, held the same views as its predecessor with respect to both the Philippines and Korea. In a jocular vein, Taft doubted that Japan would accept the Philippines even as a present unless accompanied with a dowry of a million dollars or more. But he abandoned all pretense of humor when he again explained the reasons for American determination to retain those islands. On the broad question of immigration,

46. W. H. Taft to Theodore Roosevelt, Oct. 18, 1907, Roosevelt MSS.
47. *Ibid.*
48. Copy of conference between William Howard Taft and Marquis Saionzi, Oct. 1, 1907, contained in Taft MSS. The copy was prepared by Sutemi Chinda and given to the secretary of war on the same day.

Count Saionzi assured Taft that the Imperial government would be prepared to meet the situation in a most conciliatory spirit but at the same time "wished to have it clearly understood that Japan could not possibly agree to any arrangement that would require of her any concession incompatible with her dignity as a nation in an absolutely equal footing with other powers." [49]

Taft had two more interviews with prominent Japanese political figures before his departure. The first was with his old friend Count Katsura, now out of office. Katsura, offering renewed assurances of peace, promised support in the mutual quest for amity. In a reminiscing mood, he recalled that the conversation between them in 1905 "had done much to secure acquiescence in Russian peace and to maintain friendly relations between both countries in recent strain." After this visit with the "elder statesman," as Taft described Katsura, there remained just one additional function—an audience with the emperor. On October 2, 1907, the emperor received Taft and expressed friendly sentiments toward the president of the United States and the American people and a personal expression of thanks for what Taft had said in his Tokyo speech.[50]

Taft summed up his impressions of all these conversations and offered several significant comments to the president. As to the immediate question of immigration, he reported that a treaty of reciprocal exclusion was impossible and cautioned Roosevelt not to attempt such an arrangement because the effect would be to offer a gratuitous insult to a proud people.[51] No jingo, Taft deplored rampant emotionalism as a substitute for thought and had done the best that he could to soothe Japanese feelings. He indicated his conviction that the Japanese government was most anxious to avoid war with the United

49. Ibid.
50. W. H. Taft to Theodore Roosevelt, Oct. 18, 1907, Roosevelt MSS.
51. Ibid. The author was unable to locate a single letter or memorandum in which President Roosevelt indicated his feelings about Taft's report on the immigration issue. However, it is reasonable to infer that this report strengthened the president in the moderate policy that he was already following on the immigration question.

States, for the Japanese were in no financial condition to undertake such a project.

Taft related that Hayashi had told him, speaking as an individual rather than as foreign minister, that many in the government wished to annex Korea, but financial limitations plus the opposition of influential figures such as Marquis Ito made such action impossible. Taft observed mildly that the Japanese were too preoccupied with Korea and its manifold problems to go beyond the present lines of policy.

The concluding portion of Taft's remarks dealt with Japan's interest in China.[52] In view of the United States policy of the Open Door, which meant the upholding of China's administrative and territorial integrity so as to assure equal opportunity for all countries including the United States to trade with China, Taft's remarks seem surprisingly naive. He saw no connection between Japan's stranglehold over Korea and its possible effects on China proper. Further, in discussing the question of war with the United States, he observed blandly of Japan: "Their attention is centered on China; their army has been increased by one division, not to fight with us, but because of China. They are determined to secure a predominance in China affairs and to obtain every commercial concession possible and believe it essential to retain their armament to meet contingencies." [53]

None of these startling developments seemed to disturb Taft's equanimity. During 1907, as they contemplated the possibility of war with Japan, American officials were gravely concerned over the vulnerability of the Philippines to attack.[54] In August of that year, the general board of the Navy reminded President Roosevelt that Japan would make the

52. W. H. Taft to Theodore Roosevelt, Oct. 18, 1907, *ibid.*
53. *Ibid.*
54. Braisted, "The Philippine Naval Base Problem, 1898–1909," 33. Renewed disturbances in California and in Japan during the summer of 1907 led President Roosevelt and his military advisors to re-examine their strategic plans for the entire Pacific area. For an expert analysis of the problems facing the Roosevelt administration and the actions taken, see William R. Braisted, "The United States Navy's Dilemma in the Pacific, 1906–1909," *Pacific Historical Review*, XXVI (Aug., 1957), 235–244.

conquest of the Philippines her principal objective, because their capture would provide Japan with a needed and valuable pawn in any subsequent peace negotiations.[55] Deeply worried, the president informed Taft on August 21, 1907, that he thought the Philippines should be given their independence as quickly as possible. He had reached this conclusion, Roosevelt explained, because the American people had refused to provide fortifications or a navy adequate for their protection. As matters stood, the Philippines formed "our heel of Achilles," and, therefore, a statement of the American determination to grant them independence in the near future "would remove a temptation from Japan's way." [56]

In marked contrast, Taft remained confident that Congress would provide the necessary funds for an adequate fortification of Manila and Subic Bays and successfully persuaded Roosevelt not to take any drastic steps toward the granting of independence to the Philippines. Moreover, after a successful visit to Japan in the fall of 1907, he viewed an attack by the Japanese upon the Philippines as a remote possibility.[57] The problems with Japan which had appeared so perplexing seemed capable of friendly solution.[58] In part, Taft's lack of insight about Japan's rise to the position of a great power may be attributed to his lack of historical perspective. Trained in the law, he was always the painstaking lawyer, tackling each problem in vacuo. This was his great strength—and his tragic weakness.

55. Braisted, "The Philippine Naval Base Problem, 1898–1909," 33. Braisted brings out in masterly fashion the conflicts within the Roosevelt administration on this question and the manner in which it was finally resolved.

56. Theodore Roosevelt to W. H. Taft, Aug. 21, 1907, Taft MSS.

57. W. H. Taft to Theodore Roosevelt, July 26, 1907, and Aug. 31, 1907, Roosevelt MSS; Theodore Roosevelt to W. H. Taft, Sept. 5, 1907, Roosevelt, Letters, V, 784; W. H. Taft to Theodore Roosevelt, Oct. 18, 1907, Roosevelt MSS.

58. On October 25, 1907, less than a month after Secretary Taft's second visit to Japan, Viscount Aoki, the Japanese ambassador to the United States, approached President Roosevelt with a proposal for a common declaration of friendly intention and cooperation. From their luncheon conversation on this proposal grew the Root-Takahira executive agreement of November 30, 1908, which supplemented the Taft-Katsura "agreed memorandum." Jessup, Root, II, 34–35.

CHAPTER VII

William Howard Taft's Vision of China: Origins of a Presidential Policy

BETWEEN 1900 AND 1912, the United States was confronted with many problems in determining Far Eastern policy, one of the most crucial and perplexing being relations with China. President Roosevelt's basic idea in Asia was to employ American power in such ways as would give the United States a key position there. In the power complex of the Far East, the president viewed China as a sleeping giant whose influence was negligible. He felt only contempt for the Chinese, a "backward people" by his standards, deficient in the qualities that signified civilization to him, lacking the fighting spirit that he admired so strongly in the Japanese. However, to prevent dislocations of power, Roosevelt accepted the prevailing fiction of China's independence and territorial and administrative integrity.[1] Yet in his handling of specific issues that arose between the United States and China, the president engaged in a senseless bullying of the feeble Manchu regime, and followed a policy that was scarcely distinguishable from the gunboat diplomacy of some of his predecessors.[2]

1. Beale, *Theodore Roosevelt and the Rise of America to World Power*, 181; John Morton Blum, *The Republican Roosevelt* (Cambridge, 1954), 134.
2. The story of the American China Company and the president's handling of its relations with China, and the manner in which he dealt with China's boycott of American goods, which was organized in 1905, throw a revealing light on the essen-

Although a trusted and valued member of the Roosevelt administration, William Howard Taft was not in complete sympathy with its Asian outlook. When he became president in 1909, Taft altered prevailing China policy by returning more definitely to the principles of the Open Door policy.[3] He believed that the United States should take its rightful place as a major power in the commercial and financial world and stressed the importance of the employment of the dollar abroad to promote national policies. Taft brought to the presidency a richer and more varied background of direct contact and personal experience with the Far East than any of his predecessors, or than any secretary of state. In the years 1900 through 1904, he had served first as president of the Second Philippine Commission and then as civil governor of the Philippines. Subsequently, as secretary of war from 1904 until early 1909, he had made two visits to Japan and to China and had traveled by train from Vladivostok down through Manchuria to Port Arthur and hence by the trans-Siberian railway to Moscow and Saint Petersburg. The origin of the Taftian Dollar Diplomacy policies toward China, with their different concept of the Open Door, can be traced in part to the years from 1900 through 1908 in which William Howard Taft acquired experience in foreign affairs and formulated opinions about them.

Taft's first recorded interest in China dates to the Boxer Rebellion, and was concerned with the Chinese treatment of foreign nations.[4] On July 9, 1900, he wrote to his wife: "The

tial character of Roosevelt's imperialism in China. Beale, *Theodore Roosevelt and the Rise of America to World Power*, 199–252.

3. William Howard Taft's change of pace disturbed Theodore Roosevelt, who wrote him as follows in 1910: "The 'open door' policy in China was an excellent thing, and will I hope be a good thing in the future, so far as it can be maintained by general diplomatic agreement; but as has been proved by the whole history of Manchuria, alike under Russia and under Japan, the 'open door' policy, as a matter of fact completely disappears as soon as a powerful nation determines to disregard it, and is willing to run the risk of war rather than forego its intention." Theodore Roosevelt to William Howard Taft, Dec. 22, 1910, Philander C. Knox Papers (Division of Manuscripts, Library of Congress). The entire letter is revealing.

4. In June, 1900, the Boxers cut the railroad line between Tientsin and Peking, murdered the German minister and the secretary of the Japanese legation, and then besieged the foreigners in Peking. Under murderous attack, 920 foreigners and ap-

news from China . . . is horrible. The Democrats have just adopted a platform in which they denounce militarism and foreign entangling alliances but say nothing about the Philippines. I don't understand this unless they are afraid to define any policy about them. If so, it is a strange confession of weakness. The people will be in no humor to hear about militarism when our representatives in China are being murdered." [5]

He was convinced that the United States would have to participate in suppressing the condition of lawless violence that prevailed there, for it was inconceivable that the government could "avoid alliances, entangling or otherwise, which would be the result of a joint movement to establish order in that kingdom, with which we now have so important trade relations." [6] The legations at Peking were relieved on August 14, 1900, and Taft expressed confidence that the American people, despite the critical opposition of William Jennings Bryan, would approve the active role played by the United States government in this exciting episode. Taft believed that the "ultimate effect" of the uprising by the Boxer societies would be to alert the American people to the necessity of maintaining a regular army of "respectable size" to cope with such emergencies. He did not grasp the crucial point of the affair—that the Boxers represented the "first stirrings of Chinese nationalism." [7]

proximately 1,000 Chinese Christians sought and obtained refuge in the legation area. There they defended themselves as best they were able until relief arrived. In another part of the city, some Catholic priests and a large number of Chinese were also under fire in the besieged French cathedral. Between June 24 and July 24, 1900, a total of 221 foreigners, mostly missionaries and members of their families, were massacred in Peking by the artillery fire of the Boxers. An expeditionary force of over 19,000 men, organized by all of the major powers, finally crushed the uprising, entering Peking in August, 1900. Lawrence H. Battistini, *The United States and Asia* (New York, 1955), 57.

5. W. H. Taft to Helen H. Taft, July 9, 1900, Taft MSS.
6. W. H. Taft to Annie G. Roelker, July 10, 1900, *ibid.*
7. Tyler Dennett, *Americans in Eastern Asia: A Critical Study of the Policy of the United States with Reference to China, Japan and Korea in the 19th Century* (New York, 1922), 655; W. H. Taft to Charles P. Taft, Sept. 6, 1900, Taft Papers. The United States contributed 2,500 men to the expeditionary force that crushed the Boxer uprising. Battistini, *The United States and Asia,* 57; W. H. Taft to Helen H. Taft, July 19, 1900, Taft MSS; Van Alstyne, *American Diplomacy in Action,* 331.

Almost five years passed before Taft again expressed any opinion about China. On June 15, 1905, the secretary of war delivered the commencement address at Miami University of Ohio.[8] On that occasion he said:

> Ever since the Boxer war, when America was able to show her friendship for China and her disinterestedness and freedom from the land-grabbing spirit of some other nations, China has regarded the United States as her best friend. One of the great commercial prizes of the world is the trade with the four hundred million Chinese. Ought we to throw away the advantage which we have by reason of Chinese natural friendship for us and continue to enforce an unjustly severe law, and thus create in the Chinese mind a disposition to boycott American trade and to drive our merchants from Chinese shores, simply because we are afraid that we may for the time lose the approval of certain unreasonable and extreme popular leaders of California and other coast states.[9]

Although he upheld the exclusion of Chinese laborers, Taft condemned the "unreasonable demands" of the "deeply prejudiced" leaders and people of the West Coast. These outbursts of irrational hatred militated against a decent understanding between the two peoples and gave serious offense to the Chinese people, especially those elements, including the merchants and the students, which Taft desired to placate. The result of such emotionalism had been the retaliation by the Chinese in the form of a general boycott against American trade, and now it would be the function of diplomacy to strive for the lifting of the boycott. It was the duty of the members of the Congress and the executive to "insist on extending justice and courtesy to a people from whom we are deriving and are likely to derive such immense benefit in the way of international trade." [10] There was nothing in Taft's remarks which showed, however, that he saw

8. Address by William Howard Taft at the 81st Annual Commencement of Miami University of Ohio on June 15, 1905, Taft MSS.
9. *Ibid.*
10. *Ibid.*

any real connection between the maintenance of China's territorial integrity in the face of an expanding Japan, and the ability of the United States to procure the prize of Chinese trade.

Three months later, after the completion of an official mission in the Philippines, Taft, as secretary of war, was ordered on September 2, 1905, to attempt to end the boycott that the Chinese had imposed upon American business. This mission was not of great importance, but it did provide the setting for the further elaboration of his views on China.[11] On September 4, 1905, at Canton, China, at a banquet tendered him by the Chinese viceroy there, Taft delivered a speech defining American attitudes toward China. He stressed the following points: (1) that the United States "by her statesmen, her government, and her Congress had always set her face like steel" against the division of the Chinese empire; (2) that "the preservation of the Chinese Empire was basic" to the friendship of the two nations; (3) that the United States wished from China only "her friendship and her trade association"; and (4) that China in her attempts to modernize her economy and government would have the "sympathy" and encouragement of the United States.[12]

Taft's knowledge of China began to expand, and his views to become more explicit, during the course of a sojourn in Japan, China, and Russia as part of his world tour in 1907.

11. Beale, *Theodore Roosevelt and the Rise of America to World Power*, 234–237; W. H. Taft to Theodore Roosevelt, Sept. 4, 1905, Roosevelt MSS. A concise account of this rather informal diplomatic mission is in Beale.

12. Address by William Howard Taft at a banquet tendered by the Viceroy in Canton, China, on September 4, 1905. Contained in Taft MSS. It should be remembered that these remarks came less than two months after the agreed memorandum of July 27, 1905, between Secretary Taft and Count Taro Katsura of Japan—a memorandum which may have given considerable encouragement and impetus to future Japanese expansion in Korea and Manchuria. This agreement lacked the formality of a ratified treaty and was binding—if it was binding at all—only on the Theodore Roosevelt administration. In a brilliant analysis, Raymond A. Esthus argues effectively that the Taft-Katsura conversation and accompanying memorandum was not a "secret pact" or "agreement," but rather a frank exchange of views. See Raymond A. Esthus, "The Taft-Katsura Agreement—Reality or Myth?," *Journal of Modern History*, XXXI (March, 1959), 46–51.

While in Tokyo in September and October, 1907, he met Thomas F. Millard, Far Eastern representative of the *New York Herald.* Millard had strong convictions about the Japanese and their threat to the United States interests. Millard increased Taft's sympathy for China and in a memorandum submitted to Taft, at the latter's request, set forth a detailed account of the entire situation of American trade and interests in China.[13]

This memorandum, dated September 26, 1907, was exceedingly important, for its conclusions mirrored the outlook of American business interests in China and had a profound impact upon Taft's thinking. Millard developed the following major themes: (1) that American trade with China was second only to Great Britain and could assume and hold a commanding position if American goods were allowed "to enter China on equal terms with the commodities of other nations, and with a little encouragement" from the United States government; (2) that the key element restricting American enterprise in China was "the general doubt among Americans residing and doing business there, or contemplating any important undertakings, as to the policy of our government"; and (3) that Japan and Russia intended to retain Manchuria and this would be "the beginning of a process of dismemberment which will result in the subdivision of the Empire among foreign nations, among which the United States will not be included." [14]

What then did Millard want Taft to do? If Taft were disposed to say anything which might allay the growing fears of Americans in China, and reassure them as to the Far Eastern policy of their government, this would have a salutary effect: not only would Americans be reassured and national interest served, but other nations would know where the United

13. Charles Vevier, *The United States and China 1906–1913: A Study of Finance and Diplomacy* (New Brunswick, N.J., 1955), 58–59; Memorandum, Thomas F. Millard to W. H. Taft, Sept. 26, 1907, "American Trade and Interests in China," Taft MSS.
14. *Ibid.*

States stood. Even more important, China would "undoubt-edly take heart from such encouragement." [15]

The impact of Millard's personality and considered judg-ments soon had their effect upon William Howard Taft. Writ-ing to the president from Yokohama, Japan, on October 5, 1907, he commented: "The truth is that the Chinese are now very favorable to us. Indeed, they are growing more and more suspicious of the Japanese and the English and the French in their desire for exclusive concessions and they turn to us as the only country that is really unselfish in the matter of ob-taining territory and monopolies. I think it, therefore, worth-while to cultivate them and accept courtesies at their hands. . . ." [16]

After his work in Japan was completed, the secretary of war moved on to Shanghai. There was no official purpose that made that visit mandatory. On October 8, 1907, at the Astor Hotel, Taft publicly expressed his newly developed ideas about the importance of China in an address before the Amer-icans of Shanghai, under the auspices of the American Asso-ciation of China.[17] His major ideas may be summarized as follows: (1) that the government of the United States had "not deviated in the slightest way" in its basic attitude since the Open Door policy was announced in 1900; (2) that the China trade was sufficiently great "to require the government of the United States to take every legitimate means to protect it against diminution or injury by the political preference of any of its competitors"; (3) that there was no disharmony between the underlying premise of the Open Door and the develop-

15. *Ibid.* As an added point, Millard ended his report with a remark that may well have fallen upon the receptive ears of a man then actively a presidential aspirant: "I believe, also, that the American people will support a government which prosecutes such a policy."

16. W. H. Taft to Theodore Roosevelt, Oct. 5, 1907, Taft MSS.

17. W. H. Taft to Charles P. Taft, Aug. 18, 1907, *ibid.*; Philip C. Jessup, *Elihu Root* (New York, 1938), II, 26; Robert H. Murray, *Around the World with Taft: A Book of Travel, Description, History* (Detroit, 1909), 16–17; address by William Howard Taft at a dinner given by the Americans of Shanghai, under the auspices of the American Association of China, on October 8, 1907, Roosevelt Papers; Helen Taft, *Recollec-tions*, 314.

ment and modernization of China; (4) that the oft-repeated statement "China for the Chinese," considered as an expression of nationalism, offered no obstacle to improved relations with the United States, for all the expression meant was that China "should devote her energies to the development of her immense resources, to the elevation of her industrious people, and to the enlargement of her trade and to the administrative reform of the Empire"; (5) that the removal of frictions in the administration of laws restricting Chinese entrance into the United States had improved relations between the two countries; and (6) that the improvement of American justice, as symbolized by the Circuit Court of China, would improve relations between the two countries in the future.[18]

Secretary Taft's speech elicited an enthusiastic response from the American colony at Shanghai, whose members were aware of the strong possibility that the secretary of war might well succeed Theodore Roosevelt in the presidency. The one-day stop at Shanghai, with its "unexpected courtesies," also left an imprint on the secretary.[19] In a letter to President Roosevelt, dated October 10, 1907, he depicted in glowing terms the vast improvement in Chinese-American relations:

> The waiver of the Chinese indemnity, the establishment of the United States Circuit Court and the amelioration of the administration of the immigration laws have created a revulsion of feeling so that there never was a time when the Chinese were more friendly than today, and this friendliness has another cause in the suspicion and fear that they entertain toward Japan and Russia and possibly England. They know that we do not wish to take any of their territory and that we don't ask any exclusive privileges.[20]

18. Address by William Howard Taft at a dinner given by the Americans of Shanghai, under the auspices of the American Association of China, on October 8, 1907, Roosevelt Papers. The secretary's remarks here were those of a man more concerned with appearances than with realities.

19. Vevier, *The United States and China 1906–1913*, 59; Helen Taft, *Recollections*, 313–314; W. H. Taft to Theodore Roosevelt, Oct. 10, 1907, Roosevelt MSS.

20. W. H. Taft to Theodore Roosevelt, Oct. 10, 1907, Roosevelt MSS. Taft enclosed a copy of the Shanghai speech with this letter, expressing confidence that it "reflects your views."

Although the Shanghai address was not an official declaration of United States policy, the effects of this utterance, coming from so highly placed an official of the Roosevelt administration, were far-flung. In particular, it gave encouragement to Willard Straight, then American consul-general at Mukden. Ambitious and devoted to the interests of the United States, Straight worked untiringly to introduce American goods and capital into Manchuria and was anxious to direct the attention of his government to the importance of China. Straight's idea was that Chinese officials in Manchuria were receptive to investments in the banks, railroads, and mines there. If American financiers were to appreciate the immense economic possibilities of Manchuria and do something about them, the position of the United States would be strengthened and the way paved for "an exclusive American interest north of the Great Wall." Above and beyond this, Straight viewed Manchuria "as a starting point," from which "the United States might extend its influence and activity to other portions of the Empire." [21]

Upon learning that Taft was on the way to Europe by way of Vladivostok and the trans-Siberian railroad, Straight saw his supreme opportunity to impress his views about Manchuria upon a highly placed official of the Roosevelt administration. An exchange of correspondence with Taft paved the way for a meeting in Vladivostok.[22]

On November 18, 1907, Straight arrived in Vladivostok and had a long conversation with Taft. The secretary said that Japan did not wish to fight the United States at that time, and stated frankly that he had them "sized up." Taft attributed much of the Japanese secrecy to an effort to conceal their weaknesses. He felt that the Japanese were "good bluffers."

21. Charles Vevier, The United States and China 1906–1913, 59–60, and "The Open Door: An Idea in Action, 1906–1913," Pacific Historical Review, XXIV (Feb., 1955), 51–52.
22. Vevier, The United States and China 1906–1913, 61; Herbert Croly, Willard Straight (New York, 1924), 249; Willard Straight to W. H. Taft, Sept. 15, 1907; W. H. Taft to Willard Straight, Oct. 10, 1907; Willard Straight to W. H. Taft, Oct. 29, 1907; and W. H. Taft to Arthur W. Fergusson, Oct. 30, 1907, Taft MSS.

Commenting on his warm reception at Shanghai, Taft felt strongly that China was "turning to us as the one disinterested friend." For his part, the secretary hoped that we might aid China in some concrete way. Straight then leaped to the opportunity. He assured Taft that the United States could take concrete action now, that "that the fruit is ripe and is ours to pluck." [23] According to Straight, Taft seemed to agree with this estimate, but the matter was not pursued further at that time.

On the following day, during the train trip from Vladivostok to Harbin, Straight and Taft talked about Manchuria. Taft was pleased to hear of the favorable reception accorded his Shanghai speech in Manchuria, and asked many questions about present conditions. He repeated many remarks of the day before and, according to Straight, "had a pretty thorough grasp of Chinese affairs." [24] When Straight suggested a loan scheme for Manchuria the idea appealed to Taft. However, the secretary was not optimistic about the chances of obtaining funds at that time, nor sanguine of the Roosevelt administration's success in interesting financiers to invest money there. Taft then listened to the reading of a memorandum on Manchuria by a Captain Reeves without any comment, asking only the length of time required to acquire a knowledge of the Chinese language.

On November 20, 1907, Straight presented his own memorandum to Taft.[25] It was a blistering indictment of Japan's conduct in Manchuria. Japanese activities there were a menace to Chinese sovereignty and the Open Door. The fate of Korea had been a warning to China, and Japan's recent pacts with Russia and France had only made the danger more clear. Now, in desperation, the Chinese empire was seeking financial aid that would carry with it a strong measure of dip-

23. Croly, *Willard Straight*, 250; Willard Straight Diary, Nov. 18, 1907, Straight MSS.
24. *Ibid.*
25. *Ibid.* Memorandum, Willard Straight to W. H. Taft, n.d., "Manchurian Affairs," National Archives Record Group 59: General Records of the Department of State, Numerical File, 1906–10, 2413/97–99.

lomatic support to offset Japan. Specifically, China desired "by attracting foreign capital, to create a community of interests in Manchuria." Moreover, other nations looked to the United States for action in Manchuria. The position of the United States, as the leading exponent of the Open Door policy, was "a peculiarly happy one," for there was no suspicion of "ulterior political motives." Any "concrete expression of our professed interest would be appreciated," Straight asserted, and if it were given to China by associating the United States with the leaders of the progressive movement there, "our trade with this Empire and our influence on the Pacific should be vastly augmented." [26]

What form should this "concrete expression" of interest assume? Willard Straight recommended a loan to China by Anglo-American bankers or an international loan that included France as well as Great Britain and the United States.[27] In any arrangement, he stressed, American funds would play a part. Taft, however, was not enthusiastic for international loans for China. Undaunted, Straight suggested using the remitted funds from the American share of the indemnity levied on China as a result of the Boxer Rebellion as security for a Manchurian loan. After listening to Straight's exposition of Manchuria's financial requirements, the secretary observed that "the first move toward securing an American loan with the indemnity as a security must come from China." [28]

Taft stated that the information Straight had given him was valuable. Straight's impression was that if Taft became president of the United States "he would take up the Imperial line." [29] In a letter to Maurice Casenave, written after his return to Mukden, Straight stated:

26. *Ibid.*
27. *Ibid.*
28. *Ibid.* Early in 1907, it became quite clear that the American share of the indemnity levied on China as a consequence of the Boxer Rebellion was excessive. Therefore, the United States government, in June, 1907, decided to remit all funds in excess of approximately $11,500,000. Vevier, *The United States and China 1906–1913*, 62; Willard Straight Diary, Nov. 20, 1907, Straight MSS.
29. *Ibid.*

. . . the President and the Secretary of State will be inclined, if they accept the advice which I think Mr. Taft will give, to regard Manchuria as a fair field and not as one that must be approached either with the acquiescence, or with special regard for the sensibilition [sic], of the Japanese.

The opportunity of meeting and talking with Mr. Taft was most fortunate. He was in a very receptive frame of mind and, I think, is unusually well informed about the entire Eastern situation. I was surpised at the amount of information he possessed.[30]

However, Straight admitted that when he touched on the subject of American participation in an international loan to China, he received "little encouragement"; nevertheless, Straight became more convinced that Taft had "made up his mind that we were in this game to stay." [31]

The next country on the secretary's itinerary was Russia. On December 3, 1907, Taft reached Saint Petersburg. The same afternoon at 2:00 P.M., he had a long interview with the new minister for foreign affairs of Imperial Russia, Alexander Izvolski.[32] According to the secretary, Izvolski asked bluntly how the United States liked the state of affairs in the Far East now that "you helped Japan to whip us?" Taft stoutly denied that the United States had helped Japan to defeat Russia. This did not mollify Izvolski, who countered by stating that the sympathy of the American people was "all with Japan," and indicated that that was what he had meant by his previous remarks.[33] Izvolski saw the significance of the Russo-Japanese War in the decline of Russian influence in the Far East and in the consequent decline of Russian ability

30. Willard Straight to Maurice Casenave, Dec. 4, 1907, Straight MSS.

31. *Ibid.* and Willard Straight to Captain Reeves, Dec. 4, 1907.

32. Montgomery Schuyler to Elihu Root, Dec. 7, 1907, Taft MSS; a diligent search of the Taft Papers and other source materials failed to reveal any information—in the form of a letter, document, or report written at the time—indicating what was said during this interview. This represented a departure for Taft from his usual practice of preparing careful memoranda of all official business. But at a much later date, Taft did allude to the subjects discussed during the interview and his memory of them seemed quite precise.

33. Address by William Howard Taft before the Buffalo Club of Buffalo, New York, on Jan. 4, 1917, Taft MSS.

to help in the maintenance of the Open Door, and expressed his personal view that the Open Door was now likely to close. Unfortunately, Taft did not indicate how he responded to Izvolski's commentary.

However, in a short but remarkable speech delivered before the American colony in Saint Petersburg on the evening of December 4, 1907, Taft showed the impact of his travels through Russia. He pointed out that in times past "a very great business" had flourished between the United States and Russia and hoped that the future would bring an increase in this trade relationship. Dating the traditional friendship between the two countries from the United States Civil War, he expressed the devout hope that this friendship would "increase and become stronger." Although conceding that the two countries were widely divergent in their histories and in their cultural and national characteristics, he felt that there were certain "parallels in their career that ought to produce a sympathetic feeling between them." The immense extent of the two countries, and the difficulties of administration rising therefrom, were important points in common. After calling attention to the fact that the United States "starting from the Middle West was reaching with iron rails to the Pacific Ocean," he paralleled the expansion of Russia in the previous decade to the American development.[34] This he saw in the tremendous expansion from Moscow to Vladivostok. From his own trip, Taft was convinced that there were vast stretches of Siberia from the Pacific to the Ural mountains which urgently needed industrious men to make them flourish. In a striking comparison with the United States he noted, "the country is like the Dakotas or Nebraska and will support a population of millions. The opportunities for development, therefore, of Russia toward the Pacific on the one hand are quite like the actual development in the United States towards the Pacific on the other." [35]

34. Speech by William Howard Taft at a banquet given him by the American colony in St. Petersburg, Russia, on Dec. 4, 1907, Taft MSS.
35. *Ibid.*

Taft rhapsodized upon the vistas of potential Siberian development, for there was a tremendous expanse of territory, almost isolated from Europe, containing "large cities with unpronounceable names, flourishing villages, a thoroughly healthy, strong, warm blooded and contented people." He was impressed by the flow of immigrants to Siberia to take up the new land offered gratuitously to them by the government. He looked forward to a growth in Siberia that would "make that one of the most prosperous and healthily populated parts of the globe" and which would "bring Russian and American civilization closer and closer together." Taft avowed a strong feeling of friendship for Russia because his father, Alphonso Taft, had been United States minister to Saint Petersburg for two years during the reign of Czar Alexander III. This feeling had been heightened by the "boundless hospitality" that he had received on this current visit.[36]

On Wednesday morning, December 5, 1907, Secretary Taft had an audience with his Imperial Majesty, Czar Nicholas II.[37] The interview covered a wide range of topics. Taft spoke first of having dined at the military club in Vladivostok where he had been shown the czar's signature made at the time the czar had gone there to drive the first spike in the trans-Siberian railroad. As Taft recalled it, that reference "seemed to awaken a pleasant recollection" on the part of the czar. The two men then discussed the trans-Siberian railway, its cost, and the time consumed in its building. Taft expressed his personal interest in the railway "as a great work for the benefit of mankind quite like that which the United States was carrying on at the Panama Canal." The secretary felt that the railway was a work which he "was afraid would not for a long time be profitable," but expressed certainty that good effects

36. Ibid.
37. Montgomery Schuyler to Elihu Root, Dec. 7, 1907, Taft Papers. In an official memorandum dictated by Taft apparently for his own use, the secretary appears to have been powerfully impressed by the magnificence of the Russian court. He described in great detail the splendor of the scene, replete with accounts of the hall where they dined after their interview, and furnished an elaborate description of the entire setting. Memorandum dictated by William Howard Taft of conference between Czar Nicholas II and William Howard Taft, n.d., Taft MSS.

other than "mere profit" would justify the work.[38] Expressing his pleasure at seeing the richness of the Siberian country, Taft recalled that Secretary of State William Seward had endured great criticism for having purchased Alaska from the czar's grandfather for $7,000,000. Such criticism had been based upon the alleged valuelessness of that cold, bleak territory, but Seward's faith had been justified since Alaska had returned to the United States manyfold the original price. The czar, for his part, stated that the criticism was not restricted to the United States; there were many Russian people who took sharp issue with the government for having sold Alaska.

Then followed a desultory discussion about the army. The czar was curious about the scope of Taft's official duties as secretary of war. Taft was happy to furnish an explanation and this gave him the opportunity to say that his hurried trip through Russia was dictated by the accumulation of business in Washington that called for his immediate attention. The czar reacted sympathetically and then furnished an insight in Russian thinking which may have sounded strange to a civilian secretary of war: "Yes, but after all, of course, you love the army as I do." [39]

The remainder of the secretary's world tour was without special incident, for he did not pay official calls upon the

---

38. *Ibid.*
39. *Ibid.* However, the two men found common ground in their experiences with religious difficulties and discussed them at some length. Taft related details of his previous visit to Rome to settle with the Pope the Friar Lands question and other matters relative to the Philippines. The czar then recounted some of his troubles with the Pope over Poland "where they had Polish Bishops who insisted on getting into politics." The czar then discussed the matter of the "Douma," and the problem of how far "uneducated people were able to take part in the government." This gave Taft the opportunity to make some comparisons between the Russian Duma and the Philippine Assembly, which the secretary had just opened. The czar seemed very much interested in the Philippine experience, and when Taft spoke of the limitation on the electorate which the United States had imposed, the czar remarked that the Philippine electorate was more narrow than accorded by the Russians. For that reason the czar felt that the Philippine plan was better. Apparently Taft did not feel constrained to point out that the czar was comparing the basis of representation in a colonial possession with that of a sovereign nation proper. Memorandum dictated by William Howard Taft of his conference with Czar Nicholas II, n.d., Taft MSS.

heads of state in France, Germany, and Great Britain, in accordance with instructions from President Roosevelt. On December 7, 1907, Taft boarded the S.S. *President Grant* at Hamburg, Germany, and made the long voyage home to the United States.[40]

In the spring of 1908, Taft made a number of speeches on the Far East. By this time he had become an ardent enthusiast for the possibilities of trade and commerce with the nations of the Far East, especially China. In general, he favored the maintenance of peace, enforced by a strong United States navy, the Open Door in China, and the minimizing of unnecessary frictions by discouraging irresponsible war talk and emotional appeals to racial prejudice.[41] Judging from his speeches, the secretary was a man with a mission—the promotion of American commerce and trade in China.

Taft propounded the new doctrine most cogently in an address before the board of trade at Lowell, Massachusetts, on February 19, 1908.[42] After describing the rise of the United States as a colonial power, Taft traced the steps by which the United States had put itself in a position where it was "entitled to be consulted with respect to the foreign relations toward that great Empire of China with her 400 teeming millions." There were two main reasons, he explained, for the United States interest in China. First, because the United States was "generally interested in the improvement and civ-

40. W. H. Taft to Theodore Roosevelt, Nov. 17, 1907; W. H. Taft to Charlemagne Tower, Nov. 20, 1907, *ibid.*; Pringle, *Taft*, I, 333.
41. Address by W. H. Taft before the Lowell Board of Trade, Lowell, Mass., Feb. 19, 1908; address by W. H. Taft before the Chamber of Commerce, Trenton, N.J., March 23, 1908; address by W. H. Taft at the Real Estate Exchange banquet, Boston, Mass., March 31, 1908; address by W. H. Taft before the Board of Trade, Columbus, Ohio, April 2, 1908; address by W. H. Taft before the Commercial Club, Chicago, Ill., on April 4, 1908, Taft MSS.
42. Address by W. H. Taft before the Lowell Board of Trade, Lowell, Mass., Feb. 19, 1908, Taft MSS. Whenever the secretary had to deliver a series of speeches on the same broad topic, he prepared with great care a master address which expressed his ideas most clearly and effectively. The speeches that followed were in essence variants from the master model. The master address on the Far East was presented before the Lowell, Massachusetts, Board of Trade on February 19, 1908. Taft's procedure in preparing public addresses was admirably suited for a period that lacked such effective media of mass communications as movies, radio, and television.

ilization of the world anywhere." Second, because the United States wanted to extend her trade "legitimately in every direction." [43] Here, the influence of Thomas Millard was evident, for Taft incorporated the contents of his memorandum almost verbatim in the speech.

Turning then to John Hay's policy of the Open Door, the secretary extolled it as "a doctrine in which we have the utmost interest as a trading nation" and one we were "bound to maintain." [44] After explaining in detail the transition that China was making to become a modern country, Taft set forth the direction of recommended United States policy. Specifically, he was determined to refute the prevalent idea that trade with a so-called backward nation was impossible, since the lower living standards of such nations would offer a source of unfair competition to American business and labor. He was quite explicit:

> The more civilized they become the more active their industries, the wealthier they become, and the better market they will become for us. Our best markets the world over are in those countries in which there is the greatest prosperity and the greatest advance, and therefore, even though it may change somewhat the character of the demand in China, should China progress industrially, you can be sure that with the six or eight hundred millions to which they may increase, the wealth of that country will be showered upon us in taking from us those things which they cannot produce.[45]

Taft was confident of ultimate United States trade supremacy and moral influence in China, because the lack of any American territorial ambitions in China would impress the Chinese people, and because the progressive Chinese would have an increased role in that nation's future development. The people were represented by and under the guidance of Chinese graduates of American universities who had forged

43. Address by W. H. Taft before the Lowell Board of Trade, Lowell, Mass., Feb. 19, 1908, Taft MSS.
44. *Ibid.*
45. *Ibid.*

to the front in the politics of China. They could be counted upon to pursue "a progressive—not a radical—but a progressively conservative policy with that great Empire." [46] Despite the apparent rosiness of China's future position, Taft was aware that other nations soon might challenge the principles of the Open Door policy:

> All nations came in and agreed that it was a good doctrine. Whether there are any nations who would be willing to depart from that now or not I cannot say; but conditions change, nations are subject to temptations as are individuals, and the question which we have to determine is, whether we shall maintain ourselves in such a condition that we may enforce a fair and impartial doctrine as that in conjunction with other nations, it may be, in order to preserve our foreign trade. Diplomacy accomplishes much, but a diplomat who represents a nation that does not hesitate to say what it believes to be right, and then has back of it the means of defending that right is a diplomat in a position of advantage.[47]

The speech at Lowell thus presented a concept of positive diplomacy. In the subsequent months, Taft was to be engaged with the tasks inherent in winning a presidential nomination and then with the greater problems of winning a presidential election. In November, 1908, William Howard Taft was elected to the office of the presidency of the United States. Willard Straight had once remarked that if ever Taft succeeded "in entering the White House as Master thereof," one could anticipate "great things" in the future for Manchuria.[48] It was to prove a true prophecy. The time was now drawing near to translate concept into action.

46. *Ibid.*
47. *Ibid.*
48. Willard Straight to Captain Reeves, Dec. 4, 1907, Straight MSS.

CHAPTER VIII

The Apprenticeship in Foreign Affairs: Summary and Conclusions

INTERPOSED BETWEEN two presidential giants in American politics, William Howard Taft has been treated most unkindly by history. Overshadowed by a colorful, magnetic predecessor in Theodore Roosevelt and by an inspiring, vibrant successor in Woodrow Wilson, Taft's entire career has suffered from undue neglect. In the best of circumstances, he was certainly no colorful figure; it is understandable, therefore, that his life work was not likely to attract serious and sustained attention from historians. Moreover, historians in their predilections have a greater affinity for liberal personalities, whereas Taft, of course, was pre-eminently a conservative. But all of history is a continuing process and it may well be that Taft was in some important aspects more clearly a mirror of his times than either Roosevelt or Wilson.

Certainly no man ever served his country more faithfully over a sustained period of time. No man ever gave more of himself in public service than Taft, who once wrote to his family while in Cuba on a diplomatic mission for Theodore Roosevelt: "If only I was not under such a strain this would be a most interesting place to visit. . . . If mental worry kept me down I should have lost 50 pounds in this crisis." [1] In

1. W. H. Taft to Helen H. Taft, Sept. 29, 1906; W. H. Taft to Charles P. Taft, Oct. 4, 1906, Taft MSS.

such important public capacities as judge of the Superior Court of Ohio, solicitor general of the United States, United States circuit judge for the Sixth Judicial Circuit, president of the Second Philippine Commission, civil governor of the Philippines, secretary of war, president of the United States, professor of law at Yale University and chief justice of the United States Supreme Court, Taft's half-century of public service is most reminiscent of the long and purposeful career of John Quincy Adams.

Before turning to the central issues raised by this study and the conclusions that flow therefrom, it is mandatory to speak briefly of the man himself, of the influence exercised by his family, and of the impact of the times that produced him. William Howard Taft and his gargantuan frame—after 1900 he weighed at his most slender 250 pounds—was the delight of all enterprising cartoonists. Nor did the man, renowned for his high good humor, do anything to discourage their prolific efforts. Taft's geniality, ready smile, and bubbling laughter presented an outward picture of Falstaffian affability. But all this was on the surface. The outgoing appearance was in reality a mask which concealed a complex, deeply sensitive, and inwardly troubled man, beset by profound doubts and uncertainties. Taft's basic dilemma dating from the year 1900 stemmed from two divergent ambitions: above all else, he desired a judicial career with its capstone a place on the United States Supreme Court—a post marvelously suited to his innate capacities and inherent temperament. Yet the overwhelming compulsion of events and circumstances drove him inexorably to a public career deeply intertwined in the public questions of the day.

Of vital importance in understanding Taft is the place that he occupied in relation to his own family. His father, Alphonso Taft, secretary of war and attorney-general in the cabinet of President Ulysses Simpson Grant, was a highly successful lawyer who had rounded out his career with service in the diplomatic corps. A self-made man, his entire career was substantial but undistinguished. Like so many men of all periods, Alphonso Taft was determined to lay a solid foundation for his children, and it was notable that Taft, the elder, seemed to have transferred many of his own unfulfilled ambitions to his son, William Howard. His mother, Louise Taft, was a striking woman of stout intellectual fiber who wielded an enormous influence over William Howard throughout a large part of his career. Mrs. Alphonso Taft seemed to understand her son better than anyone else and she counseled and influenced the judicial career which she keenly felt to be best suited to his qualities of mind and peculiarities of temperament. William Howard was the third of five boys, the sons of Alphonso Taft, who had married twice. William Howard, Henry Waters, Horace Dutton, and their sister, Fannie Louise, were born of the second union, while Charles Phelps and Peter Rossen were born of Alphonso Taft's first marriage to Fanny Phelps.

William Howard Taft seems definitely to have been the favorite child of the family, and this seeming favoritism shown to the child of destiny did not arouse any animosity on the part of his brothers. There appeared to have been a kind of general deference to William Howard, and all efforts were bent to the promotion of his career. Taft's brothers, each in his own way, contributed powerfully to the advancement of his fortunes. All of the Taft brothers were destined for careers in the professions and all achieved what is commonly regarded as the fruit of success.

The impact of the times that produced him was also significant.

William Howard's closest fraternal relationship was with his younger brother, Horace. Horace, a schoolmaster, maintained an intimate personal correspondence with his older brother and sought to influence William Howard generally in a more liberal direction. Horace, a Mugwump, was, in effect, the keeper of his brother's conscience. Experiencing a vicarious satisfaction in the progression of William Howard's public career, Horace, removed from the hurly-burly of public life, never lost touch with his more famous brother. William, for his part, listened to his brother's counsel, and was in part shaped by it. Remote from the rapacity of the Gilded Age and alienated by it, Horace entertained views that were somewhat heretical for a Republican. These he imparted to his older brother and they were of some influence in shaping his thinking. Horace's estimate of the abilities of William Howard Taft was accurate and incisive: "My brother was a hard worker, had a clear, strong mind, and, though certainly not brilliant, was outstanding in ability." [2]

To underscore his brother's enormous vitality, Horace has pointed out that in the Philippines "he did an amount of work that would have crushed an ordinary man and that required a great deal of physical exertion." [3] William Howard Taft's innate generosity and genuine concern for the welfare of those who were close to him was put down by Horace as one of his most endearing attributes. And the Taftian sense of humor was legendary. Here was a man who could and would tell a joke which made himself the butt, and there was much of the humane and of the compassionate in his interpersonal relationships.

The impact of Taft's brothers, Charles Phelps and Henry Walters, was also important. It was Charles Phelps, a prominent lawyer and newspaper publisher in Cincinnati, who provided the necessary financing so that William Howard could assume various governmental posts. This was true for an age-old reason in American history—the inadequacy of governmental salaries and hence the utter impossibility of maintaining the required standard of living on such limited stipends. Although he exercised less influence intellectually than Horace, Charles Phelps's voice was that of a more orthodox conservative. The role of Henry Walters is more difficult to define. His main usefulness in relation to Taft's public life stemmed from a wide and apparently intimate acquaintance with the key public figures of the day. And Henry was most ambitious for his brother's preferment. Behind the scenes he

2. Taft, *Memories and Opinions*, 107.
3. *Ibid.*, 108.

played a most unostentatious but highly effective role in advancing his brother's career. Henry seemed to enjoy the role of the inobtrusive arranger of great events; he undertook representations with Secretary Root and even with President Roosevelt on behalf of William Howard when necessity arose. The point is that the combined services of all the Taft brothers presented a formidable team and a unique one devoted to the single purpose of advancing a political career. But it is also a tribute to Taft on the personal level that he was able to command such unselfish devotion and generosity.

William Howard's wife, Nellie, played a role of much greater importance than just the traditional, conventional wife of a public figure. She was genteel, charming, bright, and altogether consumed by one overpowering obsession. She, above all else, and more than anyone else in the family, sought for her husband the biggest prize of all, the presidency of the United States. Mrs. Taft, a loyal helpmate, accompanied her husband on many of his far-flung journeys, such as those to the Philippines and Panama. Taft loved her dearly and seemed to serve her in many interesting ways. Despite the eminence of her husband's various positions, and the demands they made upon his time, Mrs. Taft insisted and successfully upon the performance of some rather routine tasks. Thus it was that Taft undertook such prosaic correspondence as that related to answering social courtesies and renewing his wife's magazine subscriptions.

The impact of the times that produced him was also significant. What then were the moving forces of the period and where did Taft stand in relation to them? Born in Cincinnati, Ohio, on September 15, 1857, and growing to manhood and receiving his education in the post–Civil War period, it is not strange that he should have been shaped by the climate of those times. Although strongly Republican by birth and tradition, he rebelled briefly while in college against the sordid aspects of Republican rule. Thus, as a sophomore at Yale in 1876, he delivered an oration on the vitality of the Democratic party. Even then there was a judicial quality to the turn of his remarks, but the apparent motivation for this speech was Taft's revulsion against such men as James G. Blaine and Roscoe Conkling, whom Taft identified as spoils' politicians. And Taft's innate honesty compelled him to view with grave misgivings the resolution of the disputed election of 1876 when Hayes was awarded the presidency.

In the main, the period between 1865 and 1900, called the Gilded Age, was the period of rising American industrialism. The main forces of the period were those of a developing capitalism and the countervailing forces identified with the Populist and Progressive movements. There is little doubt that Taft accepted the basic premise of American capitalism, and when he offered any views at all they were in opposition to the liberal currents of the day. For example, starting in 1890, Taft established an essentially unpopular position with the labor movement by his frequent issuance of injunctions. For the Pullman strikers of 1894 his hostility was ferocious; he viewed the actions of labor with alarm, as did so many of his confreres in the conservative circles of Cincinnati. Taft expressed strong views in relation to Eugene V. Debs in the famous Pullman strike; he favored the use of federal troops to support the injunction and did not hesitate to say that he preferred a fight to the finish with labor rather than accede to any ephemeral settlement. All of this would seem to make Taft appear as thoroughly reactionary, yet such was not the case. As has so often been true in the past and as can be seen again today, it is impossible to catalog as either conservative or liberal the decisions of an honest judicial mind. Thus, in some instances, Taft supported the positions taken by the American labor movement, and in the most important decision that he ever rendered, the Addystone Pipe case of 1898, Taft reinvigorated the Sherman anti-trust law which had languished through deliberate nonenforcement by two administrations. He was by no means an apologist for trusts and combinations in restraint of trade. He always felt that there were limits to be set upon monopolistic tendencies, and he strongly disapproved of the expression of opinions by the courts that encouraged such tendencies.

There was also something of the aristocrat about Taft. While favoring the development of American business, he was less than sanguine of the role of businessmen as direct actors in political life. He had not been convinced that the ability of a man to prosper in business was any sure qualification for public offices. From his earliest period, Taft had been fundamentally prepared for a career of public service. Having been thoroughly trained by a family of prestige in Cincinnati, Taft always esteemed himself as one who owed public service. The concept of *noblesse oblige* was inherent in his character and is important to an understanding of the man. In a sense he belongs to that period of the lawyer statesmen which gave the nation such men as Elihu Root and Charles Evans Hughes. Perhaps Taft's concept of government may have put emphasis upon the idea of government for the people, rather than by the people. There was a strong touch of paternalism in his evolving convictions—this was compounded of eminent fairness, but firm control. In his love for order, tradition, form, and symmetry, Taft tended to look with favor upon the British who embodied these qualities in their highest manifestation. It would be most inaccurate to say that he was an Anglophile, per se; he considered himself a patriotic American, above all else, but it is notable that the jingoism of the 1890s met with his contemptuous disdain.

Taft's thinking on a wide range of public questions, although inclined to the conservative side, was always tempered by his judicial outlook. Here is another essential key to a correct understanding of the man. Given his extreme aversion to demagoguery in any form, it is perhaps understandable that Taft was not and never could have become a truly first-rate politician. Dominated by his powerful judicial consciousness of a high order, Taft never seemed at home in the murky waters of politics. His mind could not comprehend such casuistry as that entailed in distinguishing good trusts from bad trusts; nor could he espouse causes in which he had little faith in order to capture votes and then abandon them. There was a kind of bulldog tenacity and rugged, simple honesty to the man—to such an extent that his friends often gasped in despair while their emotional attachment to him increased.

Such were the elements that comprised Taft's political chemistry and which bore heavily upon his formative concepts of foreign policy. In the life of every public figure there is at least one major turning point. In Taft's life, such a climacteric, to use Churchill's word, took place because of the acquisition of the Philippine Islands, as a consequence of United States participation in the Spanish-American War. It was this circumstance that led to Taft's first assignment in the field of foreign affairs—president of the new Philippine Commission. As Taft's biographer, Pringle, has pointed out, Taft knew as much and as little about the Philippines as the average American. This was hardly strange, for the America of the turn of the century was one that had been almost exclusively concerned with the problems of building the new nation. Taft accepted the new responsibility of his Philippine assignment with extreme reluctance for many reasons; he was opposed by temperament and by principle to the annexation of the Philippines; he lacked detailed knowledge of the problems he would have to face; he dreaded his own uncertain future, in a position which had been a graveyard for public figures in the past; and finally, and perhaps most important, he had grave misgivings about abandoning a position on the circuit court which he enjoyed and which promised every expectation of ultimate accession to the Supreme Court of the United States.

It is significant that Taft rationalized his competence for the new position by arguing that the task urgently called for a good attorney since, as he saw it, the mission required the reshaping of the government. Thus, at the very beginning of his service in the field of foreign affairs, Taft's frame of reference was exceedingly narrow. Although he did not regard the task at hand as a simple one, he did not initially grasp the manifold complexities that it was to entail. Political, social, economic, and governmental matters associated with a strange people remote from the American experience were to pose problems very far removed from the normal duties of a circuit court judge in Cincinnati. Considering all of these factors, the fact that Taft did so well was a tremendous tribute to his latent ability.

And there can be no doubt that his abilities were enormous. After he became civil governor, Taft labored ceaselessly in solving the complex problems concerning colonial administration in the Philippines. Lord Curzon best characterized Taft's work when he said: "Taft was the first Saxon to love the Malay—and the Malay returned it." [4] During the period that William Howard Taft was in the Philippines from 1900 until late 1903 enormous improvements in the government and economy were carried out with energy and intelligence: his administration created a civil service system that was fair and worked; his administration established a court system with a simplified, understandable procedure, civil and criminal, and honest, fair-minded judges were appointed to the bench; under his administration, the first insular bureaus (health, agriculture, and forestry) commenced operations; his administration established an educational system, designed to provide every Filipino child with a free public education; under his administration, a postal savings bank was founded to encourage habits of industry and thrift; his administration passed a public land act which enabled and encouraged every Filipino to acquire a free homestead; his administration separated church and state in the Philippines and purchased the large agricultural estates of the Friar orders; his administration carried out an enormous amount of construction in public buildings, docks, harbors, and roads;

4. Cotton, *William Howard Taft*, 53–54.

and a native constabulary was organized over the sustained and vehement objections of the military which suppressed brigandage and lawlessness.[5]

The question arises: why was Taft chosen for this assignment? Initially, a man of proven integrity was urgently needed and it was mandatory that such an individual be politically eligible. The position itself, however, was not a major plum for anyone, and Elihu Root, secretary of war under President McKinley, and a major figure in the administration, may have unconsciously sensed this when he alluded to Taft's acceptance as a sacrifice. But Root was most anxious to attach this type of man to the administration and may well have felt that the Philippine mission would serve as a proving ground. The president was anxious to have the American experiment in the Philippines succeed and felt that in Taft he had a man who would sustain public confidence. This was so because Taft seemed to embody those qualities of devotion to duty, ability, unimpeachable integrity, and even more—a sense of mission without ambition for personal preferment and without the danger of exceeding instructions.

Taft had formed some ideas in embryo, ideas which represented his first serious thoughts upon the Philippines, during the course of his preparation for the voyage. In somewhat doctrinaire fashion, he placed his trust and hopes in the benefits that would accrue to the Filipinos through the granting of all the constitutional guarantees of individual liberty contained in the state and federal constitutions within the United States. However, from the very outset, he realized that the task at hand was far broader than the narrow limits of written charters. It is noteworthy that this outlook accurately reflected a basic American dogma of the period—that the United States constitutional system, which had evolved under its own peculiar origins, was capable of being applied to peoples with vastly different backgrounds and totally different customs and government.

5. Tongko, *The Government of the Republic of the Philippines*, 14; Williams, *The United States and the Philippines*, 121–131; Cotton, *William Howard Taft*, 54–55.

As Taft moved further from Cincinnati and the narrow gambit of his previous experience, his horizons broadened. Thus, a three-day stopover in the Hawaiian Islands convinced him native peoples were not necessarily identical with Americans, and that the successful application of a governmental system required patience and a conservative approach, if any lasting progress was to be achieved. By a conservative approach Taft meant not only the absence of a sharp break with the past, but also a step-by-step progression into the future. Reflecting his own personal bias, the concept of a conservative approach entailed also administrators who were immune from the temptations of courting favor with the native element, by making extensive concessions unwarranted by actual conditions.

On one essential point, Taft had become adamant even before actually arriving in the Philippines: re-election of President McKinley was essential to the success of the commission's efforts. This was true by his logic because the re-election of McKinley would convince all the Filipinos that the policy of maintaining the sovereignty of the United States in the Philippines would be permanent. The maintenance of United States sovereignty, in Taft's view, would engender greater native support for the commission. In contrast, the possible election of William Jennings Bryan would be an unmitigated disaster, because Bryan was committed to independence for the islands. Such a policy could only produce turmoil and anarchy, the preconditions for a subsequent annexation by the United States. Taft's parallel here was what happened in Hawaii, to wit, internal disorganization encouraged by the policies of the Cleveland administration followed by the subsequent annexaction to the United States, under the Republicans. Taft's formative thinking was shaped and reinforced by a chance meeting with William Jennings Bryan, shortly before he left the mainland. The Great Commoner had made a poor impression on Taft, by imputing to Taft views which he, Taft, did not hold, and by indulging in a display of what Taft felt to be demagoguery. The impression of Bryan that Taft carried away from this meeting persisted for a long period of time and there can be no question that the interview buttressed Taft's first conceptions of Philippine policy. From the outset, Taft was vigorously opposed to what he considered to be the United States army practice of treating the Filipinos as inferior people. In particular, he was genuinely distressed by reports that the army, because of the exigencies of the irregular war then being conducted against Filipino rebels, and due also to the apparently deep-seated prejudices of the army wives, was adopting a conscious policy of racial discrimination in the islands. Such a policy, in Taft's view, was sheer lunacy, because it effectively precluded the formation of an effective government for the islands. An effective government would perforce require native participation, a development hardly to be expected where natives were being treated as rank inferiors and unfit for the responsibilities they were to some day assume. Much of Taft's subsequent success in working with the Filipino leaders can be attributed to this very basic outlook. In many ways Taft was ideally suited to the arduous duties which lay ahead of him. He was as patient as he was large in frame. He was tolerant. He could be stubborn when stubbornness was a virtue. Above all else, he had a vast capacity for affection. Taft began almost immediately to grow fond of the Filipinos, who seemed by every conceivable standard to differ widely from himself. "His most important discovery—the one which may, in itself, have determined the success of his career as a colonial governor—was that the Filipinos were proud and sensitive and quick to resent any implication of being an inferior race." [6] Taft did not limit his personal association with the Filipinos to the relatively few and prosperous mestizos of Manila. Throughout his administration, he went on frequent journeys into the interior. He attended elaborate banquets given by local and provincial officials and faithfully ate all the courses. He went to their fiestas and danced with their

6. Pringle, *Taft*, I, 174.

wives—his vast bulk dominating the hall.[7] Still in some ways Taft's attitude toward his wards is reminiscent of the six-teenth-century Spaniards' treatment of Indians as irrespon-sible children and the later Western concept of Orientals as the "white man's burden." Taft thought of the Filipinos as children who needed direction and the guidance of whom was a sacred trust laid upon the United States for civilization. Moreover, it is important in considering the future success of American administration in the Philippines to point out that Taft had the complete cooperation of General MacArthur in striving for the elimination of attitudes of hostility on the part of the Americans toward the Filipinos.

A basic pillar in Taft's thought about the Philippines was the imperative need to substitute civilian government for military administration as soon as possible. The army, he firmly believed, was a necessary evil but not the agent to en-courage the establishment of a well-ordered civil govern-ment. To his mind, "government by shoulder-straps" was no substitute for ordered rule under civilians. Moreover, army rule was inherently distasteful to the Filipinos. The struggle for the replacement of military government by civilian gov-ernment was to bring Taft into a head-on clash with General MacArthur.

Taft's earlier and rather rosy preconceptions about the uni-versality of the American constitutional system were to un-dergo some profound alterations after he had spent a month in the Philippines. The basic and crucial issue, one that over-shadowed all others, was the independence question. To Taft, the idea that the Filipinos could govern themselves suc-cessfully at this stage of their evolution was ill-founded. In many respects, he found them to be "nothing but grown up children," and this conclusion convinced him that the Fili-pinos needed a prolonged and vigorous preparation in the art of government, one that would extend for at least half a cen-tury. Even the educated Filipinos, in Taft's view, had pro-

7. *Ibid.*, 180.

found limitations because of a complete absence of practical experience in the workings of a democratic society.

Despite Taft's misgivings about the capacity of the Filipinos for self-rule, he favored a pattern which gave representation to the natives in a popular assembly. Such an assembly was to be held in check, however, by a legislative council appointed by the governor and by a qualified veto power directly vested in the governor. That this design recapitulated the British colonial practice may have been more than mere coincidence, for Taft was a great admirer of the British and all their works and believed that both nations faced in some degree similar problems in their colonial possessions.[8]

The basic issue that had to be resolved in the Philippines was the nature of the government itself—in short, whether that government was to be civilian or military. The question, in turn, was complicated by the presence of a sharp divergence of personalities between a flamboyant general and a strong-willed judge. At first, it appeared that few complications would ensue from a relationship that augured well for an amicable resolution of all outstanding difficulties. But it was soon to become apparent that an ambitious general who had been, in effect, America's first pro-consul was not disposed to divest himself of such power and glory voluntarily. Lord Acton's dictum never had a more suitable application. MacArthur may well have been under the illusion that his adversary was little more than an affable, prosaic, civilian official dispatched to perform a political function. More than that, MacArthur seemed at first to feel that he might mollify the judge by making inconsequential concessions, throwing him a bone, so to speak, when occasion dictated and then having his own way the remainder of the time. It would have been easy for anyone to have underestimated Taft's character, but outward appearances are frequently deceiving. There was in Taft a hard core of granite, a kind of bulldog tenacity which made him a very formidable opponent. Moreover, all

8. W. H. Taft to Helen H. Taft, Aug. 12, 1902, Taft MSS.

available evidence suggests that Taft's influence in Washington, in particular with Secretary of War Elihu Root, was very great. An inestimable advantage enjoyed by Taft was his control of the purse strings, and the judge was soon to make effective use of that advantage.

Taft's basic disenchantment with MacArthur came as a consequence of what he viewed as the general's political ineptness, as well as what Taft saw as MacArthur's reluctance to accede to the civilian commission. The difference in outlook between the two men was profound. To the general, all of the Filipinos were unrelenting enemies of the American forces. Thus, the task he envisaged was one of conquering eight million "recalcitrant, treacherous and sullen people." Taft, on the other hand, notwithstanding his deep pessimism about the immediate capabilities of the Philippine people, yet clung stubbornly to the conviction that there was some basis in the people for the ultimate establishment of responsible government. Given this outlook, it is not surprising that Taft was to counsel a steady course toward civilian government. The road he had always held was a long one, but he was ever in favor of planting the first halting steps along that road. MacArthur instinctively grasped, though it did not become evident to him immediately, that the ultimate end could only mean the diminution of military authority. The loss of influence and prestige that MacArthur was to suffer provoked him into stating to Taft that the office of military governor had been "mediatized."

Taft demonstrated no little artistry in dealing with his egotistical adversary. Never disposed to move precipitously, Taft bided his time until he was sure of his power. He would wait until the island had been effectively pacified; until the transfer of the reins of government could be smoothly accomplished with a minimum of friction; until the commission itself was prepared to assume new responsibilities; and finally, until MacArthur's removal could be effected as painlessly as possible. Moreover, events worked in Taft's favor. The enactment of the Spooner Amendment in March, 1901, was the handwriting on the wall. This fact was quite clear to the general for the normalizing of governmental functions which the Spooner Amendment enjoined could only mean the eventual triumph of civil government. It was at this juncture that MacArthur was provoked to a statement of his true position—he stated frankly that in his view the instructions of President McKinley for the guidance of the commission were "an unconstitutional interference" with the prerogatives of the military governor. Taft, in turn, was to express utter amazement at such a novel interpretation of the Constitution of the United States. It was a contest between a bulldog and a terrier, with the end result never in doubt.

At this stage in Taft's development, his conceptions were primarily administrative and political rather than diplomatic in a strict sense. In contrast to MacArthur's thinking, which was tactical and strategic, Taft was concerned with the political relationship between the Philippines and the United States. It was self-evident that the type of administration followed by the American government in the islands would in large measure determine the nature of that relationship. Basically, Taft's premises were Hamiltonian. The last, best hope for the Philippines lay in the creation of a large and influential conservative element among the educated people to serve as the basis for the government. Coequal in importance with this was the development of an intelligent public opinion among the broad masses of the people. It was not always clear just how Taft was to achieve these worthy objectives, but it was upon these conceptions that Taft was to assume the burdens involved in ruling the Philippines. It was in actuating these conceptions that Taft achieved his enormous reputation as a great colonial administrator. But beside this, he was profoundly paternalistic.

Before turning away from the Philippine Islands, it should be noted that on July 2, 1902, the United States Congress passed the first organic act for the Philippines.[9] Until then, all

9. Pratt, *America's Colonial Experiment*, 198.

provisions for government in the Philippines had been made under the authority of the president of the United States, acting at first under his war powers and, after March 2, 1901, under a blanket grant of authority by Congress, the "Spooner Amendment" to the Army Appropriation Act of 1901. The Organic Act ratified and approved all action previously taken by the president and the Second Philippine Commission, including the letter of instructions of April 7, 1900, written by Secretary Elihu Root. It declared the inhabitants of the islands who had been Spanish subjects on April 11, 1899, and who continued to reside there to be citizens of the Philippine Islands and entitled to the protection of the United States. The one exception to this ruling were those who had elected to retain their Spanish allegiance. It embodied the bill of rights contained in Secretary Root's instructions. It continued the judicial machinery established by the commission—supreme court, courts of first instance, and municipal courts—with the proviso that justices of the supreme court should in future (like the governor and members of the commission) be appointed by the president of the United States with the consent of the United States Senate, the judges of the courts of first instance by the governor with the consent of the commission. Judgments of the Supreme Court of the Philippines might be appealed to the United States Supreme Court in cases involving the United States Constitution or statutes of the United States or in which the amount at issue exceeded $25,000. There was no provision for a United States court for the Philippines.

An important feature of the Organic Act of 1902—a feature for which Governor Taft was primarily responsible—was the provision for an elective assembly.[10] It stipulated that within two years of the completion of a census of the islands (which was to be taken as soon as peace should have been restored), the president should direct the commission to call a general election for the choice of members of an assembly, which

10. *Ibid.*, 199.

thereafter should constitute the lower house of the Philippine legislature, with the commission serving as the upper house. Areas inhabited by Moros and other non-Christian tribes were not to be represented in the assembly and were to continue under the authority of the commission. Suffrage qualifications were to be those that were already in effect in municipal elections. Elections were to be biennial, sessions annual.

The property and rights acquired by the United States from Spain (excepting military or other reservations designated by the president of the United States) were placed under the control of the government of the Philippines to be administered for the benefit of the inhabitants.[11] The Organic Act contained detailed regulations for the disposal of mineral lands and limited grants of agricultural land from the public domain to sixteen hectares (about forty acres) for an individual and 1,024 hectares (about 2,500 acres) for a corporation. The act empowered the government to purchase the lands of the religious orders and to dispose of such lands as part of the public domain; to permit municipalities to issue bonds for public improvements; and to grant franchises, subject to amendment or repeal by the United States Congress. All laws passed by the legislature had to be reported to Congress, which reserved the right to annul them.

The first census of the Philippines was taken in 1903.[12] The first assembly was elected in 1907, and from that year to the passage of the Jones Act in 1916 the legislative power in the Philippines was exercised by the bicameral legislature provided for by the act of 1902—elected assembly and appointed commission. In 1908 a fourth Filipino member was added to the commission, which from then until 1913 consisted of five Americans and four Filipinos. In 1905, the title of the chief executive had been changed from civil governor to governor general.

11. *Ibid.*, 199–200.
12. *Ibid.*, 200.

Reflecting back on the years from 1901 to 1913, a distinguished historian and scholar of American colonial government has written:

> It was in the years from 1901 to 1913 that American civilization made its strongest impact upon the Philippines. Volumes could well be devoted to the useful reforms and achievements of that period, which here can only be alluded to in a few sentences. A democratic system of local and provincial government was established, capped by the semi-democracy of the Philippine legislature. An excellent judicial system was organized, and for the first time the Filipino without money or influence could hope for justice in the courts. A civil service system based on merit was instituted. An impressive beginning was made in public education, with primary schools established in most communities, a high school in each province, vocational schools, normal schools, and a new University of the Philippines in Manila. Church and state were separated, religious freedom was guaranteed, and American Protestant churches engaged in missionary activities on a modest scale and with moderate success. The Friar Lands (some 400,000 acres) were purchased from the Church and sold in small units and on easy terms, for the most part to former tenants. The friars themselves, Spaniards who had been cordially hated by the Filipinos, were largely replaced by American and native clerics. Land titles were regularized and natives were encouraged to acquire homesteads from the public domain. Modern sanitation and medical techniques were introduced and a vigorous scientific attack was made upon diseases of man and beast. A Bureau of Agriculture promoted improved farming methods, and appropriate legislation fostered the development of forest and mineral resources. Transportation was greatly improved by both land and water; an efficient native constabulary was trained; the Moros and "wild tribes" were brought into a state of comparative industry and order. All of these reforms (except the few that involved activity by the army or navy of the United States) were paid for from Philippine revenues, but the Philippine tax rate remained but a small fraction of the federal tax rate in the United States, and

the bonded indebtedness of the Philippine government in 1913 was only $16,000,000.[13]

William Howard Taft presents the unusual spectacle of a man who had to be pushed from post to post, always from a lower position to a higher one. He seemed to be rather immobile and to cling to that which was familiar. The uncertainty of change seemed to hold terrors for him. Thus it was that it took a combination of the not inconsiderable persuasive powers of an Elihu Root and a Theodore Roosevelt, coupled with pressure from members of his own family, to dislodge Taft from the Philippines. His next assignment was that of secretary of war, but for purposes of tracing the evolution of his thinking in foreign affairs, it must be remembered that he assumed the burden of unofficial troubleshooter abroad for the Roosevelt administration, both by chance and by design. By the tenets of strict governmental administration, which would involve a proper delegation of work, Taft should never have played a prominent role in the conduct of American foreign policy. But Theodore Roosevelt was not one to adhere to the precepts of the rule book. In Taft he found a man ideally suited to his purposes—utterly loyal, completely trustworthy, and magnificently thorough. Circumstances also were to play no small part in creating this role for Taft. The illness of Secretary of State John Hay in the spring of 1905 coupled with the absence of Theodore Roosevelt from the capital meant in actual practice that Taft was acting secretary of state. It was his ability to do so many varied things and to do them well that led Theodore Roosevelt to explain that all would proceed smoothly in Washington while he took a needed vacation because he had "left Taft sitting on the lid." [14]

With the possible exception of John Quincy Adams, it is difficult to suggest the name of another public figure who had a more exacting and rigorous training in foreign affairs before assuming the burdens of the presidency than William How-

13. *Ibid.*, 200–201.
14. *New York Times*, April 4, 1905, p. 1.

ard Taft. It is an interesting sidelight that the two main regional areas in which Taft helped to execute policy—Latin America and the Far East—were the same areas that were to engage his attention during his presidency. Thus, if one wishes to comprehend the underlying philosophy of the Taft administration, he must examine the roots of Taft's concepts as they developed during his tenure as secretary of war.

Taft's first connection with Latin America began with his assignment to expedite the completion of the Panama Canal. As much of the work basic to the fulfillment of this task was legal and administrative, it was a burdensome and irksome assignment to the dynamic personality of Theodore Roosevelt, but rather congenial to the more placid and painstaking character of Taft. One is amazed at the broad range of subject matter that Taft was compelled to handle in carrying out this assignment. Demonstrating a prodigious capacity for the mastery of detail and for understanding the core of the problems, Taft undertook to straighten out all problems incident to the completion of the canal. These involved not only technical matters as related to engineering, but also complex political problems concerned with relations between the Panamanian government and the people. At great length, Taft analyzed the currency, tariff, and related economic problems of Panama, and made detailed recommendations concerning exceedingly intricate matters. His patience with such detail was monumental.

The most striking fact that emerges from a study of Taft's labors in Panama lies in the basic attitude that he developed toward Latin-American countries. In his mind, the Latin-Americans could not be compared with the Filipinos. In fact, he seemed to resent bitterly any attempt to make a comparison. He once described the countries of Latin-America as "dirty, so-called republics." Although this mental image was of some importance, nevertheless, Taft clung to the basic formulas deriving from his experience in the Philippines. Once again, the real hope for the establishment of a stable government for the isthmus lay in the development of a strong conservative leadership of the educated and merchant classes supported by an intelligent electorate. Implicit in this concept of an intelligent electorate was one that would perceive the eminent wisdom and superiority of sound conservative doctrine. Taft came to believe that Roosevelt's policy toward Panama from its inception was based upon a sense of justice toward all parties concerned and would be vindicated by history.

In contrast to his paternalistic outlook toward the Philippines, Taft was iron-handed in his approach to Panama. He would exercise restraint in avoiding any unnecessary friction with the Panamanians, but he did not propose to be in any way deflected from his course by reason of over-sensitivity to Panamanian feelings. He made it clear that such sovereignty as still remained with Panama was purely "titular." In a striking manifestation of nationalism, Taft by his actions showed that he was not prepared to see a vital interest of the United States sacrificed upon the altar of what he considered to be a meaningless abstraction—that abstraction being the ideal of self-government for the Panamanians. It is significant that Taft did not feel constrained to evaluate the broad political and social repercussions which his determined actions might well produce. There was no feeling of doubt or concern over any possible legacy of suspicion and resentment which United States conduct might leave to future generations. However, by this time, Taft had acquired considerable finesse in dealing with foreign officials and his conduct of policy questions in Panama bears testimony to this acquisition.

The geographical distance between Panama and Cuba does not accurately measure the conceptual distance between Taft's approach to the two areas. In the case of Panama, Taft sought to minimize any potential troublemaking by the Panamanian government. He was, above all else, concerned with the protection and furtherance of an American "vital interest," namely, the completion of the canal. Taft's role in the Cuban intervention of 1906 was to expand to a much greater degree his conceptions of what the interests of the United States in the Caribbean area were. From the very outset, Taft saw the destruction of foreign property in Cuba as the crucial question at issue because such destruction would make intervention imperative on the part of the United States. In due course this was to become the key question with Taft and to provide the frame of reference for guiding action by the government of the United States.

Characteristically, Taft had been reluctant to assume the Cuban assignment. He frankly conceded the limitations of his knowledge, and it may well have been that he was reluctant to court an adventure whose failure would have interfered seriously with his presidential aspirations. Taft's concern about the Cuban situation had a strong foundation in the extreme deterioration that had occurred there. A revolution had broken out in the summer of 1906, but it was not the simple type of outbreak so common to the past. In 1906, economic conditions in the island were in desperate straits. This, in turn, had produced a chronic and widespread unemployment which had always been the stuff of which revolutions are made. Moreover, an additional factor of some magnitude was now present. There was in Cuba at this time from $75,000,000 to $100,000,000 of foreign investments in sugar, of which American citizens held a large percentage. Given the lack of popular support for the government of Cuba, it is a reasonable presumption that American nationals should have been extremely concerned about the safety of their investments and might well have felt that the United States government offered the only hope for them in an otherwise impossible situation.

Under the Platt Amendment, the government of the United States had the necessary authority to intervene in Cuba to preserve Cuban independence, to maintain a stable government there, and to guarantee the fulfillment of international obligations. Considering all of these factors, there was an almost airtight case for intervention. Despite the exigencies of the situation, it is most significant that President Roosevelt dreaded the prospects of intervention because such action

might well provide useful political ammunition to the opposition, and the Congressional elections of 1906 were in the
offing. Distressed by the turn of events, the president instructed his secretary of war to intervene without the appearance of a full-scale intervention. Taft was to struggle with the
resolution of this problem. The ways of the politician were
always strange and devious to him. Something of a literalist,
who combined a blunt straightforward approach to matters of
state, he was never skilled in the art of making things appear
as other than what they actually were.

A day after his arrival in Cuba, in a personal letter to his
wife, Taft expressed the view that the Cuban people were
unfit for self-government. The record of the Cuban government had been abysmal and the hostility of the people was a
normal protest against such a state of affairs. Without any vestige of popular support for the government, Taft almost de-
spaired of resurrecting a government so bankrupt in integrity
and ability. And if peace could not be restored there was a
very real danger that "some 200 million of American property
and investment might go up in smoke."

Almost from the beginning Taft had believed that intervention was inevitable, and events were to justify his opinion.
What proved far more significant, however, was the expanding conceptions that Taft formulated while in Cuba. With reference to the actual intervention, he fell back upon a legal
formula characteristic of a corporation attorney justifying his
client's actions. Thus, the government of the United States
undertook the assignment of making the Cuban government
function just as "a receiver carries on the business of a corporation or a trustee the business of his ward." New conditions permitted new actions and suspension of old opera-
tional methods. Taft was not blind to the novelty of the
situation, but there was no trace of uncertainty in the righ-
teousness of his course.

Far more significant, however, was Taft's formula for the
future good of Cuba. In Taft's judgment what was needed
among the Cubans was "a desire to make money, to found

great enterprises, and to carry on the prosperity of the beautiful island and the young Cubans ought most of them to begin in business." However, the day in which the business elements in Cuba would play an influential role in the country lay in the future. With his practical mind, Taft was concerned with what would happen in the interim. The proper development of Cuba during that transitory stage would call for foreign capital. It was in this light, if in no other, that Taft could find some good words for the old order in Cuba, for the leadership of the old order had perceived the necessity for importing foreign capital and convincing the outside world of the "essentially conservative character of the government." Such an assurance was absolutely imperative, for it provided the necessary security which paved the way for the entry of such capital.

In all of the foregoing, one discerns in embryonic form the origins of what later came to be inextricably linked with William Howard Taft—Dollar Diplomacy. Actually, some of these concepts Taft had begun to formulate, and in a far different context, while serving in the Philippines. Then Taft believed that foreign capital was a necessary prerequisite for future development and growth, but the emphasis was different. In all policy decisions related to the Philippines, Taft had a central motivation—that all policies undertaken and measures enacted must, first and foremost, serve the needs of the Philippine people. To the work in the Philippines Taft had brought a sense of dedication, of idealism, and of purpose. The same could not be said for Cuba, where the welfare of the Cuban people was not the central objective. To be sure, it was involved in all policy consideration, but only as one factor among many.

It is in the Far East that we see the culmination of Taft's developing conceptions about foreign affairs. The pattern followed a familiar course. In the summer of 1905, Taft was scheduled to visit the Philippines in order to survey the progress that was being made, and to educate a large Congressional delegation as to the responsibilities the United

States had assumed there. President Roosevelt instructed Taft to pay a courtesy call to Japan en route, and this was to prove of vast significance, perhaps even more than the president had originally envisaged. Japan, at this time, was a rising power, and the United States, in terms both of its public officials and its private citizens, had encouraged and supported that rise. Taft, who was favorably disposed toward the Japanese, mirrored the sentiments of the times. He felt that the Japanese had as their purpose the achievement of the status of a great power which he did not, at first, fear; in fact, he believed such status to be modeled upon the European ideal. He also held that the Japanese were more friendly to the United States than any other country. Yet in all of this there were reservations.

Taft's early acceptance of the Japanese seemed at variance with his own stated view that they were bent upon self-aggrandizement "at the expense of anybody." Nevertheless, Taft, apparently acting upon his own authority, negotiated the Taft-Katsura agreement of 1905. This understanding, supported by President Theodore Roosevelt, in plain language meant that Japan was to have a free hand in Korea in return for a guarantee of the safety of the Philippines. That Taft could make such an agreement is understandable in the light of his prior thinking. Before arriving in Japan, he had expressed confidence that Japan would look to the United States for friendship, especially in view of the forthcoming peace conference at Portsmouth—"in any negotiations that might stem from the Russo-Japanese War." Far more revealing was his bland afterthought that Japan would "have her hands full" in developing Korea and the Lia Tung peninsula. Such preoccupation would bring an inevitable respite to the United States in the Philippines. Given such preconceptions and an essentially one-track mind that focused upon the protection of the Philippines, the Taft-Katsura agreement appears only as a logical sequel. Whether Taft exceeded his instructions, if any, is an open question. In any event, President Roosevelt quickly confirmed his position. In this instance

Taft most certainly reflected the thinking of the Roosevelt administration.

In 1907, Taft was once again to visit Japan as a special representative of the president. The difficulties between the United States and Japan over Japanese immigration to the United States and the developing anti-Japanese sentiment on the United States West Coast provided the setting and the reason for this mission. Taft was basically sympathetic to the Japanese position on immigration. He deplored the manifestations of racism then so rampant. In Japan, however, he found that it was an utter impossibility to secure a treaty which would cover the hotly disputed question. However, his second mission did lessen the war tensions between the two countries which had grown up since the more tranquil and amicable arrangement of 1905. By this time, Taft was less sanguine of Japan's benevolent intentions than he had been two years earlier. But he did not believe that war was imminent, as, in his opinion, Japan was in no financial position to undertake such a course of action.

In his reports to Washington, Taft wrote approvingly about Japanese policy in Korea. Moreover, he seemed unconcerned about the threat that Japan posed to China and the maintenance of the Open Door. In fact, his brief comments were directed to the theme that Japan was preparing to fight China and not the United States. In this connection, Taft seemed rather oblivious of the dangers to the policy of the Open Door. He recognized that the Japanese were a threat to the integrity of China and he was interested in the preservation of the Open Door, but somehow he did not seem to have made the connection. In any event, the whole matter held no urgency for him. A practical man with a pragmatic approach, the secretary was concerned with the easing of tensions with the Japanese and the safeguarding of immediate United States interests in the Far East. These interests, clearly, were the safety and security of the Philippine Islands.

Taft's somewhat provincial horizons were to be extended during the course of a sojourn to China as part of his world tour in 1907. Two years before, as this study has shown, Taft had visited Canton, China, in an attempt to end the boycott that the Chinese were then imposing. At that time he had expressed the usual sentiments of official America about the importance of amicable relations between the United States and China. The speech was filled with pious protestations of United States interest in and concern over the preservation of the Chinese empire. In an allusion that was rather unusual for the normally candid Taft, the secretary of war pontificated that the United States had always "set her face like steel" against any dismemberment of China. This remark was made a scant two months after the conclusion of the Taft-Katsura agreement which, in effect, encouraged Japanese territorial expansion at China's expense. However, in that address, Taft did recur to what was now becoming a stronger theme of his, namely, that of the importance of trade. At this time, Taft's interest in promoting an expanded China trade was not correlated with the trend of events in the Far East—in other words, the potential menace posed by Japan to the furtherance of any such trade expansion was apparently ignored or not properly understood by the secretary of war.

The turning point in relation to Taft's outlook vis-à-vis China coincided with a meeting with Thomas F. Millard, Far Eastern representative of the *New York Herald* in Tokyo during September and October of 1907. Millard was a strong protagonist of China; he was alarmed over what he feared as the threat of the Japanese to the United States interests in China. At Taft's request, Millard prepared a memorandum which set forth a detailed account of the total situation in China, with particular reference to the status of American trade with that country. Millard was an enthusiast for China and foresaw enormous possibilities for trade provided that the United States government properly appreciated the problems involved, and provided the United States gave proper support to the maintenance of Chinese integrity in the face of the developing Japanese threat. Millard did not shrink from the harsh realities of the situation and pinpointed Manchuria as the potential trouble spot. If Japan and Russia retained their positions of influence in that province, as seemed highly probable, the way would be paved for the eventual dismemberment of the entire Chinese empire. In the ultimate disintegration of China which these events portended, the United States would, in effect, be frozen out. Millard was convinced that a high spokesman for the Roosevelt administration should allay the fears of the Americans in China and set forth with unmistakable clarity a vigorous policy of support for the Open Door.

The ideas in Millard's thesis had a profound impact upon Taft, whose conceptions of China were exceedingly tentative up to this point. In a letter to President Roosevelt, dated October 5, 1907, Taft seemed to echo the sentiments expressed by Millard. As Taft saw it, the Chinese were very favorably disposed to the United States as the only country devoid of selfish ambitions in that area and were growing increasingly suspicious of the other foreign powers whose aspirations seemed limitless. Whatever may have been the original reasons for Taft's visit to China, there was now a new dimension present in the secretary's expanding conceptions of that country's importance.

On October 8, 1907, Taft gave public expression to his newly developed ideas in an address before the Americans of Shanghai, under the sponsorship of the American Association of China. This speech ranks as one of the most important that Taft made during the years with which this study is concerned. Dealing comprehensively with the entire question of American policy toward the Far East, the secretary was blunt and forthright. The speech itself, in terms of the ideas contained within it, showed to a startling degree the influence of Millard. At the very outset, Taft made it absolutely clear that the United States had no intention under any circumstances of selling the Philippine Islands. It should be pointed out that there had been for some time past persistent rumors to the effect that the United States was giving active consideration to the possibility of selling those islands. The source of this rumor is one of the minor mysteries of history, but its persistent repetition had gained for it a certain measure of credence at this time. The Japanese in broaching the subject to Taft in prior conferences may well have been testing the determination of the United States to remain in the Far East. Having demolished this myth, Taft turned directly to the question of the Open Door. He stated flatly that the United States government "had not deviated in the slightest way in its basic attitude since the policy was announced in 1900." This statement was far more indicative of a guide to Taft's future course than it was a true statement of past performance.

It was at this time and at this point that Taft's thinking expanded and enabled him to cross the bridge which connected the Open Door with the possibility of an expanded United States-China trade. Up to this time, he had not made the connection, and had tended to deal with the questions as though they were abstractions, and separate ones at that. Leaving no room for misunderstanding, Taft made it clear that there could be no opportunity for American trade in the absence of an independent China and that the efforts of the United States would be directed toward the wholehearted support of Chinese independence. Moreover, the legitimate interests of American businessmen and merchants in China deserved and would receive United States governmental support. If American traders lost out in China because of the superior skills of their competitors under circumstances of fair competition, that was one thing; but "if American businessmen lost out due to a departure from the policy of the Open Door then the United States Government had the right to protest."

How far was the United States prepared to go in the protection and preservation of the China trade? If Taft's remarks were an accurate barometer, the United States government would revise its faltering policy of the past, when a kind of indifference was its distinguishing characteristic despite verbal protestations to the contrary. The United States was now in the game to stay. Looking into the future, Taft predicted an even greater importance for foreign trade. This was predicated upon the assumption that the United States as a growing commercial nation, more and more involved in world affairs, would need and seek outlets for trade and commerce that were commensurate with her swiftly changing position. This being the case, it would be a tragic error for the United States to acquiesce in the foreclosure of areas of trade that would loom more importantly in the future. The new element in the secretary's expanding outlook was the role of the United States government—that of supporter and protector of American foreign trade. A positive policy was in the process of formulation which would receive its official expression when Taft became president.

In a prophetic vein, Taft foresaw the inevitable development and modernization of China. This was all to the good, for it would further support a flourishing and expanding trade. Taft did not fear such a development as did many of his fellow countrymen, who were apparently worried that such a development would pose the inevitable competition to American business and industry. On the contrary, Taft saw the flaw as being in trade with a backward nation which could offer little of permanent stability in the long run. These views are a significant reflection of the man's basic economic philosophy. At heart, Taft was a devout adherent of classical conservatism, with its emphasis upon maximizing the area of competition. There was perhaps a correlation between Taft's thinking in matters of domestic economics and his thinking in foreign affairs. Here a consistent philosophy seemed to underlie both. At home the government would assume the function of the impartial umpire dedicated to preserving conditions of true competition. Hence when the specter of monopoly at home diminished the area of competition, the government's function, as he saw it, was to curtail the monopoly and if necessary to dissolve it, in order to restore the area of free competition. Projecting this philosophy to foreign affairs, it was the government's imperative duty to see to it that trade opportunities remained open for American nationals. Here foreign powers had taken the role of the monopoly, thus causing Americans to lose out because of unfair conditions of competition. It was the duty of the United States government, therefore, to redress the balance.

Taft's Shanghai speech received an understandably favorable reception among Americans in the Far East. This was particularly true for Willard Straight, then American consul general in Mukden, a man who also held strong views respecting China. Straight was further to influence Taft's thinking along the lines already set by Millard. Straight's thesis was that Manchuria offered great opportunities for American capital and that the Chinese officials there would welcome American participation in that area. Straight felt that American penetration into Manchuria would accomplish two objectives of crucial importance: it would weaken the control over Manchuria exercised by Japan, and it would provide the United States with a starting point for the eventual economic penetration of the entire Chinese empire.

Taft's thinking was intensified by Straight because the latter seized the opportunity to impress his views upon the secretary. It was at Vladivostok on November 18, 1907, that Straight first met Taft, and in the following days he received ample opportunity to air his views. Taft proved receptive to Straight's ideas, but the net effect of the interview in terms of any concrete action was negligible. Straight had merely fortified a position which Taft had already formulated. It was at this time that Taft first expressed a fundamental change in his estimate of the Japanese. Whereas in previous years he seemed to have been complacent about the Japanese, he was now much less sanguine. Although he did not believe that the Japanese desired to fight the United States, he saw the Japanese in the unsympathetic role of "bluffers," playing a sinister game of power politics, hiding what they lacked to present an illusion of strength. Significantly, Taft concentrated his attention upon the future relationship between China and the United States, for he was now convinced that the former was "turning towards us as the one disinterested friend."

Taft's brief visit in Saint Petersburg probably increased his apprehension about the Japanese, although there is no direct evidence to support this conclusion. Taft's journey through Manchuria and later through Siberia made a profound impression upon him. He now became alive to the existence of a hitherto unknown part of the world, whose immensity and potentiality seemed to stagger his imagination.

Although it may seem a minor consideration, the extreme cordiality of the Russian government left its mark upon Taft. He was now far more disposed to view that country in a friendly light than at any time in the past. Nor did the Russian minister for foreign affairs hesitate to make a strong presentation of the Russian viewpoint. He pointedly asked Taft how the United States felt now about conditions in the Far East and particularly about Japan, the country the United States had helped in the Russo-Japanese War. Although Taft denied any favoritism by the United States in that episode, the strong tenor of the Russian's comments and their significance were not without their effect upon him. Thus, the secretary's horizons were further broadened and the perspective in which he viewed events in the Far East was further changed.

Upon his return to the United States, Taft made a number of speeches about the Far East. These speeches revealed his widening conceptual approach to international problems. For the first time, Taft enunciated a doctrine of foreign policy that transcended the merely pragmatic approach to individual issues as they arose. The total effect of these speeches was to adumbrate a kind of coherent philosophy that summed up Taft's thinking in relation to foreign affairs. It was now possible to turn to Taft's utterances and to state that this is what the man truly represented—here is where he stood. He had gone to the Philippines to reshape the government; to Panama, to make the dirt fly; to Cuba, to establish law and order; to Japan, to reduce international tension; to China, to end a boycott and to satisfy apparently a deep-seated curiosity about that country. The sum total of these experiences was to produce a definite framework for his conceptions of foreign policy.

All of the foregoing were embodied in Taft's speeches in 1908. In general, Taft's approach could be summed up in these terms. He had become an enthusiast for the possibility of Chinese trade and commerce. A developing nation like the United States must be alert to the prospects and opportunities of increasing trade. But trade could hardly flourish in an atmosphere of war, uncertainty, and absorption of China by foreign powers. It was, therefore, the responsibility of the United States government to uphold the Open Door in China to the end that American businessmen would be able to compete in an honest race. While he was most anxious to avoid international conflict, Taft was not oblivious to the need for a strong United States navy which could render the American position more secure.

The years of the Taft presidency are associated in the field of foreign affairs with the concept of Dollar Diplomacy as practiced in the Far East and in Latin America. Taft's outlook toward these regions, as this study has indicated, did not develop in a vacuum. The years from 1900 through 1908 were the years of apprenticeship in which Taft acquired experience in the field of foreign affairs, and formulated opinions about them. As president, Taft was to be preoccupied in the sphere of foreign relations with Latin America and the Far East—the two areas where he had undertaken all of his diplomatic relations in the period since 1900. He thus arrived at the presidency with a preparation unusual for his times and with a set of preconceptions about the problems with which he would have to grapple. If the future could have been anticipated, Taft could scarcely have received a better training.

William Howard Taft brought to the presidency a fine legal mind, an integrity of granite, energy of astounding proportions, and a capacity for detail that was truly monumental. His predilections were conservative. He was not adverse to change as long as that change was gradual, moderate, and bounded by a traditional frame of reference. A product of his times, he mirrored in his outlook the powerful forces of an expanding America, and as president he was soon to be the spokesman in the field of foreign affairs. Perhaps even more than Theodore Roosevelt or Woodrow Wilson, William Howard Taft faithfully reflected the main currents of his times.

Bibliographical Essay

THE BIBLIOGRAPHICAL STRUCTURE of this study is inherent in the body of the work. The backbone of this monograph is the William Howard Taft Papers. These papers are on deposit in the Manuscript Division of the Library of Congress, Washington, D.C. However, in order to acquire a balanced perspective about my subject, to deepen still further my knowledge about his life and times, and to provide the proper setting for a detailed and analytical study of his intellectual growth, I found it necessary to make extensive use of other important collections of private papers, to utilize such materials at the National Archives in Washington, D.C., as proved relevant to my topic, and to explore countless other sources of information, too numerous and varied to mention here. A word about the Taft Papers is in order. A voluminous collection, by estimate of the librarians, the sixth or seventh largest on deposit in the Library of Congress, it comprises hundreds of thousands of letters and other memoranda. However, for the purposes of this study, I shall speak only of those parts of the collection relevant to the topic itself. The most valuable single section of the papers is the "Letterpress Books," covering the years 1890 to 1921. Located in 144 separate containers, these documents comprise most of the important letters written by William Howard Taft and memoranda of various kinds. Arranged chronologically and prepared apparently by the Taft family, they are a joy for the historian. The first twenty-four containers cover the time span of this work and were indispensable. Although there is an excellent index to the Taft Papers, there is no substitute for turning the pages if one wishes to make a careful and detailed study of the man.

Next in importance to the "Letterpress Books" is the "Family Correspondence" section of the Taft Papers—a section which covers the years 1810 to 1914. This portion of the Taft Collection, officially listed as having thirty-one boxes, although there are thirty-five containers in all, deals with letters sent and received by William Howard and various members of his family. These letters are invaluable in delineating Taft's personality and in providing a revealing insight into family relationships. Included here are substantial amounts of the correspondence of Alphonso Taft, William Howard Taft's father, as well as correspondence among William Howard and his three brothers, Charles P., Horace D., and Henry W.

Of almost equal importance to these two sections of the Taft Papers, although not comparable in size, is that part devoted to the correspondence between Taft and Theodore Roosevelt. As Taft served under President Roosevelt while in the Philippines and as his secretary of war, undertaking numerous missions in that capacity, and because of the fact that their association was close, there was a substantial amount of correspondence. Found in seven containers, consisting of letters sent and received, and chronologically arranged on a day by day basis, the material here is informative and vastly illuminating.

The "Addresses and Articles" of William Howard Taft comprise yet another significant section of the papers. Prepared with loving care, again apparently by the Taft family, this section totals forty-two volumes boxed in twenty-one containers. The years of this study are covered in Volumes I through XIII. Although the addresses and articles are extensive in coverage, they do not include all of the speeches delivered by William Howard. Several of the most important of the addresses for the period under investigation were found in other parts of the papers.

Finally, there is the "General Correspondence," a classification common to all manuscript collections in the Manuscript Division of the Library of Congress. This section, consisting mainly of letters received, although some carbon copies of letters sent are included, contains innumerable miscellaneous items all of which taken together spell out a more complete picture of the man. The years covered by the general correspondence run from 1877 to 1916 and are found in 285 separate containers. The years 1877 to 1909 are covered in 178 boxes.

Next in importance to the Taft Papers for the purposes of this study were the Theodore Roosevelt Papers, also available at the Manuscript Division of the Library of Congress. This imposing collection, which is housed not only at the Library of Congress but also at the Widener Library of Harvard University, is one of the great collections of American history. One section of the Roosevelt Papers at the Library of Congress covers the years 1901 to 1909, and within this portion of the Roosevelt Papers is contained the Taft Correspondence in two boxes.

Three other collections must be mentioned briefly. The writer examined with care the Elihu Root Papers, the William McKinley Papers, and the Willard Straight Papers. The first two are on deposit at the Manuscript Division of the Library of Congress, while the Straight Papers are available at the Collection of Regional History and University Archives of Cornell University. As Elihu Root was secretary of war while Taft served in the Philippines, and secretary of state during much of the time that Taft was secretary of war, the importance of these papers is obvious. Although Root and Taft were good friends and admired each other, the relationship was not as close as that which existed between Taft and Theodore Roosevelt.

The McKinley Papers were examined for the years 1900 to 1901, for it was President McKinley who first projected Taft into public life by appointing him to the presidency of the Second Philippine Commission and subsequently as the first governor general of the Philippines. I found that Taft and McKinley held a strong admiration for each other, but the McKinley Papers were disappointing in that they contained little that was enlightening or stimulating.

Of more significance were the Willard Straight Papers for the light they shed upon the formulation of Taft's attitudes toward and ideas about Manchuria and China. Straight was American consul general at Mukden, Manchuria, in 1907 when Taft visited Vladivostok as part of a world tour. The value of this collection is enhanced by a revealing diary kept by Willard Straight. This diary proved most helpful to the investigator by providing an important link in the chain that defined Taft's total philosophy. Willard Straight, a

219

young man in his twenties at this time, possessed unusual vitality, brilliance, and an enthusiasm which permeated the letters he wrote.

Finally, I examined the John Hay Papers in the hopes that they might add to my knowledge of Taft. Unfortunately, this quest was to prove fruitless. Hence, there are no references in the body of this study to the John Hay Papers. In summary, therefore, the best source of knowledge about Taft, as one would expect, was Taft himself. This study has attempted to permit Taft to speak for himself through his own writings and experiences.

Selected Bibliography

1. MANUSCRIPT COLLECTIONS

Cornell University Library
  Willard Straight Papers
Library of Congress
  William McKinley Papers
  Theodore Roosevelt Papers
  Elihu Root Papers
  William Howard Taft Papers

2. RECORDS IN THE NATIONAL ARCHIVES

Record Group 59: General Records of the Department of State, Numerical File, 1906–10.

3. GOVERNMENT DOCUMENTS

House Document I, 56th Cong., 1st Sess., *Papers Relating to the Foreign Relations of the United States, with the Annual Message of the President,* December 5, 1899. Washington, D.C.: Government Printing Office, 1900.
Senate Document 331, 57th Cong., 1st Sess., *Affairs in the Philippine Islands.* Washington, D.C.: Government Printing Office, 1902. 3 vols.

Senate Document 357, 61st Cong., 2nd Sess. Malloy, William M. *Treaties, Conventions, International Acts, Protocols and Agreements between the United States of America and Other Powers, 1776–1909.* Washington, D.C.: Government Printing Office, 1910. 2 vols. with supplementary volume 1910–23.

4. AUTOBIOGRAPHIES, BIOGRAPHIES, LETTERS, AND MEMOIRS

Barker, Charles E. *With President Taft in the White House: Memories of William Howard Taft.* Chicago, Ill.: A. Kroch and Son, 1947.

Beale, Howard K. *Theodore Roosevelt and the Rise of America to World Power.* Baltimore, Md.: The Johns Hopkins Press, 1956.

Bishop, Joseph Bucklin. *Theodore Roosevelt and His Time: Shown in His Own Letters.* New York: Charles Scribner's Sons, 1920. 2 vols.

Blum, John Morton. *The Republican Roosevelt.* Cambridge, Mass.: Harvard University Press, 1954.

Burton, David H. *Theodore Roosevelt: Confident Imperialist.* Philadelphia: University of Pennsylvania Press, 1968.

Chessman, G. Wallace. *Theodore Roosevelt and the Politics of Power.* Boston, Mass.: Little, Brown and Co., 1968.

Cotton, Edward H. *William Howard Taft: A Character Study.* Boston, Mass.: Beacon Press, Inc., 1932.

Cowboys and Kings: Three Great Letters by Theodore Roosevelt. With an Introduction by Elting E. Morison. Cambridge, Mass.: Harvard University Press, 1954.

Croly, Herbert. *Willard Straight.* New York: Macmillan Co., 1924.

Davis, Oscar King. *William Howard Taft: The Man of the Hour: His Biography and His Views on the Great Questions of Today.* Philadelphia, Pa.: P. W. Ziegler Co., 1908.

Dawes, Charles G. *A Journal of the McKinley Years.* Edited and with a foreword by Bascom N. Timmons. Chicago, Ill.: Lakeside Press, R. R. Donnelley and Sons Co., 1950.

Dennett, Tyler, *John Hay: From Poetry to Politics.* New York: Dodd, Mead and Co., 1934.

———. *Roosevelt and the Russo-Japanese War: A Critical Study of American Policy in Eastern Asia in 1902–1905, Based Primarily* upon *the Private Papers of Theodore Roosevelt.* Garden City, N.Y.: Doubleday, Page and Co., 1925.

Duffy, Herbert S. *William Howard Taft.* New York: Minton, Balch and Co., 1930.

Dunn, Robert Lee. *William Howard Taft American.* Boston, Mass.: The Chapple Publishing Co., Ltd., 1908.

Einstein, Lewis. *A Diplomat Looks Back.* Edited by Lawrence E. Gelfand with a foreword by George F. Kennan. New Haven, Conn.: Yale University Press, 1968.

Garraty, John A. *Henry Cabot Lodge: A Biography.* New York: Alfred A. Knopf, 1953.

Glad, Paul W. *The Trumpet Soundeth: William Jennings Bryan and His Democracy, 1896–1912.* Lincoln: University of Nebraska Press, 1960.

Griscom, Lloyd C. *Diplomatically Speaking.* New York: Literary Guild of America, Inc., 1940.

Harbaugh, William Henry. *Power and Responsibility: The Life and Times of Theodore Roosevelt.* New York: Farrar, Straus and Cudahy, 1961.

Harrington, Fred Harvey. *God Mammon and the Japanese: Dr. Horace N. Allen and Korean-American Relations, 1884–1905.* Madison: University of Wisconsin Press, 1944.

Hechler, Kenneth W. *Insurgency: Personalities and Politics of the Taft Era.* New York: Russell and Russell, Inc., 1964.

Hicks, Frederick C. *William Howard Taft: Yale Professor of Law and New Haven Citizen: An Academic Interlude in the Life of the Twenty-Seventh President of the United States and the Tenth Chief Justice of the Supreme Court.* New Haven, Conn.: Yale University Press, 1945.

Hill, Howard C. *Roosevelt and the Caribbean.* Chicago, Ill.: University of Chicago Press, 1927.

Howe, M. A. De Wolfe. *George von Lengerke Meyer: His Life and Public Services.* New York: Dodd, Mead and Co., 1920.

Hunt, Frazier. *The Untold Story of Douglas MacArthur.* New York: Devin-Adair Co., 1954.

Jessup, Philip C. *Elihu Root.* New York: Dodd, Mead and Co., 1938.

Kohlsaat, H. H. *From McKinley to Harding: Personal Recollections of Our Presidents.* New York: Charles Scribner's Sons, 1923.

Lee, Clark, and Richard Henschel. *Douglas MacArthur.* New York: Henry Holt and Co., 1952.

Leech, Margaret. *In the Days of McKinley.* New York: Harper and Bros., 1959.

Leopold, Richard W. *Elihu Root and the Conservative Tradition.* Boston, Mass.: Little, Brown and Co., 1954.

Letters of Grover Cleveland 1850–1908. Edited by Allan Nevins. Boston, Mass.: Houghton Mifflin Co., 1933.

The Letters of Theodore Roosevelt. Edited by Elting E. Morison. Cambridge, Mass.: Harvard University Press, 1951–54. 8 vols.

Link, Arthur S. *Woodrow Wilson and the Progressive Era, 1910–1917.* New York: Harper and Bros., 1954.

Lockmiller, David A. *Enoch H. Crowder: Soldier, Lawyer, and Statesman.* Columbia: University of Missouri Press, 1955.

———. *Magoon in Cuba: A History of the Second Intervention, 1906–1909.* Chapel Hill: University of North Carolina Press, 1938.

Mason, Alpheus Thomas. *William Howard Taft: Chief Justice.* New York: Simon and Schuster, 1964, 1965.

Manners, William. *T. R. and Will: A Friendship that Split the Republican Party.* New York: Harcourt, Brace and World, Inc., 1969.

McHale, Francis. *President and Chief Justice: The Life and Public Service of William Howard Taft.* Philadelphia, Pa.: Dorrance and Co., 1931.

Miller, Francis Trevelyan. *General Douglas MacArthur: Fighter for Freedom.* Philadelphia, Pa.: John C. Winston Co., 1942.

Morgan, H. Wayne. *William McKinley and His America.* Syracuse, N.Y.: Syracuse University Press, 1963.

Mowry, George E. *The Era of Theodore Roosevelt 1900–1912.* New York: Harper and Bros., 1958.

Murray, Robert H. *Around the World with Taft: A Book of Travel, Description, History.* Detroit, Mich.: F. B. Dickerson Co., 1909.

Olcott, Charles S. *The Life of William McKinley.* Boston, Mass.: Houghton Mifflin Co., 1916. 2 vols.

Pringle, Henry F. *The Life and Times of William Howard Taft.* New York: Farrar and Rinehart, Inc., 1939. 2 vols.

———. *Theodore Roosevelt: A Biography.* New York: Harcourt, Brace and Co., 1931.

Ross, Ishbel. *An American Family: The Tafts—1678 to 1964.* Cleveland, Ohio: World Publishing Co., 1964.

Rovere, Richard H., and Arthur M. Schlesinger, Jr. *The General and the President: And the Future of American Foreign Policy.* New York: Farrar, Straus and Young, 1951.

Scholes, Walter V. and Marie V. *The Foreign Policies of the Taft Administration.* Columbia: University of Missouri Press, 1970.

Selections from the Correspondence of Theodore Roosevelt and Henry Cabot Lodge, 1884–1918. Edited by Henry Cabot Lodge. New York: Charles Scribner's Sons, 1925. 2 vols.

Spielman, William Carl. *William McKinley Stalwart Republican.* New York: Exposition Press, Inc., 1954.

Taft and Roosevelt: The Intimate Letters of Archie Butt, Military Aide. Garden City, N.Y.: Doubleday, Doran and Co., Inc., 1930. 2 vols.

Taft, Horace Dutton. *Memories and Opinions.* New York: Macmillan Co., 1942.

Taft, William Howard. *Four Aspects of Civic Duty.* New York: Charles Scribner's Sons, 1907.

———. *Our Chief Magistrate and His Powers.* New York: Columbia University Press, 1916.

———. *Popular Government: Its Essence, Its Permanence and Its Perils.* New Haven, Conn.: Yale University Press, 1913.

———. *Present Day Problems: A Collection of Addresses Delivered on Various Occasions.* New York: Dodd, Mead and Co., 1908.

———. *The Presidency: Its Duties, Its Powers, Its Opportunities and Its Limitations.* New York: Charles Scribner's Sons, 1916.

Taft, Mrs. William Howard. *Recollections of Full Years.* New York: Dodd, Mead and Co., 1914.

Thayer, William Roscoe. *Theodore Roosevelt: An Intimate Biography.* New York: Grosset and Dunlap, 1919.

Theodore Roosevelt: An Autobiography. New York: Charles Scribner's Sons, 1927.

Varg, Paul A. *Open Door Diplomat: The Life of W. W. Rockhill.* Urbana: University of Illinois Press, 1952.

Wheeler, Post, and Hallie Erminie Rives. *Dome of Many-Coloured Glass.* Garden City, N.Y.: Doubleday and Co., Inc., 1955.

William McKinley 1843–1901: Chronology—Documents—Bibliographical Aids. Edited by Harry J. Sievers, S. J. Dobbs Ferry, N.Y.: Oceana Publications, Inc., 1970.

5. Books

American Imperialism in 1898. The Quest for National Fulfillment. Edited by Richard H. Miller. New York: John Wiley and Sons, Inc., 1970.

Bailey, Thomas Andrew. *A Diplomatic History of the American People.* 4th ed. New York: Appleton-Century-Crofts, 1950.

———. *America Faces Russia: Russian-American Relations from Early Times to Our Day.* Ithaca, N.Y.: Cornell University Press, 1950.

———. *Theodore Roosevelt and the Japanese-American Crises: An Account of the International Complications Arising from the Race Problem on the Pacific Coast.* Stanford, Calif.: Stanford University Press, 1934.

Battistini, Lawrence H. *Japan and America: From Earliest Times to the Present.* New York: John Day Co., 1954.

———. *The United States and Asia.* New York: Frederick A. Praegar, 1955.

———. *The Rise of American Influence in Asia and the Pacific.* Lansing: Michigan State University Press, 1960.

Bau, Mingchien Joshua. *The Open Door Doctrine in Relation to China.* New York: Macmillan Co., 1923.

Beisner, Robert L. *Twelve against Empire: The Anti-Imperialists, 1898–1900.* New York: McGraw-Hill Book Co., 1968.

———. *The Latin American Policy of the United States: An Historical Interpretation.* New York: Harcourt, Brace and Co., 1943.

Bernstein, David. *The Philippine Story.* New York: Farrar, Straus and Co., 1947.

Bullard, Arthur. *Panama: The Canal, the Country and the People.* New York: Macmillan Co., 1913.

Buss, Claude A. *The Far East: A History of Recent and Contemporary International Relations in East Asia.* New York: Macmillan Co., 1955.

Callcott, Wilfrid Hardy. *The Caribbean Policy of the United States, 1890–1920.* Baltimore, Md.: The Johns Hopkins Press, 1942.

Campbell, Charles S., Jr. *Anglo-American Understanding, 1898–1903.* Baltimore, Md.: The Johns Hopkins Press, 1957.

Chapman, Charles E. *A History of the Cuban Republic: A Study in Hispanic American Politics.* New York: Macmillan Co., 1927.

Coolidge, Archibald Cary. *The United States as a World Power.* New York: Macmillan Co., 1912.

Damon, Ethel M. *Sanford Ballard Dole and Hawaii.* Palo Alto, Calif.: Pacific Books, 1957.

Daniels, Roger. *The Politics of Prejudice: The Anti-Japanese Movement in California and the Struggle for Japanese Exclusion.* Berkeley: University of California Press, 1962.

Dennett, Tyler. *Americans in Eastern Asia: A Critical Study of the Policy of the United States with Reference to China, Japan and Korea in the Nineteenth Century.* New York: Macmillan Co., 1922.

Dennis, Alfred L. P. *Adventures in American Diplomacy, 1896–1906.* New York: E. P. Dutton and Co., 1928.

Dictionary of American Biography. Edited by Allen Johnson, Dumas Malone, *et al.* New York: Charles Scribner's Sons, 1936. 22 vols.

Dulles, Foster Rhea. *America's Rise to World Power, 1898–1954.* New York: Harper and Bros., 1955.

———. *China and America: The Story of Their Relations since 1784.* Princeton: Princeton University Press, 1946.

———. *Forty Years of American-Japanese Relations.* New York: Appleton-Century Co., Inc., 1937.

———. *The Imperial Years.* New York: Thomas Y. Crowell Co., 1956.

———. *The Road to Teheran: The Story of Russia and America, 1781–1943.* Princeton, N.J.: Princeton University Press, 1944.

Dunn, Arthur Wallace. *From Harrison to Harding: A Personal Narrative, Covering a Third of a Century 1888–1921.* New York: G. P. Putnam's Sons, The Knickerbocker Press, 1922. 2 vols.

Ekirch, Arthur A., Jr. *The Civilian and the Military.* New York: Oxford University Press, 1956.

———. *The Decline of American Liberalism.* New York: Longmans, Green and Co., 1955.

Elliott, Charles Burke. *The Philippines to the End of the Commission Government: A Study in Tropical Democracy.* Indianapolis, Ind.: Bobbs-Merrill Co., 1916.

———. *The Philippines to the End of the Military Regime: American Overseas.* Indianapolis, Ind.: Bobbs-Merrill Co., 1917.

Ellis, L. Ethan. *A Short History of American Diplomacy.* New York: Harper and Bros., 1951.

Esthus, Raymond A. *Theodore Roosevelt and Japan*. Seattle: University of Washington Press, 1966.

Expansion and Imperialism. Edited by A. E. Campbell. New York: Harper and Row, 1970.

Faulkner, Harold U. *Politics, Reform and Expansion 1890–1900*. New York: Harper and Bros., 1959.

Fish, Carl Russell. *American Diplomacy*. 4th ed. New York: Henry Holt and Co., 1923.

Fitzgibbon, Russell H. *Cuba and the United States: 1900–1935*. Menasha, Wis.: Collegiate Press, George Banta Publishing Co., 1935.

Forbes, W. Cameron. *The Philippine Islands*. Boston: Houghton Mifflin Co., 1928.

Friend, Theodore. *Between Two Empires: The Ordeal of the Philippines, 1929–1946*. New Haven, Conn.: Yale University Press, 1965.

Ginger, Ray. *Age of Excess. The United States from 1877 to 1914*. New York: Macmillan Co., 1965.

Grant, A. J., and Harold Temperley. *Europe in the Nineteenth and Twentieth Centuries*. 6th ed. London: Longmans, Green and Co., 1952.

Griswold, A. Whitney. *The Far Eastern Policy of the United States*. New York: Harcourt, Brace and Co., 1938.

Grunder, Garel A., and William E. Livezey. *The Philippines and the United States*. Norman: University of Oklahoma Press, 1951.

Guggenheim, Harry F. *The United States and Cuba: A Study in International Relations*. New York: Macmillan Co., 1934.

Halle, Louis J. *Dream and Reality: Aspects of American Foreign Policy*. New York: Harper and Bros., 1958, 1959.

Hayden, Joseph Ralston. *The Philippines: A Study in National Development*. New York: Macmillan Co., 1942.

Healy, David F. *The United States in Cuba, 1898–1902*. Madison: University of Wisconsin Press, 1963.

Higham, John. *Strangers in the Land: Patterns of American Nativism, 1860–1925*. New Brunswick, N.J.: Rutgers University Press, 1955.

Hofstadter, Richard. *The Age of Reform: From Bryan to F.D.R.* New York: Alfred A. Knopf, 1956.

Jones, Chester Lloyd. *Caribbean Interests of the United States*. New York: Appleton-Century, 1916.

————. *The Caribbean since 1900*. New York: Prentice-Hall, Inc., 1936.

Julien, Claude. *America's Empire*. New York: Pantheon Books, 1971.

Kalaw, Maximo M. *Philippine Government: Its Development, Organization and Activities*. Manila: Published by the Author, 1948.

Kennan, George F. *American Diplomacy, 1900–1950*. Chicago, Ill.: University of Chicago Press, 1951.

Kirk, Grayson L. *Philippine Independence: Motives, Problems, and Prospects*. New York: Farrar and Rinehart, Inc., 1936.

Klein, Ernest L. *Our Appointment with Destiny: America's Role on the World Stage*. New York: Farrar, Straus and Young, 1952.

Latané, John Holladay, and David W. Wainhouse. *A History of American Foreign Policy*. New York: Odyssey Press, 1940.

Latané, John Holladay. *America as a World Power, 1897–1907*. New York: Harper and Bros., 1907.

————. *The United States and Latin America*. Garden City, N.Y.: Doubleday, Page and Co., 1922.

LaFeber, Walter. *The New Empire: An Interpretation of American Expansion, 1860–1898*. Ithaca, N.Y.: Cornell University Press, 1964.

Link, Arthur S., with the collaboration of William B. Catton. *American Epoch. A History of the United States since the 1890's*. 2nd ed., rev. New York: Alfred A. Knopf, 1963.

Link, Arthur S. *Wilson the Diplomatist: A Look at His Major Foreign Policies*. Baltimore, Md.: The Johns Hopkins Press, 1957.

Liss, Sheldon B. *The Canal: Aspects of United States Panamanian Relations*. Notre Dame, Ind.: University of Notre Dame Press, 1967.

March, Alden. *The History and Conquest of the Philippines and Our Other Island Possessions*. New York: Arno Press, 1970.

May, Ernest R. *Imperial Democracy: The Emergence of America as a Great Power*. New York: Harcourt, Brace and World, Inc., 1961.

McCain, William D. *The United States and the Republic of Panama*. Durham, N.C.: Duke University Press, 1937.

McCormick, Thomas J. *China Market: America's Quest for Informal Empire, 1893–1901*. Chicago, Ill.: Quadrangle Books, Inc., 1967.

McDonald, Forrest. *The Torch Is Passed: The United States in the Twentieth Century*. Reading, Mass.: Addison-Wesley, 1968.

McKinley, Albert Edward. *Island Possessions of the United States*. Philadelphia, Pa.: George Barrie's Sons, 1907.

Merk, Frederick. *Manifest Destiny and Mission in American History: A Reinterpretation*. New York: Alfred A. Knopf, 1963.

Millett, Allan R. *The Politics of Intervention: The Military Occupation of Cuba, 1906–1909*. Columbus: Ohio State University Press, 1967.

Millis, Walter. *Arms and Men: A Study in American Military History*. New York: G. P. Putnam's Sons, 1956.

Morgenthau, Hans J. *In Defense of the National Interest: A Critical Examination of American Foreign Policy*. New York: Alfred A. Knopf, 1952.

Munro, Dana G. *Intervention and Dollar Diplomacy in the Caribbean, 1900–1921*. Princeton, N.J.: Princeton University Press, 1964.

———. *The United States and the Caribbean Area*. Boston, Mass.: World Peace Foundation, 1934.

Nearing, Scott, and Joseph Freeman. *Dollar Diplomacy: A Study in American Imperialism*. New York: B. W. Huebsch and Viking Press, 1925.

Nelson, M. Frederick. *Korea and the Old Orders in Eastern Asia*. Baton Rouge: Louisiana State University Press, 1946.

Neu, Charles E. *An Uncertain Friendship: Theodore Roosevelt and Japan, 1906–1909*. Cambridge, Mass.: Harvard University Press, 1967.

Neumann, William L. *America Encounters Japan: From Perry to MacArthur*. Baltimore, Md.: The Johns Hopkins Press, 1963.

Osgood, Robert Endicott. *Ideals and Self-Interest in America's Foreign Relations: The Great Transformation of the Twentieth Century*. Chicago, Ill.: University of Chicago Press, 1953.

Perkins, Dexter. *The American Approach to Foreign Policy*. Cambridge, Mass.: Harvard University Press, 1952.

———. *The Evolution of American Foreign Policy*. New York: Oxford University Press, 1948.

———. *Hands Off: A History of the Monroe Doctrine*. Boston: Little, Brown and Co., 1941.

Plesur, Milton. *America's Outward Thrust: Approaches to Foreign*

Affairs 1865–1890. De Kalb: Northern Illinois University Press, 1971.

Pratt, Julius W. *A History of United States Foreign Policy*. New York: Prentice-Hall, Inc., 1955.

———. *America's Colonial Experiment: How the United States Gained, Governed, and in Part Gave Away a Colonial Empire*. New York: Prentice-Hall, Inc., 1950.

———. *Challenge and Rejection: The United States and World Leadership, 1900–1921*. New York: Macmillan Co., 1967.

———. *Expansionists of 1898: The Acquisition of Hawaii and the Spanish Islands*. Baltimore, Md.: The Johns Hopkins Press, 1936.

The Record of American Diplomacy: Documents and Readings in the History of American Foreign Relations. Edited by Ruhl J. Bartlett. 3rd ed. New York: Alfred A. Knopf, 1954.

Rhodes, James Ford. *The McKinley and Roosevelt Administrations: 1897–1909*. New York: Macmillan Co., 1922.

Riencourt, Amaury de. *The American Empire*. New York: Dial Press, Inc., 1968.

Rippy, J. Fred. *The Caribbean Danger Zone*. New York: G. P. Putnam's Sons, 1940.

Schuman, Frederick L. *International Politics: The Destiny of the Western State System*. 4th ed. New York: McGraw-Hill Book Co., 1948.

Sears, Louis Martin. *A History of American Foreign Relations*. 2nd ed. New York: Thomas Y. Crowell Co., 1935.

The Shaping of American Diplomacy: Readings and Documents in American Foreign Relations, 1750–1955. Edited with commentary by William Appleman Williams. Chicago: Rand McNally and Co., 1956.

Storey, Moorfield, and Marcial P. Lichauco. *The Conquest of the Philippines by the United States, 1898–1925*. New York: G. P. Putnam's Sons, 1926.

Stuart, Graham H. *Latin America and the United States*. 5th ed. New York: Appleton-Century-Crofts, 1955.

Tarsaidze, Alexandre. *Czars and Presidents: The Story of a Forgotten Friendship*. New York: McDowell, Obolensky, Inc., 1958.

Threshold to American Internationalism: Essays on the Foreign

Policies. Edited with a prologue by Paolo E. Coletta. New York: Exposition Press, Inc., 1970.

Tolentino, Arturo M. *The Government of the Philippines*. Manila: R. P. Garcia Publishing Co., 1950.

Tompkins, E. Berkeley. *Anti-Imperialism in the United States: The Great Debate 1890–1920*. Philadelphia: University of Pennsylvania Press, 1970.

Tongko, Primo L. *The Government of the Republic of the Philippines*. Rev. ed. Manila: R. P. Garcia Publishing Co., 1953.

Trani, E. P. *The Treaty of Portsmouth: An Adventure in American Diplomacy*. Lexington: University of Kentucky Press, 1969.

Treat, Payson J. *Diplomatic Relations between the United States and Japan, 1895–1905*. Stanford, Calif.: Stanford University Press, 1938.

———. *Japan and the United States, 1853–1921*. Boston, Mass.: Houghton Mifflin Co., 1921.

Van Alstyne, Richard W. *American Crisis Diplomacy: The Quest for Collective Security, 1918–1952*. Stanford, Calif.: Stanford University Press, 1952.

———. *American Diplomacy in Action*. 2nd ed. Stanford, Calif.: Stanford University Press, 1947.

———. *The Rising American Empire*. Oxford: Basil Blackwell, Ltd., 1960.

Varg, Paul A. *The Making of a Myth: The United States and China 1897–1912*. East Lansing: Michigan State University Press, 1968.

Vevier, Charles. *The United States and China 1906–1913: A Study of Finance and Diplomacy*. New Brunswick, N.J.: Rutgers University Press, 1955.

Warburg, James P. *The United States in a Changing World: An Historical Analysis of American Foreign Policy*. New York: G. P. Putnam's Sons, 1954.

Weinberg, Albert K. *Manifest Destiny: A Study of Nationalist Expansion in American History*. Baltimore, Md.: The Johns Hopkins Press, 1935.

White, John A. *The Diplomacy of the Russo-Japanese War*. Princeton, N.J.: Princeton University Press, 1964.

Williams, D. R. *The United States and the Philippines*. Garden City, N.Y.: Doubleday, Page and Co., 1926.

Williams, William Appleman. *American Russian Relations, 1781–1947*. New York: Rinehart and Co., Inc., 1952.

————. *The Roots of the Modern American Empire: A Study of the Growth and Shaping of Social Consciousness in a Marketplace Society*. New York: Random House, 1969.

————. *The Tragedy of American Diplomacy*. Cleveland, Ohio: World Publishing Co., 1959.

Wolff, Leon. *Little Brown Brother: How the United States Purchased and Pacified the Philippine Islands at the Century's Turn*. Garden City, N.Y.: Doubleday and Co., Inc., 1961.

Worcester, Dean C. *The Philippines Past and Present*. New York: Macmillan Co., 1930.

Young, Marilyn B. *The Rhetoric of Empire: American China Policy, 1895–1901*. Cambridge, Mass.: Harvard University Press, 1968.

Zabriskie, Edward H. *American-Russian Rivalry in the Far East: A Study in Diplomacy and Power Politics, 1895–1914*. Philadelphia: University of Pennsylvania Press, 1946.

Zebel, Sydney H. *A History of Europe since 1870: With a Background Chapter Dealing with Events from 1815 to 1870*. Chicago: J. B. Lippincott Co., 1948.

6. PERIODICALS

Ameringer, Charles D. "Philippe Bunau-Varilla: New Light on the Panama Canal Treaty," *Hispanic American Historical Review*, XLVI (Feb., 1966), 28–52.

Bailey, Thomas A. "The Root-Takahira Agreement of 1908," *Pacific Historical Review*, IX (March, 1940), 19–36.

————. "Was the Presidential Election of 1900 a Mandate on Imperialism?," *The Mississippi Valley Historical Review*, XXIV (June, 1937), 43–52.

Berthoff, Rowland T. "Taft and MacArthur, 1900–1901: A Study in Civil-Military Relations," *World Politics*, V (Jan., 1953), 196–213.

Blake, Nelson Manfred. "Ambassadors at the Court of Theodore Roosevelt," *The Mississippi Valley Historical Review*, XLII (Sept., 1955), 179–206.

Braisted, William R. "The Philippine Naval Base Problem, 1898–1909," *The Mississippi Valley Historical Review*, XLI (June, 1954), 21–40.

————. "The United States Navy's Dilemma in the Pacific,

1906–1909," *Pacific Historical Review*, XXVI (Aug., 1957), 235–244.

Burton, D. H. "Theodore Roosevelt: Confident Imperialist," *Review of Politics*, XXIII (July, 1961), 356–377.

Campbell, Charles S. "The Anglo-American Crisis in the Bering Sea, 1890–1891," *The Mississippi Valley Historical Review*, XLVIII (Dec., 1961), 393–414.

———. "The Bering Sea Settlements of 1892," *Pacific Historical Review*, XXXII (Nov., 1963), 347–367.

Chay, Jongsuk. "The Taft-Katsura Memorandum Reconsidered," *Pacific Historical Review*, XXXVII (Aug., 1968), 321–326.

Coker, William S. "The Panama Canal Tolls Controversy: A Different Perspective," *The Journal of American History*, LV (Dec., 1968), 555–564.

Coletta, Paolo E. "Bryan, McKinley, and the Treaty of Paris," *Pacific Historical Review*, XXVI (May, 1957), 131–146.

———. "McKinley, the Peace Negotiations, and the Acquisition of the Philippines," *Pacific Historical Review*, XXX (Nov., 1961), 341–350.

Conroy, Hilary. "Japanese Nationalism and Expansionism," *The American Historical Review*, LX (July, 1955), 818–829.

Coxe, John E. "The New Orleans Mafia Incident," *Louisiana Historical Society*, XX (Oct., 1937), 1067–1110.

Cramer, Frederick H. "The Pacific: Sea of Decision: II. The Western Condominium (1800–1900)," *Current History*, XX (March, 1951), 151–157.

———. "The Pacific: Sea of Decision: III. The United States Supreme (1900–1950)," *Current History*, XX (April, 1951), 193–201.

Curry, Roy Watson. "Woodrow Wilson and Philippine Policy," *The Mississippi Valley Historical Review*, XLI (Dec., 1954), 435–452.

Curtin, Philip D. "The United States in the Caribbean," *Current History*, XXIX (Dec., 1955), 364–370.

Dennett, Tyler. "President Roosevelt's Secret Pact with Japan," *Current History*, XXI (Oct., 1924), 15–21.

Esthus, Raymond A. "The Changing Concept of the Open Door 1899–1910," *The Mississippi Valley Historical Review*, XLVI (Dec., 1959), 435–454.

Eyre, James K., Jr. "Japan and the American Acquisition of the Philippines," *Pacific Historical Review*, XI (March, 1942), 55–71.

———. "Russia and the American Acquisition of the Philippines," *Mississippi Valley Historical Review*, XXVIII (March, 1942), 539–562.

Farrell, John T. "Background of the 1902 Taft Mission to Rome. I," *The Catholic Historical Review*, XXXVI (April, 1950), 1–32.

———. "Background of the Taft Mission to Rome. II," *The Catholic Historical Review*, XXXVII (April, 1951), 1–22.

Florinsky, Michael T. "Russia and the United States," *Current History*, XXVIII (Feb., 1955), 108–113.

Friedlander, Robert A. "A Reassessment of Roosevelt's Role in the Panamanian Revolution of 1903," *The Western Political Quarterly*, XIV (June, 1961), 535–543.

Godwin, Robert K. "Russia and the Portsmouth Peace Conference," *American Slavic and East European Review*, IX (Dec., 1950), 279–291.

Grenville, J. A. S. "Great Britain and the Isthmian Canal, 1898–1901," *The American Historical Review*, LXI (Oct., 1955), 48–69.

Harrington, Fred H. "The Anti-Imperialist Movement in the United States, 1898–1900," *Mississippi Valley Historical Review*, XXII (Sept., 1935), 211–230.

———. "Literary Aspects of American Anti-Imperialism, 1898–1902," *New England Quarterly*, X (Dec., 1937), 650–667.

Heidingsfield, Myron S. "Cuba: A Sugar Economy," *Current History*, XXII (March, 1952), 150–155.

Hess, Stephen. "Big Bill Taft," *American Heritage*, XVII (Oct., 1966), 32–37, 82–86.

Karlin, Jules A. "The Indemnification of Aliens Injured by Mob Violence," *Southwestern Social Science Quarterly*, XXV (March, 1945), 235–246.

———. "The Italo-American Incident of 1891 and the Road to Reunion," *Journal of Southern History*, VIII (May, 1942), 242–246.

La Feber, Walter. "The Background of Cleveland's Venezuelan Policy: A Reinterpretation," *The American Historical Review*, LXVI (July, 1961), 947–967.

Lasch, Christopher. "The Anti-Imperialists, the Philippines, and the Inequality of Man," *Journal of Southern History*, XXIV (Aug., 1958), 319–331.

Leuchtenburg, William E. "Progressivism and Imperialism: The

Progressive Movement and American Foreign Policy, 1898–1916," *The Mississippi Valley Historical Review*, XXXIX (Dec., 1952), 483–504.

Livermore, Seward H. "The American Naval-Base Policy in the Far East, 1850–1914," *Pacific Historical Review*, XIII (June, 1944), 113–135.

——. "American Strategy Diplomacy in the South Pacific, 1890–1914," *Pacific Historical Review*, XII (March, 1943), 33–52.

——. "Theodore Roosevelt, the American Navy, and the Venezuelan Crisis of 1902–1903," *The American Historical Review*, LI (April, 1946), 452–471.

Magsaysay, Ramon. "Roots of Philippine Policy," *Foreign Affairs*, XXXV (Oct., 1956), 29–36.

May, Ernest R. "The Far Eastern Policy of the United States in the Period of the Russo-Japanese War: A Russian View," *The American Historical Review*, LXII (Jan., 1957), 345–351.

McCormick, Thomas. "Insular Imperialism and the Open Door: The China Market and the Spanish-American War," *Pacific Historical Review*, XXXII (May, 1963), 155–169.

Minger, Ralph Eldin. "From Law to Diplomacy: The Summons to the Philippines," *Mid-America*, LIII (April, 1971), 103–120.

——. "Panama, the Canal Zone, and Titular Sovereignty," *The Western Political Quarterly*, XIV (June, 1961), 544–554.

——. "Taft, MacArthur, and the Establishment of Civil Government in the Philippines," *The Ohio Historical Quarterly*, LXX (Oct., 1961), 308–331.

——. "Taft's Missions to Japan: A Study in Personal Diplomacy," *Pacific Historical Review*, XXX (Aug., 1961), 279–294.

——. "William H. Taft and the United States Intervention in Cuba in 1906," *The Hispanic American Historical Review*, XLI (Feb., 1961), 75–89.

——. "William Howard Taft's Forgotten Visit to Russia," *The Russian Review*, XXII (April, 1963), 149–156.

Morgan, W. Wayne. "William McKinley as a Political Leader," *Review of Politics*, XXVIII (Oct., 1966), 417–432.

Neu, Charles. "Theodore Roosevelt and American Involvement in the Far East, 1901–1909," *Pacific Historical Review*, XXXV (Nov., 1966), 433–449.

Patterson, John. "Latin American Reactions to the Panama Revolution of 1903," *Hispanic American Historical Review*, XXIV (May, 1944), 342–351.

Pilapil, Vincente R. "The Cause of the Philippine Revolution," *Pacific Historical Review*, 34 (Aug., 1965), 249–264.

Plesur, Milton. "Across the Wide Pacific," *Pacific Historical Review*, XXVIII (Feb., 1959), 73–80.

———. "The Years from Hayes to Harrison," *The Historian*, XXII (May, 1960), 280–295.

Pratt, Julius W. "Manifest Destiny and the American Century," *Current History*, XXIX (Dec., 1955), 331–336.

Romulo, Carlos P. "The American Dilemma: Democracy and Empire," *Current History*, XXIX (Dec., 1955), 325–330.

Snowbarger, Willis E. "Pearl Harbor in Pacific Strategy, 1898–1908," *The Historian*, XIX (Aug., 1957), 361–384.

Stuart, Graham H. "Immigration and Foreign Policy," *Current History*, XXIX (Nov., 1955), 279–284.

Tannenbaum, Frank. "The American Tradition in Foreign Relations," *Foreign Affairs*, XXX (Oct., 1951), 31–50.

Thompson, Carol L. "America in the Far East: I. The Treaty of Portsmouth," *Current History*, XIX (Sept., 1950), 144–150.

———. "Isolation and Expansion," *Current History*, XXI (Nov., 1951), 258–262.

———. "The Period of Growth," *Current History*, XXV (Oct., 1953), 197–202.

Thorson, Winston B. "American Public Opinion and the Portsmouth Peace Conference," *The American Historical Review*, LIII (April, 1948), 439–464.

Tompkins, E. Berkeley. "Seylla and Charybdis: The Anti-Imperialist Dilemma in the Election of 1900," *Pacific Historical Review*, XXXVI (May, 1967), 143–162.

Uhlig, Frank, Jr. "The Great White Fleet," *American Heritage*, XV (Feb., 1964), 30–34, 35–43, 103–106.

Van Alstyne, Richard W. "United States: New American Relationship," *Current History*, XXII (March, 1952), 161–165.

Varg, Paul. "Alternatives in the Far East," *World Affairs Quarterly*, XXVI (Oct., 1955), 247–254.

Vevier, Charles. "American Continentalism: An Idea of Expansion, 1845–1910," *The American Historical Review*, LXV (Jan., 1960), 323–335.

———. "The Open Door: An Idea in Action, 1906–1913," *Pacific Historical Review*, XXIV (Feb., 1955), 49–62.

Whitaker, Arthur P. "The United States in Latin America since 1865," *Current History*, XXVIII (March, 1955), 154–159.

Williams, William Appleman. "Brooks Adams and American Expansion," *New England Quarterly*, XXV (June, 1952), 217–232.

———. "The Frontier Thesis and American Foreign Policy," *Pacific Historical Review*, XXIV (Nov., 1955), 379–395.

Yanaga, Chitoshi. "Japan: Nationalism Succeeds and Fails," *Current History*, XIX (Aug., 1950), 67–72.

Zornow, William F. "Funston Captures *Aguinaldo*," *American Heritage*, IX (Feb., 1958), 24–29, 107.

7. NEWSPAPERS

Dyer, Brainerd. "Today in History," Los Angeles *Times*, June 6, 1956.

———. "Today in History," Los Angeles *Times*, Aug. 15, 1956.

New York *Times*, Feb. 7, 1900; March 30, 1900; July 5, 1901; Aug. 19, 1901; April 4, 1905; Sept. 6, 1912.

Index